Dallas Dish

Dallas Dish
JUNIOR LEAGUE OF DALLAS

Copyright ©2005
Junior League of Dallas, Inc.
8003 Inwood Road
Dallas, Texas 75209
800-931-8821

www.jld.net

Photography: © Dave Carlin, Greg Booth and Associates
Food Styling: Brooke Leonard

This cookbook is a collection of favorite recipes,
which are not necessarily original.

Library of Congress Catalog Number: 2005920292

ISBN: 0-9617677-1-5

Edited, Designed, and Manufactured by
Favorite Recipes® Press
An imprint of

FRP.

P.O. Box 305142
Nashville, Tennessee 37230
800-358-0560

Art Director: Steve Newman
Project Editor: Debbie Van Mol, RD

Manufactured in the United States of America

First Printing: 2005   30,000

 Casual Plate

 Gourmet Plate

 Typical Texas plate

Dallas Dish

JUNIOR LEAGUE OF DALLAS

Introduction 6

Cookbook Committee 6

Dallas: Then and Now 7

Contents

Beverages 8

Appetizers 22

Soups & Sandwiches 58

Salads 84

Sides 110

Main Dishes 140

Desserts 176

Breads & Brunch 224

Basics 258

Vegetable Saucery 273

Equivalents 274

Herbs 276

Acknowledgments 277

Testers 277

Contributors 278

Index 280

Order Information 288

Cookbook Committee

Chairman	Traci Schuh
Chairman-Elect	Mary-Elizabeth Carrell
Copy Editor	Christina Nihira
Design	Susan Harvey
Marketing	Denise Duggan
Recipes	Marcy Feldman
Retail	Ellen Bryant
Sustaining Advisor	Denise Stewart

Committee Members

Kelly Baisden	Lisa Grissom
Heather Basso	Nicole Kapioltas
Anne Bentley	Cari Kaye
Martha Blue	Jeanette Mann
Ashley Boisture	Betsy Massey
Julie Buxton	Melissa McRoberts
Katherine Coker	Hilary Miller
Charlotte Corn	Carey Mosley
Mersine Defterios	Katherine Quest
Aimee Dunlow	Misty Quinn
Sally Dutter	Stacey Shield
Maryann Denton	D'Ann Shippy
Kathleen Elliott	Mary Kat White
Laurie Ewing	Erin Willis
Tiffany Finn	Liana Yarckin
Shannan Humphries	

A special thank-you to...
Mary Meier, President 2003-2004
Pam Perella, President 2004-2005
Christie Carter, President 2005-2006

6

Introduction

The Junior League of Dallas is pleased to present an array of culinary delights that is certain to appeal to both the basic cook and the seasoned chef. Drawing from Dallas' vibrant heritage, we introduce food that is richly diverse, elegant and enjoyable.

Recipes in this book were contributed by Junior League members, their relatives and friends, plus famous local chefs and restaurants. All recipes, ranging from traditional fare to more unusual dishes, were tested and perfected by our toughest critics, a team of more than one hundred volunteers.

We give you the inside scoop on the place we call home, offering new twists on old favorites. Other recipes introduce unique ingredients or fresh cooking techniques.

We also created a series of variations throughout the book by using several basic recipes and expanding them to include casual, gourmet and typical Texan versions. The results are dynamic and certain to fit any occasion.

Please be our guest and enjoy a terrific meal featuring Texas flavors and hospitality.

Dallas: Then and Now

Dallas carries the mystique of oil, cowboys and sophistication. The city's impressive skyline rises to prominence amid the sloping prairies of north Texas. A major hub for telecommunications, insurance, medicine and banking, it is the ninth largest city in the country with over one million residents. Nearly five million people call the Dallas-Fort Worth Metroplex home.

Dallas will forever be remembered as the city where, in 1963, President John F. Kennedy was assassinated. It also received notoriety in the 1980s when the fictional Ewing family called South Fork Ranch home on the hit television drama *Dallas*.

Long known as one of the country's fashion capitals, Dallas has solid retail roots. Neiman Marcus opened in 1907 in downtown and operates one of its busiest stores at NorthPark Center in central Dallas. That mall, built in 1965, was the first covered shopping center in the United States. When not shopping, locals visit the sixty lakes and 50,000-plus acres of public parks found within a one-hundred-mile radius of the city.

It's always the season for sports, given the Metroplex boasts six professional sports teams. The Dallas Cowboys (football), Dallas Mavericks (basketball), Dallas Stars (hockey), Texas Rangers (baseball), FC Dallas (soccer) and Dallas Desperados (arena football) all make their home here.

Indoor recreation is easily found at the Dallas Arts District, which features the century-old Dallas Museum of Art, Crow Collection of Asian Art, Latino Cultural Center and Nasher Sculpture Center. Beyond this urban arts area, the city offers numerous museums, galleries, professional and community theaters, plus local symphony and chamber orchestras, ballet troupes and opera organizations.

The sun shines in Big D. There are 137 days of sunshine, on average, each year. The average annual rainfall is 33.3 inches and the average temperature is 65.4 degrees Fahrenheit. Typically, July is the warmest month, while January is the coldest.

Doctors and nurses are always busy at the county's highly regarded public health facility, Parkland Hospital. They deliver more that 16,000 babies each year, making it the busiest birthing center in the country.

Dallas/Ft. Worth Airport, which opened to traffic in 1974, is jointly owned by the cities of Dallas and Fort Worth and is operated by the DFW Airport Board. It is the second largest airport in the United States in terms of land mass and the fifth busiest in terms of traffic in the world. The supersonic Concorde jet made its first U.S. landing at DFW, and the NASA Space Shuttle *Atlantis* and its transport jet landed in 1989, making DFW the first commercial airport to host a space shuttle landing.

An important tradition is the Texas State Fair, which is held every October in Fair Park and draws millions of visitors. The fair is a one-hundred-year-old institution and features livestock exhibits, a rodeo, football and America's biggest ferris wheel, the Texas Star. One of the staples served is the famous corny dog, a recipe included in the Anniversary Edition of The Dallas Junior League Cookbook, fondly referred to as the Blue Book.

The city often receives national attention for developing cooking trends and styles. Dallacites know and appreciate good cuisine. In fact, the city has four times more restaurants per person than New York City. The types of food span the globe, with a concentration in Tex-Mex eateries and steakhouses.

Beverages

THE DISH ON DALLAS

Dallas is home to the frozen margarita, which was invented in the early 1970s by restaurant owner Mariano Martinez. He used his father's recipe of tequila, lime juice, orange liqueur, and simple syrup. He perfected this slushy cocktail by using a modified, soft-serve ice cream machine to prevent the alcohol from freezing.

Nectarine Basil Lemonade recipe on page 16.

The Best Margarita

fine kosher salt

1 lime wedge

1/2 cup (about) crushed ice

2 ounces fresh lime juice, chilled

1 1/2 ounces premium tequila

1/2 ounce fresh lemon juice, chilled

1/2 ounce Triple Sec

1 lime wedge

Pour kosher salt into a shallow bowl. Rub the rim of a margarita glass with 1 lime wedge and rotate the rim gently in the salt to cover evenly. Combine the crushed ice, lime juice, tequila, lemon juice and liqueur in a cocktail shaker and shake to mix.

Strain the cocktail into the salt-rimmed glass and garnish with 1 lime wedge. You can easily make the blended variety by processing 1/4 to 1/2 cup ice with the remaining liquid ingredients in a blender. Serves 1.

tinted sugar

1 1/2 ounces peach schnapps

1 peach slice

PEACH MARGARITA

Rim a Champagne glass with tinted sugar or a large-grained sugar instead of salt as directed above. Prepare The Best Margarita, substituting peach schnapps for the Triple Sec, and strain into the sugar-rimmed glass. Omit the lime wedge garnish and garnish with the peach slice, allowing the slice to float in the glass.

2 1/2 ounces prickly pear purée, chilled

1/2 ounce orange liqueur

1 lime wedge

PRICKLY PEAR MARGARITA

Rim the margarita glass with salt as directed above. Prepare The Best Margarita, omitting the Triple Sec and adding the Prickly Pear purée and orange liqueur. Strain into the salt-rimmed glass and garnish with the lime wedge.

10

The prickly pear cactus, Texas' state plant, is found in the drier areas of south and central Texas. The fruit (tunas) it bears normally ripens and is ready for harvest from July to September. Tunas are eaten raw, while their juicy pulp is processed into preserves, syrups, fermented juice, or tea. Most of these items can be found in gourmet groceries, liquor stores, or online. There is a legend that the coyote brushes the spines off the fruit with his tail before consuming the fruit.

Mexitini

2 ounces silver/white tequila

1 ounce Cointreau

1 to 2 ounces Sprite

1 ounce orange juice without pulp

juice of ½ lime without pulp

margarita salt (optional)

2 or 3 jalapeño-stuffed olives

Combine the tequila, liqueur, soda, orange juice and lime juice in a cocktail shaker and shake to blend. Moisten the rim of a Mexican-style martini glass with the shell of the lime and dip the rim in margarita salt to cover.

Strain the cocktail into the salt-rimmed glass and garnish with the olives skewered on cactus-shaped swizzle picks or umbrella picks. Serves 1.

F*amilarize yourself with cocktail lingo.*

On the Rocks—*Over ice.*

Straight Up—*Stirred or shaken over ice and served in a chilled glass.*

Rocks on the Side—*You get the same rocks it was made in.*

Frozen—*A weaker but larger slushy-type cocktail.*

Neat—*It is not chilled but is served straight from the bottle and should be served in the appropriate glass.*

Mist—*Served over crushed ice.*

Shaken—*Made in a cocktail shaker.*

Frappé—*A cocktail made with a shaker or a mixing glass containing two-thirds ice. The drink changes color, density, and sometimes taste. Once the cocktail has been prepared, it is often necessary to filter it with a cocktail strainer.*

D*on't overdress a drink. If you manage to tantalize both the eye and the palate, you will have a successful cocktail.*

Bloody Mary

1 (32-ounce) bottle Bloody Mary mix
1 tablespoon horseradish
1 tablespoon Dijon mustard
5 dashes of Tabasco sauce
8 dashes of Worcestershire sauce
5 pinches of celery salt
8 twists from black pepper mill
juice of 5 lemon wedges
6 lime wedges
celery salt
9 ounces vodka or gin
6 pickled okra

Combine the Bloody Mary mix, horseradish, Dijon mustard, Tabasco sauce, Worcestershire sauce, 5 pinches of celery salt, the black pepper and lemon juice in a large pitcher and mix well.

For each serving, moisten the rim of a glass with 1 lime wedge and dip the rim in celery salt. Fill the celery salt-rimmed glass with ice, 1/6 of the Bloody Mary mixture and 1 1/2 ounces vodka and stir. Garnish with pickled okra. Serves 6.

Bloomer Droppers

3 ripe peaches, peeled and chopped
1 cup crushed ice
1 (6-ounce) can frozen pink lemonade
    concentrate
1 lemonade can vodka
1/4 teaspoon sugar

Combine the peaches, ice, lemonade concentrate, vodka and sugar in a blender and process until slushy. Pour into glasses and serve immediately. Serves 6.

Creative beverage garnishes attract drinkers. For sweet drinks, try fruits like pineapple, mango, and kiwifruit. Use pearl onions, cucumber slices, cherry tomatoes, stuffed olives, and sprigs of mint for more flavorful drinks. Creamy drinks can be garnished with a dusting of grated nutmeg or ground cinnamon. To craft a frosted rim, moisten the rim with water or lime juice and dip in sugar. For a colored rim, substitute a syrup or liqueur for the water or lime juice. For a salted rim, moisten with a lemon slice and dip in salt.

Classic Vodka Martini

1 tablespoon blue cheese or
    Gorgonzola cheese, softened
1/4 teaspoon heavy cream
1 pitted green olive
1 cup crushed ice
2 ounces vodka, chilled
1/4 ounce dry vermouth, chilled

Mix the cheese and heavy cream in a bowl and spoon into a sealable plastic bag. Seal the top and trim off 1 corner of the bag. Pipe the cheese mixture into the olive and chill in the refrigerator. Vary the olive stuffing according to taste.

Place 1/2 cup of the ice in a cocktail shaker and the remaining 1/2 cup ice in a martini glass. Pour the vodka and vermouth into the cocktail shaker and shake to mix. Discard the ice in the glass and strain the martini into the chilled glass. Garnish with 1 stuffed olive. Serves 1.

2 1/2 ounces peppermint schnapps
1 peppermint stick or miniature
    candy cane

PEPPERMINT MARTINI

Prepare the Classic Vodka Martini, substituting the peppermint schnapps for the vermouth and omitting the stuffed olive. Strain the martini into a chilled glass and garnish with the peppermint stick. This is a great version for the holidays!

2 ounces sour apple schnapps
2 ounces cranberry juice
1 unpeeled Red Delicious apple,
    cut into wedges
juice of 1 lemon

RED APPLETINI

Prepare the Classic Vodka Martini, substituting the schnapps and cranberry juice for the vermouth and omitting the stuffed olive. Strain the martini into a chilled glass. Garnish with apple slices tossed with lemon juice to prevent browning.

14

Cocktails should be cold, the colder the better. This makes shaking the preferred choice of mixing. It is easier to chill a drink by shaking than by stirring.

Vodka Freeze

1 fifth vodka

1 (32-ounce) bottle cranberry juice

1 (12-ounce) can frozen orange juice
   concentrate, thawed

1 (6-ounce) can frozen lemonade
   concentrate, thawed

1 (2-liter) bottle ginger ale, chilled

lemon or orange wedges

Combine the vodka, cranberry juice, orange juice concentrate and lemonade concentrate in a freezer container and mix well. Freeze, covered, for 1 1/2 hours. Remove and stir. When frozen, the mixture will remain slushy due to the alcohol content.

To serve, fill a highball glass 1/2 full with the slush mixture and top off with the ginger ale; stir. Garnish with a lemon or orange wedge and serve immediately. Serves 12.

White Wine Sangria

1 pound seedless watermelon,
   scooped into 1-inch balls

1/4 honeydew melon, cut into
   1-inch chunks

1 star fruit, seeded and sliced

1 cup seedless green grapes

1 kiwifruit, sliced

1 lime, seeded and sliced

1 pink grapefruit, seeded, sliced and
   cut into quarters

1 tablespoon superfine sugar

3 ounces Cointreau

3 ounces brandy

1 (750-milliliter) bottle fruity white
   wine, chilled

1 cup white cranberry juice

Combine the watermelon, honeydew melon, star fruit, grapes, kiwifruit, lime and grapefruit in a large container and mix gently. Sprinkle the sugar over the fruit and stir to combine. Stir in the liqueur and brandy. Let stand at room temperature for 1 hour.

Add the wine and cranberry juice to the watermelon mixture and mix well. Taste and add additional sugar if desired. Chill, covered, until serving time. Serves 4 to 6.

The wine is open, but the cork is broken or stuck. Gently push the cork into the wine so the wine does not splash out. This technique will not alter the flavor of the wine.

Nectarine Basil Lemonade

2 cups water

1 cup fresh basil leaves

1 nectarine, chopped

3/4 cup sugar, or to taste

1 1/2 cups water

1 nectarine, thinly sliced

1 cup fresh lemon juice

fresh basil leaves

Combine 2 cups water, 1 cup basil, 1 chopped nectarine and the sugar in a small saucepan and mix well. Bring to a boil and boil until the sugar dissolves, stirring occasionally. Reduce the heat and simmer for 5 minutes longer, stirring occasionally. Let stand until cool.

Strain the nectarine mixture through a fine sieve over a pitcher, pressing hard on the solids with the back of a spoon; discard the solids. Stir in 1 1/2 cups water, 1 sliced nectarine and the lemon juice. Pour the lemonade over ice in tall glasses and garnish each serving with fresh basil leaves. Makes 6 cups.

Photograph for this recipe on page 8.

16

Add a festive touch to any beverage by dropping in colorful ice cubes. Cut small edible flowers, such as pansies, violas, or miniature roses, from your garden or simply use petals from larger edible flowers. Fill an ice cube tray half full of water and place in the freezer until frozen. Remove the tray and place one flower in each of the cube cups. Top with enough water to cover the blossoms and freeze. Remove the cubes from the trays and use immediately in beverages. Otherwise, store in the freezer for unexpected guests.

Summer Lemonade

1 cup water

1 cup sugar

6 lemons, at room temperature

4 cups ice

4 cups cold water

6 to 8 teaspoons cherry juice

6 to 8 maraschino cherries

Bring 1 cup water to a boil in a saucepan. Reduce the heat and stir in the sugar. Cook until the sugar dissolves, stirring constantly. Let stand until cool.

Roll the lemons on the counter to release the juices. Cut the lemons into halves and squeeze the juice into a measuring cup until the juices measure just over 1 cup. Place the ice in a pitcher. Mix the cooled syrup and lemon juice in a bowl and pour over the ice in the pitcher along with the cold water. Pour the lemonade over ice in glasses. Stir 1 teaspoon of the cherry juice into each serving and garnish each with 1 cherry. If the lemons are cold, briefly microwave to bring to room temperature. Serves 6 to 8.

For *Lime Phosphate,* mix one can frozen lemonade or limeade concentrate using the can instructions and substituting club soda for the water.

Orange Frosty

1 (6-ounce) can frozen orange juice
   concentrate
1 cup whole or skim milk
1 cup water
1/3 to 1/2 cup sugar, or an equivalent
   amount of sugar substitute
1 teaspoon vanilla extract
12 ice cubes, cracked

Combine the orange juice concentrate, milk, water, sugar and vanilla in a blender and process at medium speed until blended. Add the ice gradually, processing constantly at high speed until slushy. Pour into glasses and serve immediately. Serves 4.

Sunshine Punch

2 cups water
1 1/2 cups sugar
1 (46-ounce) can pineapple juice
1 (12-ounce) can frozen orange juice
   concentrate, prepared
3 cups fresh lemon juice
3 liters lemon-lime soda, chilled

Bring the water and sugar to a boil in a saucepan and boil for 5 minutes, stirring occasionally. Cool slightly and pour the syrup into a bowl. Stir in the pineapple juice, orange juice and lemon juice and freeze. Beat until fluffy and refreeze.

Just before serving, spoon the frozen mixture into a punch bowl and pour the soda over the top. Ladle into punch cups. For variety, process 4 bananas in a blender until smooth and add to the punch mixture before freezing. Serves 25.

Holiday Party Punch

1 (28-ounce) can pineapple juice
1 (12-ounce) can frozen raspberry
   lemonade concentrate, thawed
1 (6-ounce) can frozen orange juice
   concentrate, thawed
4 cups cold water
2 liters ginger ale, chilled
Ice Ring

Combine the pineapple juice, raspberry lemonade concentrate, orange juice concentrate and cold water in a punch bowl. Add the ginger ale and ice ring just before serving. Ladle into punch cups.
Makes 50 (4-ounce) servings.

1 (64-ounce) can cranberry raspberry
   juice
1 (6-ounce) jar maraschino cherries,
   drained
fresh mint leaves

ICE RING

Fill a bundt pan with the juice. Add the cherries and mint leaves and freeze for 8 to 10 hours.

Cranberry Raspberry Punch

1 (16-ounce) package sliced
   sweetened strawberries, thawed
1 (12-ounce) can frozen lemonade
   concentrate, thawed
1 (11-ounce) can frozen cranberry
   raspberry juice concentrate,
   thawed
2 liters ginger ale, chilled
2 liters club soda, chilled
1 quart raspberry or orange sherbet

Process the strawberries, lemonade concentrate and cranberry raspberry juice concentrate in a blender until smooth. Pour the strawberry mixture into a punch bowl and gently stir in the ginger ale and club soda. Top with scoops of the sherbet and ladle into punch cups immediately.
Makes 5 quarts.

Ice molds create great party sculptures. Molds are reusable and available to fit any party theme. Fill the molds with water and freeze for forty-eight hours. They can also be filled with gelatin, ice cream, or other liquids for a quick and easy entertaining solution.

Lone Star Sweet Tea

1 quart water
8 tea bags
1¹/₂ cups sugar
1 (6-ounce) can frozen lemonade
   concentrate
3 quarts water

Bring 1 quart water to a boil in a saucepan. Remove from the heat and add the tea bags. Steep for 15 to 20 minutes and discard the tea bags. Add the sugar and lemonade concentrate to the tea and stir until the sugar dissolves.

Pour the tea mixture into a large container and add 3 quarts water. Chill until serving time. Pour the tea over ice in glasses.
Makes 16 (8-ounce) servings.

Morning Cooler

1 (48-ounce) bottle cranberry juice,
   chilled
3 cups fresh tangerine juice, chilled
¹/₂ cup fresh lime juice, chilled
¹/₂ bottle dry Champagne, chilled
   (optional)
2 unpeeled tangerines, cut into
   ¹/₄-inch slices

Combine the cranberry juice, tangerine juice and lime juice in a large glass pitcher and mix well. Fill tall glasses half full with the Champagne and top off with the juice mixture. Garnish each serving with a tangerine slice. Serves 4 to 6.

Freeze some portion of the liquid tea base in ice cube trays and add to your tea to prevent dilution. The same technique can be used with tonic water.

Appetizers

THE DISH ON DALLAS

Like most of Texas, the Metroplex prides itself on its Tex-Mex cuisine. Fresh tortillas, homemade chips, and tangy salsa are standards in local eateries. Dallacites actually consume more picante sauce than any other people in the United States. We follow up chips and salsa with a platter of sizzling chicken fajitas, a Tex-Mex specialty invented in Dallas.

Tomatillo and Avocado Salsa recipe on page 49.

Tomato Basil Bruschetta

1 loaf Italian bread, cut into
   ³/₄-inch slices
3 tablespoons olive oil
3 garlic cloves
salt and freshly cracked pepper
10 Roma tomatoes, chopped
¹/₂ cup fresh basil, chopped
2 tablespoons balsamic vinegar
1¹/₂ tablespoons white wine vinegar
1 tablespoon sugar
1 tablespoon minced garlic
¹/₄ teaspoon salt
¹/₄ teaspoon freshly cracked pepper

Preheat the broiler. Brush the bread slices with the olive oil and arrange in a single layer on a baking sheet. Broil for 1 to 2 minutes or until toasted. Rub the slices with the garlic cloves and season to taste with salt and pepper.

Mix the tomatoes, basil, balsamic vinegar, white wine vinegar, sugar, minced garlic, ¹/₄ teaspoon salt and ¹/₄ teaspoon pepper in a bowl. Spread some of the tomato mixture on the warm or room temperature toasted bread slices. Serves 12.

1 pound mixed wild mushrooms
3 garlic cloves, minced
¹/₄ cup (¹/₂ stick) butter
2 tablespoons bourbon
¹/₃ cup cream
2 ounces Gorgonzola cheese
¹/₂ cup chopped prosciutto
¹/₄ cup chopped fresh Italian parsley
¹/₂ cup (2 ounces) shredded
   Parmesan cheese
salt and pepper to taste

WILD MUSHROOM BRUSCHETTA

Toast the bread slices as directed above. Preheat the oven to 350 degrees. Sauté the mushrooms and garlic in the butter in a skillet over medium heat for 8 to 10 minutes. Stir in the bourbon and cook for 30 seconds, stirring constantly. Add the cream and bring to a boil, stirring occasionally.

Stir in the crumbled Gorgonzola cheese, prosciutto, parsley and Parmesan cheese. Remove from the heat and season to taste with salt and pepper. Top each toasted bread slice with some of the mushroom mixture and arrange in a single layer on a baking sheet. Bake for 5 minutes.

8 ounces goat cheese
3 tablespoons olive oil
1 teaspoon minced fresh basil
1 teaspoon minced fresh thyme
1 cup chopped tomatoes
¹/₃ cup chopped red onion
2 tablespoons olive oil
1 tablespoon cider vinegar
1 tablespoon minced jalapeño chile
1 tablespoon chopped fresh cilantro
1 garlic clove, minced
salt and pepper to taste

SOUTH-OF-THE-BORDER BRUSCHETTA

Toast the bread slices as directed above. Mix the goat cheese, 3 tablespoons olive oil, the basil and thyme in a bowl. For the **Pico de Gallo,** mix the tomatoes, onion, 2 tablespoons olive oil, the vinegar, jalapeño chile, cilantro, garlic, salt and pepper in a bowl. Spread each toasted bread slice with some of the goat cheese mixture and top with the Pico de Gallo.

Blue Cheese Popovers

1 cup all-purpose flour

$1/2$ teaspoon kosher salt

$1/8$ teaspoon freshly ground pepper

1 cup milk

2 eggs

2 tablespoons unsalted butter, melted

$1^1/4$ ounces blue cheese, crumbled

1 tablespoon chopped fresh thyme

Mix the flour, salt and pepper in a bowl. Add the milk, eggs and butter and whisk until smooth. Whisk in the cheese and thyme. Pour the batter into an airtight container and chill for 2 to 24 hours.

Preheat the oven to 425 degrees. Generously butter miniature muffin cups. Fill each cup to the top with the chilled batter. Bake for 15 to 18 minutes or until golden brown and puffed. Serve warm. Makes 1 dozen popovers.

Because the batter for Blue Cheese Popovers must be chilled before pouring into the muffin cups, prepare one day in advance. Unlike traditional popover recipes, this simple version requires no hot pans or hot oil. Though the rise and fall of these miniature popovers is less dramatic than that of the standard size popover, the low profile product is perfect as a vehicle for canapés. Try spreading with Smoked Salmon Spread on page 53 or top with beef tenderloin and a dollop of Arugula Mayonnaise on page 78.

Gorgonzola-Stuffed Endive

1/4 cup (1/2 stick) butter

1 pound walnuts

1/2 cup packed brown sugar

9 heads endive, separated into spears

1 pound Gorgonzola cheese, crumbled

1 red bell pepper, finely chopped

Dijon Vinaigrette

Heat the butter in a sauté pan over medium heat. Stir in the walnuts. Add the brown sugar and cook until the mixture is bubbly and the walnuts are coated and caramelized, stirring frequently. Remove the walnuts to a sheet of waxed paper and let stand until cool. Break into small pieces.

Arrange the endive spears on a flat serving platter or cake stand. Fill each spear with caramelized walnuts and a sprinkling of the cheese. Top with some of the bell pepper. Pour the Dijon Vinaigrette into a wide-tipped squeeze bottle and drizzle over the stuffed spears. Makes 50 to 60 stuffed spears.

DIJON VINAIGRETTE

1/4 cup red wine vinegar

1 tablespoon Dijon mustard

1 teaspoon sugar

1/2 teaspoon salt

1/2 teaspoon freshly ground pepper

minced fresh parsley to taste

snipped fresh chives to taste

1/2 cup olive oil

Whisk the vinegar, Dijon mustard, sugar, salt, pepper, parsley and chives in a bowl. Add the olive oil gradually, whisking constantly until incorporated. Taste and adjust the seasonings. You may prepare in a blender.

Pears with Goat Cheese and Prosciutto

Serve as an appetizer on a plate drizzled with a little more of the Garlic Parmesan Dressing or surround a bowl of the dressing with the pear wedges for a large gathering.

6 pears
goat cheese
24 paper-thin slices prosciutto
Garlic Parmesan Dressing

Cut the pears into halves. Remove the seeds and scoop out a well in the center of each half using a melon baller. Tightly pack the well with goat cheese. If prepared in advance, rub the cut surfaces of the pears with lemon juice, wrap in plastic wrap and chill.

To serve, cut each filled pear half into halves. Wrap each wedge with a strip of the prosciutto. Arrange the wedges on a platter and drizzle with the Garlic Parmesan Dressing. Makes 2 dozen.

GARLIC PARMESAN DRESSING

1 envelope Garlic Parmesan salad
    dressing mix
balsamic vinegar
$1/2$ teaspoon fresh lemon or lime juice
$1/2$ teaspoon brown or coarse
    mustard
$1/8$ teaspoon Worcestershire sauce
$1/16$ teaspoon sugar

Prepare the salad dressing mix in a jar with a tight-fitting lid using the package directions and substituting balsamic vinegar for the cider vinegar. Add the lemon juice, brown mustard, Worcestershire sauce and sugar to the dressing and shake to mix. Chill until thickened.

Marinated Olives

8 ounces Greek green olives, pitted

8 ounces kalamata olives, pitted

3 ribs celery, chopped

$1/2$ cup chopped yellow bell pepper

$1/2$ cup chopped red bell pepper

$1/4$ cup olive oil

$1/4$ cup white wine vinegar

1 tablespoon dried oregano

1 large garlic clove, minced

freshly cracked pepper to taste

Pita Chips

Mix the olives, celery and bell peppers in a bowl. Combine the olive oil, vinegar, oregano, garlic and pepper in a jar with a tight-fitting lid and seal tightly. Shake to mix and pour over the olive mixture.

Marinate, covered, at room temperature for 2 days, stirring occasionally. Chill, covered, until serving time. Serve alone or spooned over feta cheese with Pita Chips. For variety, process in a food processor until puréed and use as a tapenade. Serves 8.

Make your own **Pita Chips.** *Cut 6 pita rounds into halves to form 12 pockets total and split the pockets into halves. Heat 1 cup butter, $1/2$ cup margarine and 2 finely chopped garlic cloves in a saucepan until the butter and margarine melt, stirring occasionally. The margarine prevents the butter from burning when the pita chips are baked. If desired, use a mixture of $1/2$ butter and $1/2$ margarine. Brush the cut sides of the pita rounds with the butter mixture and cut each half into 2 wedges. Arrange the wedges in a single layer on a baking sheet and sprinkle with $1/2$ cup grated Parmesan cheese and salt to taste. Bake at 350 degrees for 12 to 15 minutes or until crisp and just beginning to brown. Store in an airtight container for up to 1 week. Makes 4 dozen chips.*

Vegetarian Spring Rolls

1 pound sliced white mushrooms

1 tablespoon butter or margarine

dried basil to taste

12 rice paper wrappers

2 large carrots, julienned

1 red onion, thinly sliced

1 bunch cilantro, trimmed

1 (2-inch) piece fresh ginger,
   julienned

leaves of 3/4 bunch fresh mint

leaves of 1 bunch fresh basil

Peanut Dipping Sauce (page 31)

Ginger Dipping Sauce (page 31)

Sauté the mushrooms in the butter in a skillet and sprinkle with dried basil. Pour hot water into a large bowl and lay a tea towel on a hard surface. Submerge 1 rice paper wrapper in the hot water and let stand for 30 seconds or until soft and pliable. Remove the wrapper and place on the tea towel. Pat the top of the wrapper with another tea towel to remove any excess moisture. Do not allow the wrappers to soak in the hot water too long, as they will become too soft and will tear easily when rolled.

Spread some of the sautéed mushroom mixture on the wrapper just below the center. Top with some carrots, a few slices of onion and some cilantro. Arrange 1 slice of ginger, 1 mint leaf and 1 basil leaf on each side of the center so that when you cut the spring roll into halves each half will contain 1 basil leaf, 1 mint leaf and 1 slice of ginger. Roll as tightly as possible to enclose the filling, tucking in the sides. Cut diagonally into halves.

Arrange the rolls on a serving platter and cover with damp paper towels until serving time; do not chill. Repeat the process with the remaining wrappers. Serve with the Peanut Dipping Sauce and/or the Ginger Dipping Sauce. Makes 12 spring rolls.

Ginger Dipping Sauce

1 cup (1/8-inch slices) green
   onion tops
1/2 cup soy sauce
1/2 cup Chinese black vinegar
2 teaspoons finely chopped
   fresh ginger
1 teaspoon red pepper flakes
1 teaspoon sugar

Combine the green onion tops, soy sauce, vinegar, ginger, red pepper flakes and sugar in a bowl and stir until the sugar dissolves. Use immediately or store, covered, in the refrigerator for up to 1 week. Serve with Vegetarian Spring Rolls on page 30, Chinese dumplings or egg rolls. Makes 2 cups.

Peanut Dipping Sauce

1 cup peanut butter
3/4 cup water
1/4 cup soy sauce
1/4 cup sesame oil
3 tablespoons rice vinegar
   (not seasoned)
2 tablespoons finely chopped garlic
2 tablespoons grated fresh ginger
2 tablespoons fresh lime juice
1 tablespoon hoisin sauce, or to taste
1 1/2 teaspoons Thai chili sauce, or
   1 teaspoon dried hot red
   pepper flakes

Combine the peanut butter, water, soy sauce, sesame oil, vinegar, garlic, ginger, lime juice, hoisin sauce and chili sauce in a blender or food processor and process until smooth. Store, covered, in the refrigerator for up to 1 week. Serve with Vegetarian Spring Rolls on page 30 or with grilled chicken. Makes 2 cups.

Shrimp 'n' Caper Bites

2¹/₂ pounds deveined peeled shrimp

¹/₂ cup chopped celery

¹/₄ cup pickling spice

3¹/₂ teaspoons salt

2 white onions, thinly sliced

7 or 8 bay leaves

1¹/₄ cups vegetable oil

³/₄ cup white vinegar

2¹/₂ tablespoons capers with juice

2¹/₂ teaspoons celery seeds

2 teaspoons salt

¹/₂ teaspoon white pepper

¹/₈ teaspoon Tabasco sauce

Combine the shrimp with enough boiling water to cover in a large saucepan. Add the celery, pickling spice and 3¹/₂ teaspoons salt. Cook for 6 minutes or until the shrimp turn pink. Drain and rinse with cold water to cool.

Layer the shrimp and onions in a shallow dish and top with the bay leaves. Mix the oil, vinegar, capers, celery seeds, 2 teaspoons salt, white pepper and Tabasco sauce in a jar with a tight-fitting lid and seal tightly. Shake to mix and pour over the shrimp mixture.

Marinate, covered, in the refrigerator for 24 hours or for up to 1 week. Discard the bay leaves and let stand at room temperature for 5 minutes before serving; stir. Serves 8 to 10.

Fried Green Tomatoes

Chef Gilbert Garza, owner and chef at Suze, operates a friendly neighborhood bistro specializing in simple, homemade meals. A local favorite, it was named as one of the "ten great places for a down-to-earth meal" in USA Today.

vegetable oil for frying

3 cups panko (Japanese bread crumbs)

2 tablespoons turmeric

2 tablespoons paprika

2 teaspoons cumin

3/4 cup milk

2 eggs

2 or 3 small to medium green tomatoes

salt and pepper to taste

2 cups all-purpose flour

shaved Spanish manchego cheese

Marinara Sauce (page 265)

Pour enough oil into a skillet to measure 1 to 2 inches and heat to 350 degrees. Mix the bread crumbs, turmeric, paprika and cumin in a shallow dish. Whisk the milk and eggs in a bowl until blended. Cut the tomatoes into 1/8-inch slices and sprinkle with salt and pepper.

Coat the tomatoes with the flour, shaking off the excess. Dip the slices in the egg wash and then in the seasoned bread crumbs until totally covered. Fry in the hot oil for 1 to 1 1/2 minutes; drain. Serve with cheese shavings and Marinara Sauce. Serves 2 to 3.

Sweet Tomato Tart

3 tablespoons Quick Herbed Mustard

1 Savory Tart Crust, baked and
    slightly cooled (page 272)

8 ounces Gruyère cheese,
    thinly sliced

6 ripe tomatoes, cut into 1/4-inch
    slices

3 tablespoons brown sugar

salt and pepper to taste

fresh basil leaves

Preheat the oven to 425 degrees. Spread the Quick Herbed Mustard over the bottom of the crust and layer with the cheese and tomatoes. Sprinkle with the brown sugar and season to taste with salt and pepper.

Bake for 15 to 20 minutes or until the crust is golden brown, the cheese is melted and the tomatoes are tender. Garnish with fresh basil. Substitute mozzarella cheese for the Gruyère cheese for a more Italian flavor. Great as an appetizer, but can also be served as a side dish (great with lamb), for lunch, or as a light supper. Serves 8 to 10.

QUICK HERBED MUSTARD

1 1/2 cups Dijon mustard

1/4 cup chopped fresh basil, mint,
    thyme, chives, marjoram, rosemary
    or other herbs of choice, or to taste

1 1/2 tablespoons dry white wine

Combine the Dijon mustard, basil and wine in a bowl and mix well. Spoon into a sterilized jar and seal with a 2-piece lid. Store in a cool dark environment for up to 3 months.

34

Chiquito Risotto

**3 cups vegetable or chicken stock
(page 261)**

2 tablespoons olive oil

1 garlic clove, crushed

1 cup arborio rice

1/4 cup dry white wine

**1/2 cup oil-pack sun-dried tomatoes,
cut into strips**

**salt and freshly ground pepper
to taste**

1/2 cup heavy cream

**1/2 cup (2 ounces) grated Parmesan
cheese**

2 tablespoons butter

3/4 cup fresh basil chiffonade

vegetable oil for deep-frying

**4 ounces mozzarella cheese,
cut into 1/4-inch cubes**

1/2 cup all-purpose flour

2 eggs, beaten

**2 cups fine white bread crumbs,
minced in blender and dried**

Bring the stock to a simmer in a saucepan. Heat the olive oil in a heavy saucepan and sauté the garlic in the hot oil just until tender. Stir in the rice and cook for 2 minutes or until the rice is coated and partially transparent and begins to make a clicking noise, stirring constantly. Add the wine and cook until the liquid is absorbed, stirring constantly.

Add 1 1/2 cups of the warm stock 1 ladle at a time, cooking until the stock is absorbed after each addition and stirring constantly. Stir in the tomatoes and season to taste with salt and pepper. Continue adding the remaining 1 1/2 cups of stock 1 ladle at a time, cooking until the stock is absorbed after each addition and stirring constantly. Stir in the heavy cream and cook until the rice is al dente. Remove from the heat and stir in the Parmesan cheese, butter and basil. Let stand, covered, for 3 minutes. Stir and taste, adjusting the seasonings if desired. Spread the risotto in a shallow dish and let stand until cool.

Preheat the oven to 200 degrees. Pour enough oil into a deep skillet to deep-fry and heat to 350 degrees. Shape the risotto 1 tablespoon at a time into 1-inch balls and mold each risotto ball around a cube of mozzarella cheese. Coat the risotto balls with the flour, dip in the eggs and coat with the bread crumbs. Fry in the hot oil for 2 to 3 minutes or until golden brown. If fried too quickly, the cheese will not melt. Drain on paper towels and keep warm in a 200-degree oven.
Makes 2 dozen risotto balls.

Steak Satay with Cilantro

12 wooden skewers

3 large garlic cloves

1/2 cup fresh cilantro

3 tablespoons soy sauce

2 tablespoons olive oil

2 tablespoons fresh lime juice

1 tablespoon hot sauce

1 1/4 teaspoons ground cumin

1 1/2 pounds flank or skirt steak

salt and pepper to taste

Soak the skewers in a bowl of water for 1 hour. Process the garlic in a blender or food processor until chopped. Add the cilantro, soy sauce, olive oil, lime juice, hot sauce and cumin and process until blended.

Preheat the grill. Trim the fat from the steak and slice diagonally across the grain into 1/2-inch strips. Toss the strips with the soy sauce mixture in a shallow dish and let stand for 10 minutes, turning once or twice. Thread the steak strips on the skewers and season to taste with salt and pepper.

Arrange the skewers on an oiled grill rack and grill for 2 to 4 minutes, turning once; do not overcook. Serve with Pepper Jam on page 55 as a dipping sauce. Serves 12.

Reuben Strudel

1 (10-ounce) package shredded
   cabbage
1 sweet onion, chopped
1 garlic clove, crushed
1/2 teaspoon caraway seeds
1/2 cup Thousand Island salad
   dressing
1/2 cup (1 stick) butter, melted
1/4 cup spicy brown mustard
16 sheets phyllo pastry, thawed
2 cups (8 ounces) shredded
   Swiss cheese
1 pound corned beef, thinly sliced
   and chopped (page 82)

Preheat the oven to 425 degrees. Sauté the cabbage, onion, garlic and caraway seeds in a large nonstick skillet coated with nonstick cooking spray for 4 minutes or until the cabbage wilts. Remove from the heat and stir in the dressing. Let stand until cool. Mix the butter and spicy brown mustard in a bowl.

Unroll the phyllo and remove 1 sheet of the pastry. Arrange the sheet on a hard surface with the short side facing you. Cover the remaining sheets with waxed paper and a damp tea towel to prevent drying out. Lightly brush the sheet with the butter mixture and carefully layer with another pastry sheet. Lightly brush with the butter mixture. Cut the stack lengthwise into thirds and then crosswise into thirds to make 9 equal rectangles.

Spoon equal portions (about 1 teaspoon each) of the cabbage mixture, cheese and corned beef 1 inch from the end of the short side of each rectangle, leaving a 1/2-inch border on the long sides. Fold 1/2 inch of the long sides over the filling and starting from the end with the filling, roll into a log. Arrange the log seam side down on a baking sheet sprayed with nonstick cooking spray. Repeat the process with the remaining phyllo, remaining butter mixture, remaining cabbage mixture, remaining cheese and remaining corned beef. Lightly coat the logs with nonstick cooking spray and bake for 8 to 12 minutes or until golden brown. Serve immediately. Makes 6 dozen.

Chicken Phyllo Pockets

1/4 cup light soy sauce

1/4 cup dry sherry

2 scallions, cut into 1/2-inch pieces

2 tablespoons Chinese oyster sauce

3 thin slices fresh ginger

1 tablespoon honey

3 star anise

4 boneless skinless chicken breasts

4 ounces phyllo pastry

1/2 cup (1 stick) butter, melted

Combine the soy sauce, sherry, scallions, oyster sauce, ginger, honey and star anise in a saucepan and mix well. Simmer for 5 minutes and add the chicken, turning to coat. Reduce the heat and simmer, covered, for 20 minutes; do not allow the mixture to become too dry. Remove the cover and simmer for 15 minutes longer, turning the chicken frequently to color evenly. Remove the chicken to a cutting board using a slotted spoon and cut crosswise into thin slices, reserving the sauce.

Preheat the oven to 425 degrees. Cut the phyllo sheets into 2×10- to 2×12-inch strips. For each pocket, brush 2 strips of the phyllo lightly with the butter. Arrange 2 or 3 slices of the chicken and a small amount of the reserved sauce in a corner of 1 of the strips. Fold the corner over the chicken to form a triangle (like a flag). Continue to fold in uniform triangles until the chicken is completely wrapped with the first strip of phyllo. Lay the wrapped chicken in the corner of the second strip of phyllo and repeat the folding process.

Arrange the triangles 2 inches apart on an ungreased baking sheet and bake for 12 to 15 minutes or until golden brown. Serve warm. The prepared triangles may be stored in the refrigerator for up to 24 hours prior to baking or in the freezer for up to 1 month before baking. Makes 3 dozen.

Poached Salmon with Horseradish Sauce

1 (1-pound) skinless salmon fillet,
  boned
2 to 3 cups water
1 to 2 cups white wine
juice of 2 lemons
1/2 cup mayonnaise
1/4 cup chopped fresh Italian parsley
3 shallots, minced
3 tablespoons drained capers
2 tablespoons white wine
1 tablespoon fresh lemon juice
1 garlic clove, minced
8 ounces smoked salmon, chopped
salt and pepper to taste
Horseradish Sauce

Arrange the salmon in a large skillet or fish poacher, adding just enough of the water and 1 to 2 cups of the wine to cover. Add the juice of 2 lemons. Bring to a gentle simmer and poach the salmon for 12 to 20 minutes or just until opaque. Drain, cool and flake with a fork.

Combine the mayonnaise, parsley, shallots, capers, 2 tablespoons wine, 1 tablespoon lemon juice and the garlic in a bowl and mix well. Fold in the poached salmon and smoked salmon and season to taste with salt and pepper. Serve with assorted party crackers and/or party pumpernickel bread along with the Horseradish Sauce on the side. Serves 10.

3/4 cup mayonnaise
1/4 cup sour cream
1/3 cup minced shallots
2 tablespoons drained capers
1 tablespoon chopped fresh
  Italian parsley
1 tablespoon chopped fresh
  horseradish
1 teaspoon fresh lemon juice
11/2 teaspoons coarsely ground
  pepper

HORSERADISH SAUCE

Combine the mayonnaise, sour cream, shallots, capers, parsley, horseradish, lemon juice and pepper in a bowl and mix well. Chill, covered, for 2 to 10 hours. The flavor is enhanced if chilled overnight.

Steamed Mussels with Chorizo

4 ounces prosciutto, chopped

4 ounces chorizo, linguiça or any dry
   hot sausage, sliced

2 tablespoons olive oil

2 onions, chopped

5 garlic cloves, minced

1 green bell pepper, chopped

2 bay leaves

2 teaspoons paprika

1/4 teaspoon crushed dried chile
   pepper flakes

1/4 teaspoon ground black pepper

1/4 teaspoon Tabasco sauce

2 (14-ounce) cans peeled whole
   tomatoes

2/3 cup dry white wine

4 dozen mussels in shells (farm-
   raised, beardless)

3 tablespoons chopped fresh
   Italian parsley

3 tablespoons chopped fresh cilantro

Sauté the prosciutto and chorizo in 1 tablespoon of the olive oil in a skillet. Remove the prosciutto mixture using a slotted spoon to paper towels to drain, reserving the pan drippings.

Heat the remaining 1 tablespoon olive oil with the reserved pan drippings. Sauté the onions, garlic and bell pepper in the hot oil until the onions are tender. Stir in the bay leaves, paprika, chile pepper flakes, black pepper and Tabasco sauce. Add the undrained tomatoes and 1/3 cup of the wine and mix well. Stir in the prosciutto mixture.

Simmer over medium heat, stirring occasionally. Add the remaining 1/3 cup wine and the mussels and stir until the mussels are covered by the sauce. Steam, covered, until the mussels open. Discard any unopened mussels and the bay leaves. Stir in the parsley and cilantro and ladle into large bowls. Provide extra bowls for discarded shells. Serves 4.

Photograph for this recipe on facing page.

Designer Crab Purses

24 green onion tops, cut into 3- to 4-inch strips

12 ounces fresh crab meat, drained and shells removed, or imitation crab meat

4 ounces fat-free cream cheese, softened

1/4 cup minced green onions

2 teaspoons fresh lemon juice

1 teaspoon grated fresh ginger

1/2 teaspoon hot sauce

1/4 teaspoon salt

1/8 teaspoon pepper

24 won ton wrappers

1 egg white, lightly beaten

2 tablespoons low-sodium soy sauce

1 tablespoon water

1 tablespoon fresh lemon juice

Add the green onion strips to a saucepan of boiling water and cook for 10 seconds or until limp; drain. Combine the crab meat, cream cheese, minced green onions, 2 teaspoons lemon juice, the ginger, hot sauce, salt and pepper in a bowl and mix well.

Remove 1 won ton wrapper at a time, covering the remaining wrappers with a damp tea towel to prevent drying out. For each purse, spoon about 2 teaspoons of the crab meat mixture in the center of the wrapper. Moisten the edges of the wrapper with the egg white, gather the corners of the wrapper and crimp to seal, forming a purse. Tie 1 green onion strip around the crimped top of each purse.

Arrange 1/2 of the purses in a single layer in a vegetable steamer coated with nonstick cooking spray. Steam, covered, for 8 minutes or until tender. Remove the purses from the steamer to a platter and cover to keep warm. Repeat the procedure with the remaining purses.

Mix the soy sauce, water and 1 tablespoon lemon juice in a small bowl and serve with the purses. The purses may be steamed up to 1 hour in advance and re-steamed just before serving. For variety, substitute ground pork for the crab meat. Steam for 8 minutes and then pan-fry in a small amount of vegetable oil until golden brown on 2 sides. Makes 2 dozen purses.

Crisp Scallops and Creamed Sweet White Corn

A Dallas retail giant for nearly a century, Neiman Marcus symbolizes luxury in fashion and cuisine. The first Neiman Marcus restaurant opened in 1953 and loyal guests have enjoyed it ever since. For over ten years, Vice President and Executive Chef Kevin Garvin has overseen the restaurant's celebrated dishes.

8 jumbo sea scallops

salt and pepper to taste

1 tablespoon olive oil

1 tablespoon chopped shallots

1/2 teaspoon minced garlic

2 cups fresh or frozen white corn kernels

2 cups heavy cream

2 cups coarsely chopped fresh spinach

1 teaspoon chopped fresh thyme

Asparagus, Fennel and Radish Salad

Preheat the oven to 350 degrees. Season the scallops on all sides with salt and pepper. Heat the olive oil in a skillet until smoking and add the scallops. Cook until crisp and golden brown on top and bottom. Remove the scallops to a baking sheet using a slotted spoon, reserving the pan drippings. Bake for 3 to 4 minutes.

Sauté the shallots and garlic in the reserved pan drippings for several seconds. Add the corn and continue to sauté for several minutes. Deglaze the skillet with the heavy cream. Cook until the mixture is creamy and thick, stirring frequently. Add the spinach, thyme, salt and pepper and cook until the spinach wilts.

To serve, spoon 1/4 of the corn mixture in the center of each of 4 serving plates and arrange 2 scallops over each serving. Top each with a spoonful of the Asparagus, Fennel and Radish Salad. Serves 4.

ASPARAGUS, FENNEL AND RADISH SALAD

1/2 bunch asparagus, diagonally cut into 1/2-inch pieces

1/2 fennel bulb, cut into thin strips

2 tablespoons olive oil

1 tablespoon chopped fresh parsley

salt and pepper to taste

4 radishes, thinly sliced and soaked in ice water

splash of fresh lemon juice

Preheat the oven to 325 degrees. Combine the asparagus, fennel, 1 tablespoon of the olive oil, the parsley, salt and pepper in a bowl and toss to combine. Spread the asparagus mixture on a baking sheet and bake for 4 minutes or until the vegetables are crisp. Let stand until cool.

Drain the radishes and mix with the asparagus mixture in a bowl. Add the remaining 1 tablespoon olive oil and the lemon juice and toss to combine. Season to taste with salt and pepper. Store, covered, at room temperature until serving time.

Shrimp Wrapped in Bacon with Jalapeño

Wendy Krispin is a local caterer and restaurant owner. Featured in the book, Texas Women: Trailblazers, Shining Stars & Cowgirls, *she is listed as a caterer to the cultural crowd, cowboys, corporations, and charities. This is her most requested appetizer.*

30 wooden picks

15 thin slices lean bacon,
    cut into halves

30 deveined peeled shrimp
    (16- to 20-count)

1 jalapeño chile, cut into the largest
    pieces you can stand

Soak the wooden picks in a bowl of water for 10 minutes. Preheat the grill. Preheat the oven to 350 degrees. Wrap 1 bacon slice around 1 shrimp and 1 piece of jalapeño chile and secure with a wooden pick.

Arrange the bacon-wrapped shrimp on an oiled grill rack and grill each side until the shrimp are no longer gray. You may prepare up to this point and store in the refrigerator until just before serving or freeze for future use. Arrange the shrimp on a baking sheet and bake until the bacon is crisp and the shrimp are pink. Makes 30 appetizers.

Grilled Shrimp with Basil Pistachio Sauce

32 to 40 wooden skewers

2 pounds large shrimp, peeled and
 deveined (26/40 count)

vegetable oil

salt and freshly ground pepper
 to taste

Basil Pistachio Sauce

Soak the skewers in a bowl of water. Preheat the grill or heat a lightly oiled grill pan on high. Brush the shrimp with oil and sprinkle with salt and pepper. Thread the shrimp on the skewers and arrange on a grill rack or on a grill pan.

Grill for 1 to 2 minutes per side or until lightly charred or pink. The shrimp should be just cooked through. Serve hot with the Basil Pistachio Sauce for dipping. Serves 8.

BASIL PISTACHIO SAUCE

$1/4$ cup unsalted pistachios

$3/4$ cup coarsely chopped fresh basil

$1/4$ cup coarsely chopped fresh mint

$1/4$ cup extra-virgin olive oil

1 tablespoon fresh lime juice

1 tablespoon rice vinegar

$1/4$ teaspoon dry mustard

$1/16$ teaspoon (heaping) cayenne
 pepper

$1/2$ cup (about) ice water

salt and freshly ground black pepper
 to taste

Preheat the oven to 400 degrees. Spread the pistachios in a single layer on a baking sheet and toast for 5 minutes or until light brown. Remove to a plate and let stand until cool.

Combine the pistachios, basil, mint, olive oil, lime juice, vinegar, dry mustard and cayenne pepper in a food processor and process until puréed. Add the ice water until of the desired dipping consistency, processing constantly. Taste and season with salt and black pepper.

Chill, covered, for up to 2 days. Bring to room temperature before serving. Whisk the sauce and add additional water if needed for the desired consistency.

Hot Feta Artichoke Dip

1 (14-ounce) can artichoke hearts,
   drained and chopped
1 cup crumbled feta cheese
1 cup mayonnaise
$1/2$ cup (2 ounces) shredded
   Parmesan cheese
1 (4-ounce) jar diced pimentos,
   drained
1 garlic clove, minced
2 tablespoons chopped fresh tomato
2 tablespoons sliced green onions

Preheat the oven to 350 degrees. Combine the artichokes, feta cheese, mayonnaise, Parmesan cheese, pimentos and garlic in a bowl and mix well. Spread the artichoke mixture in a 9-inch baking dish and bake for 20 to 25 minutes or until light brown. Sprinkle with the tomato and green onions and serve warm with assorted party crackers and/or pita bread.

You may prepare 1 day in advance and store, covered, in the refrigerator. Bake at 350 degrees for 30 to 35 minutes or until light brown just before serving. Serves 6 to 10.

Texas Two-Step Guacamole

2 very ripe large avocados
2 or 3 Roma tomatoes, blanched,
   peeled, seeded and chopped
$1/4$ cup finely chopped red onion
2 serrano chiles, seeded and minced
2 garlic cloves, minced
1 tablespoon chopped fresh cilantro
juice of 1 small lime
salt to taste

Mash the avocados in a bowl with a potato masher or large fork. Fold in the tomatoes, onion, serrano chiles, garlic, cilantro and lime juice. Season to taste with salt and serve with assorted chips. Makes 2 cups.

Avocado Feta Salsa

1 large avocado, chopped

2 plum tomatoes, chopped

1/4 cup minced purple onion

1 garlic clove, minced

1 tablespoon olive oil

1 tablespoon chopped fresh parsley

1 1/2 teaspoons red wine vinegar

1/2 teaspoon chopped fresh oregano

2 ounces feta cheese, crumbled

salt to taste

Combine the avocado and tomatoes in a bowl and mix gently. Add the onion, garlic, olive oil, parsley, vinegar and oregano and toss to mix. Fold in the cheese and season to taste with salt.

Serve immediately with chips or over burgers, pasta, grilled fish or grilled chicken. Makes 2 cups.

Monterey Jack Cilantro Salsa

1 cup (4 ounces) shredded Monterey
   Jack cheese

1 (4-ounce) can chopped green
   chiles, drained

1 (2-ounce) can chopped olives,
   drained

3 or 4 green onions, chopped

2 tomatoes, chopped

1 bunch cilantro, trimmed and
   chopped

1/2 to 3/4 cup Italian salad dressing

Combine the cheese, green chiles, olives, green onions, tomatoes and cilantro in a bowl and mix well. Add the dressing until the desired consistency and mix well.

Let stand, covered, at room temperature for 1 to 2 hours before serving. Serve with tortilla chips. Serves 4 to 6.

Fiesta Salsa

2 ears of unhusked corn

2 tomatoes, seeded and chopped

2 firm ripe avocados, coarsely
   chopped

1 zucchini, seeded and chopped

$1/2$ cup chopped red onion

$1/2$ cup smooth salsa

$1/4$ cup chopped fresh cilantro

juice of 2 limes

1 serrano chile, finely chopped

2 tablespoons vegetable oil

$3/4$ teaspoon garlic salt

$1/4$ teaspoon ground cumin

Preheat the grill. Discard the outer husks from the corn and loosen the silk without removing. Dip the ears in water and arrange directly on a grill rack.

Grill for 15 minutes. Remove from the grill and discard the silk. Cut the kernels from the cob into a bowl using a sharp knife. Add the tomatoes, avocados, zucchini and onion to the corn and mix well.

Combine the salsa, cilantro, lime juice, serrano chile, oil, garlic salt and cumin in a bowl and mix well. Add the salsa mixture to the tomato mixture and toss gently. Chill, covered, for 3 to 4 hours, stirring occasionally. Serve with tortilla chips. Serves 4 to 6.

Tomatillo and Avocado Salsa

1 or 2 serrano chiles

9 small tomatillos, husks removed

$1/2$ bunch cilantro, trimmed and
　　coarsely chopped

2 garlic cloves

1 pickled jalapeño chile

1 tablespoon pickled jalapeño
　　chile liquid

salt to taste

2 avocados, cut into $1/2$-inch chunks

$1/2$ cup finely chopped white
　　Mexican onion

Fill a medium saucepan $3/4$ full of water and bring to a boil. Add the serrano chiles to the boiling water and boil for 5 minutes. Add the tomatillos to the boiling water and boil for 5 minutes longer; drain. Remove the stems from the serrano chiles.

Combine the serrano chiles, tomatillos, cilantro, garlic, jalapeño chile and jalapeño chile liquid in a food processor and process until puréed. Taste and season with salt. Chill, covered, until serving time. Stir in the avocados and onion just before serving and serve with tortilla chips. Serves 8.

Photograph for this recipe on page 22.

Cheese Ball

1 cup chopped pecans, toasted
   (page 268)
1/2 cup chopped fresh flat-leaf parsley
16 ounces cream cheese, softened
16 ounces sharp Cheddar cheese,
   shredded
6 ounces blue cheese, crumbled
1 cup finely chopped green onions
1 tablespoon Worcestershire sauce

Reserve 1/2 cup of the pecans and 1/4 cup of the parsley for the garnish. Combine the remaining 1/2 cup pecans, remaining 1/4 cup parsley, the cream cheese, Cheddar cheese, blue cheese, green onions and Worcestershire sauce in a food processor and pulse until combined and the mixture forms a ball. Coat with the reserved 1/2 cup pecans and the reserved 1/4 cup parsley. Chill, wrapped tightly with plastic wrap, for 4 to 10 hours. Serve with assorted party crackers. Serves 15 to 20.

1 (9-ounce) jar chutney
8 ounces bacon, crisp-cooked
   and crumbled
3/4 cup currants or raisins
11/2 tablespoons curry powder
1 cup shredded coconut, toasted

CHUTNEY CHEESE BALL

Reserve 4 ounces of the chutney. Combine the remaining chutney, bacon, currants, curry powder and Cheese Ball ingredients in a food processor and process as directed above. Coat with the reserved chutney and roll in the coconut, omitting 1/2 cup pecans and 1/4 cup parsley for garnish. Chill as directed above.

50

6 tablespoons Worcestershire sauce
1/4 cup brandy
2 teaspoons hot sauce
1/2 teaspoon celery salt
1/2 teaspoon garlic salt
flour tortillas (optional)

BRANDY CHEESE BALL

Combine the Worcestershire sauce, brandy, hot sauce, celery salt, garlic salt and Cheese Ball ingredients in a food processor and process as directed above. Chill as directed above, coating with the reserved pecans and reserved parsley. For a Texas twist, spread the cheese mixture on flour tortillas and roll to enclose the filling. Wrap tightly in plastic wrap and chill. Cut each roll diagonally into slices and dip 1 of the cut sides in the reserved parsley, omitting 1/2 cup pecans for garnish.

Reinvent this classic appetizer by molding the cheese ball into an updated shape. Press the cheese mixture into a springform pan or fluted tart pan lined with plastic wrap or baking parchment and chill. Invert onto a large serving platter or cake stand. Smooth the edge with a knife heated under hot tap water and sprinkle with the reserved pecans and reserved parsley. This is a much easier way for guests to enjoy an old favorite.

Avocado Caviar Mousse

2 envelopes unflavored gelatin

$1/2$ cup warm water

5 hard-cooked eggs, chopped (page 262)

1 cup chopped green onions

$1/2$ cup mayonnaise

$1/4$ cup chopped fresh parsley

salt and pepper to taste

1 large avocado, mashed

1 large avocado, chopped

1 small onion, finely chopped

3 tablespoon mayonnaise

2 tablespoons fresh lemon juice

1 cup sour cream

$1/4$ cup minced onion

4 to 6 ounces red or black caviar

Dissolve the gelatin in the warm water in a bowl. Combine the eggs, green onions, $1/2$ cup mayonnaise and the parsley with 2 tablespoons of the gelatin mixture in a bowl and mix well. Season to taste with salt and pepper and spread the egg mixture in a 9- or 10-inch springform pan sprayed with nonstick cooking spray.

Combine the avocados, 1 chopped onion, 3 tablespoons mayonnaise and the lemon juice in a bowl with 2 tablespoons of the remaining gelatin mixture and mix well. Spread the avocado mixture over the prepared layer.

Combine the sour cream, $1/4$ cup onion and the remaining gelatin mixture in a bowl and spread over the prepared layers. Chill for 6 to 10 hours. Unmold onto a serving platter and top with the caviar just before serving. Serve with melba toast rounds or assorted crackers. Serves 20 to 25.

51

Ripe avocados feel firm and give slightly to the touch. If not used within two days of purchase, they will spoil. Store under-ripe avocados at room temperature. To peel, cut avocados lengthwise into halves and scoop out the pit using a large spoon. When making guacamole, scoop the avocado out from the skin. To slice for salads or sandwiches, slice lengthwise, being careful not to cut through the skin. Run the knife under the slices and cut away from the skin. To prevent discoloration, lay plastic wrap directly on guacamole or sprinkle citrus juice over avocado slices.

Sun-Dried Tomato Spread

11 ounces goat cheese, crumbled

4 ounces cream cheese, softened

1/2 cup chopped sun-dried tomatoes

1/2 cup chopped pitted kalamata olives

3 tablespoons finely chopped fresh basil

2 tablespoons olive oil

1 tablespoon balsamic vinegar

1 tablespoon drained capers

Mix the goat cheese and cream cheese in a bowl and form the cheese mixture into the desired shape. Arrange on a serving platter.

Combine the sun-dried tomatoes, olives, basil, olive oil, vinegar and capers in a bowl and mix well. Spoon the tomato mixture over the cheese mixture and serve with assorted party crackers and/or sliced baguette. Serves 12.

Smoked Salmon Spread

8 ounces smoked salmon, chopped

1/2 cup minced red onion

1/2 cup sour cream

1/4 cup mayonnaise

1 tablespoon drained capers

2 teaspoons chopped fresh dill weed

freshly ground pepper to taste

chopped fresh parsley to taste

Combine the salmon, onion, sour cream, mayonnaise, capers and dill weed in a bowl and mix well. Spoon the salmon spread into a serving dish and sprinkle with pepper and parsley. Serve with melba toast rounds. Serves 6 to 8.

Camembert Pastry Platter

1/4 cup (1/2 stick) butter

1 cup walnut halves

1/2 cup packed light brown sugar

1/3 cup granulated sugar

1 (17-ounce) package frozen puff
   pastry, thawed in the refrigerator

1 (8-ounce) Camembert cheese
   wheel, cut horizontally into halves

3 tablespoons apricot jam

1 egg, beaten

1 teaspoon milk

2 green or Bosc pears, cut into
   thin wedges

2 ripe red d'Anjou pears, cut into
   thin wedges

3 tablespoons fresh lemon juice

8 ounces Gorgonzola cheese,
   crumbled

Preheat the oven to 350 degrees. Heat the butter in a medium saucepan over medium-high heat. Add the walnuts, brown sugar and granulated sugar to the melted butter and cook for 2 to 3 minutes or until caramelized, stirring constantly. Spread the walnuts on a sheet of waxed paper and let stand until cool.

Lay the pastry sheets on a large sheet of baking parchment and roll gently with a rolling pin until slightly flat. Place the bottom half of the Camembert cheese wheel in the center of 1 sheet of the pastry. Spread the jam over the cut side of the cheese and sprinkle with 3 tablespoons of the caramelized walnuts. Top with the remaining Camembert cheese half. Bring the 4 corners of the pastry up to the center and pinch the seams to seal. Remove to a baking sheet.

Cut leaves of various sizes from the remaining pastry sheet using decorative cutters or use a sharp knife and create your own shapes. Arrange the pastry leaves on the top of the pastry. Shape a few small pieces of the pastry into 1/4-inch balls to resemble acorns and arrange these at the center. Brush with a mixture of the egg and milk.

Bake for 40 minutes or until golden brown. Tent with foil to prevent overbrowning if needed. Cool for 5 minutes and remove to a large decorative platter. You may freeze before baking for future use. Increase the baking time to 55 minutes.

Arrange the pears around the baked cheese wheel. Drizzle the lemon juice over the pears and sprinkle with the remaining caramelized walnuts and Gorgonzola cheese. Tuck shortbread cookies, wheat crackers and/or water crackers along the edge of the platter and serve immediately. Serves 12 to 15.

Pepper Jam

3 red bell peppers, minced

3 green bell peppers, minced

3 yellow bell peppers, minced

6 fresh jalapeño chiles, seeded
and minced

6^1/$_2$ cups sugar

1^1/$_2$ cups white vinegar

6 ounces liquid pectin

Combine the bell peppers, jalapeño chiles, sugar and vinegar in a 6-quart saucepan and mix well. Bring to a hard rolling boil and boil for 1 minute. Stir in the pectin and return the mixture to a full rolling boil. Boil for 1 minute, stirring constantly.

Remove the jam mixture from the heat and skim the foam from the top. Immediately pour into hot sterilized jars, leaving a ^{1}/$_8$-inch headspace. Wipe the rims of the jars with a clean cloth and seal with 2-piece lids.

Invert the jars for 5 minutes and then turn upright. Let stand until cool. Check the seals by pressing the middle of the lid with your finger. If the lid springs up when your finger releases the lid, it is not sealed. You can also use the USDA water bath method. Refer to page 133 for canning instructions. Makes 6 to 8 (^{1}/$_2$-pint) jars.

Artichoke Stuffed with Brie

1 artichoke
2 ounces Brie cheese, cut into
   1/2-inch chunks
Whole Grain Mustard Sauce

Remove the stem of the artichoke to form a flat base and cut off approximately 1/4 to 1/3 of the top. Snip off the prickly tips of the leaves with kitchen scissors. Cook the artichoke in boiling water in a saucepan for 10 to 15 minutes or until the bottom is easily pierced with a fork. Drain and rinse with cold water to stop the cooking process.

Preheat the oven to 350 degrees. Scrape out the fuzzy choke and stuff the cheese in the artichoke and throughout the leaves. Place the artichoke on a baking sheet and bake for 10 minutes or until the cheese melts. Remove the artichoke to a serving plate and drizzle with the warm Whole Grain Mustard Sauce. Serves 2.

WHOLE GRAIN MUSTARD SAUCE

1/2 cup white wine
1 tablespoon chopped shallots
1 cup (2 sticks) butter, cut into
   1/4-inch slices
2 ounces whole grain mustard
1 tablespoon white wine vinegar
fresh lemon juice to taste
salt and pepper to taste

Combine the wine and shallots in a saucepan and cook over high heat until the shallots are tender, stirring occasionally. Add the butter gradually, stirring constantly. Remove from the heat and stir in the mustard, vinegar and lemon juice. Season to taste with salt and pepper.

Hot Onion Soufflé

1 (12-ounce) package frozen chopped
   onions, thawed
1 small onion, chopped
16 ounces cream cheese, softened
2 cups (8 ounces) grated Parmesan
   cheese
1/2 cup mayonnaise

Preheat the oven to 350 degrees. Pat the frozen onions dry with a paper towel. Combine the thawed frozen onions, 1 small onion, the cream cheese, Parmesan cheese and mayonnaise in a bowl and mix well.

Spoon the onion mixture into a baking dish and bake for 20 to 30 minutes or until heated through. Serve with assorted party crackers and/or party bread. Serves 25.

Onions outsell all other Texas crops. Most varieties of this extremely sweet onion arrived in the Lone Star State as early as 1898 from Bermuda.

Soups & Sandwiches

THE DISH ON DALLAS

Americans consume nearly three hundred million sandwiches a day. For Dallacites, the variety is wide, from chicken parmigiana subs and the traditional Cuban sandwich to the classic deli Reuben. One interesting note, in a poll of four hundred food writers from across the country, one of the top two burgers in the country is found in the Metroplex at Kincade's.

Fire and Ice Tomato Soup with Dainty BLTs recipe on page 69.

Farmer's Market Berry Soup

2 cups fresh raspberries

2 cups fresh strawberry halves

$1/2$ cup 100% cranberry
raspberry juice

$1/2$ cup sugar

$1/2$ cup dry white wine

$1/8$ teaspoon ground cinnamon

1 cup low-fat strawberry yogurt

1 cup fresh blueberries

2 teaspoons sugar

2 teaspoons 100% cranberry
raspberry juice

Combine the raspberries, strawberries and $1/2$ cup juice in a blender and process until puréed. Taste and add $1/2$ (or less) of the sugar for desired sweetness. Strain the raspberry mixture through a sieve into a medium saucepan, discarding the solids. Stir in the wine, remaining sugar and the cinnamon and bring to a boil over medium heat, stirring occasionally.

Cook for 2 minutes and remove from the heat. Pour the soup into a heatproof bowl and chill, covered, for 3 hours or longer. Stir in the yogurt.

Process the blueberries, 2 teaspoons sugar and 2 teaspoons juice in a blender until puréed. Strain the blueberry mixture through a sieve into a bowl, discarding the solids. Ladle the soup into 4 soup bowls and drizzle each serving with 1 tablespoon of the blueberry mixture. Serves 4.

Carrot Bisque

6 tablespoons butter

2 pounds small carrots, cut into
    halves or thirds

3 onions, chopped

2¹/₂ teaspoons ground ginger

1 tablespoon grated orange zest

¹/₂ teaspoon ground coriander

5 cups chicken broth

1 cup half-and-half

salt and pepper to taste

minced fresh parsley to taste

Melt the butter in a Dutch oven or stockpot over medium heat and stir in the carrots and onions. Cook, covered, for 15 minutes or just until the vegetables begin to soften, stirring occasionally. Stir in the ginger, orange zest and coriander. Add 2 cups of the broth and reduce the heat to medium-low.

Simmer, covered, for 30 to 40 minutes or until the carrots are tender, stirring occasionally. Process the carrot mixture in batches in a food processor until puréed. Return the purée to the Dutch oven and add the remaining 3 cups broth and the half-and-half. Season to taste with salt and pepper and bring to a slow boil. Ladle into soup bowls and sprinkle with parsley. Serves 6.

Authentic Texas Chili

3 or 4 beef round steaks,
   bone in if possible
1 onion, finely chopped
1 garlic clove, minced
1 (8-ounce) can tomato sauce
1 cup tomato soup
1 cup water
3 tablespoons chili powder
1 tablespoon salt
1 tablespoon paprika
1/2 teaspoon freshly ground
   black pepper
1/4 teaspoon ground cumin
1/4 teaspoon cayenne pepper
1/4 to 1/3 cup masa
1/2 cup water

Trim the fat from the beef and cut into 1/4-inch pieces. Sauté the beef in a large saucepan. Add the onion and garlic and cook until the onion is tender, stirring frequently. Stir in the tomato sauce, soup, water, chili powder, salt, paprika, black pepper, cumin and cayenne pepper.

Simmer, covered, for 1 hour, stirring occasionally; remove the cover. Simmer until the excess moisture evaporates and the beef is tender; do not allow the mixture to become too dry. Mix the flour and water in a bowl until blended and add to the chili. Cook for 5 to 10 minutes longer or until thickened, stirring frequently. Ladle into chili bowls.
Makes 2 quarts.

Steak and Big Bean Chili with Homemade Biscuits

2 pounds beef chuck steak, cut into
  $1/4$-inch cubes
$1/2$ teaspoon salt
2 tablespoons vegetable oil
1 (18-ounce) can onion soup
1 (45-ounce) can kidney beans,
  drained
1 (28-ounce) can tomato sauce
  or purée
1 (12-ounce) can cola (not diet)
1 (6-ounce) can tomato paste
1 tablespoon chili powder
2 teaspoons ground cumin
2 teaspoons baking cocoa
$1/2$ teaspoon pepper
Homemade Biscuits

Season the steak with the salt and brown on all sides in the oil in a skillet. Drain and place the steak in a slow cooker. Process the soup in a blender for 1 minute and pour over the steak. Add the beans, tomato sauce, soda, tomato paste, chili powder, cumin, baking cocoa and pepper to the slow cooker and mix well.

Simmer on Low for 6 hours or on High for 2 hours, stirring occasionally. Ladle into chili bowls and serve with the Homemade Biscuits. For **Chili Mac,** spoon the chili over hot cooked noodles and sprinkle with cheese and minced onion. Serves 4 to 6.

HOMEMADE BISCUITS

2 cups milk
$1/2$ cup vegetable shortening
$1/2$ cup (scant) sugar
1 teaspoon salt
1 envelope dry yeast
$1/2$ cup warm water
5 to 6 cups all-purpose flour

Scald the milk in a saucepan. Add the shortening, sugar and salt to the scalded milk and stir until blended. Cool to 130 degrees. Dissolve the yeast in the warm water and stir. Add the yeast mixture to the cooled milk mixture and mix well. Add the flour gradually, stirring until the mixture forms a ball.

Let rise, covered, in a warm environment until doubled in bulk and knead. Pat or roll the dough $1/2$ inch thick and cut with a round cutter. Fold the rounds over and arrange in a greased round or oblong baking dish. Let rise until doubled in bulk.

Preheat the oven to 400 degrees and bake for 10 minutes or until light brown. Serve immediately.

Wicked White Chili

2 pounds boneless chicken breasts

1 tablespoon olive oil

2 onions, chopped

4 garlic cloves, minced

2 (4-ounce) cans chopped mild green
  chiles, drained

2 teaspoons ground cumin

1¹/₂ teaspoons dried oregano

¹/₄ teaspoon ground cloves

¹/₄ teaspoon cayenne pepper

3 (15-ounce) cans Great Northern
  beans, drained

1 (14-ounce) can chicken broth

3 cups (12 ounces) shredded
  Monterey Jack cheese

salt and black pepper to taste

sour cream

salsa

chopped fresh cilantro

Combine the chicken with enough cold water to generously cover in a large heavy saucepan. Simmer, covered, for 15 minutes or until cooked through. Drain and let stand until cool. Chop the chicken, discarding the skin.

Heat the olive oil in a large saucepan over medium-high heat. Sauté the onions in the hot oil for 10 minutes or until tender. Stir in the garlic, green chiles, cumin, oregano, cloves and cayenne pepper. Sauté for 2 minutes. Add the beans and broth and bring to a boil. Reduce the heat and simmer for 45 minutes, stirring occasionally. You may prepare to this point up to 1 day in advance and store, covered, in the refrigerator. Bring to a simmer before continuing the recipe.

Add the chicken and 1 cup of the cheese to the bean mixture and mix well. Simmer until the cheese melts, stirring frequently. Season to taste with salt and black pepper and ladle into chili bowls. Serve with the remaining 2 cups cheese, sour cream, salsa and cilantro. Serves 8.

Crawfish and Corn Chowder

1/2 cup vegetable oil

1/2 cup all-purpose flour

1 onion, finely chopped

1 red bell pepper, chopped

1 tablespoon minced garlic

1 (17-ounce) can cream-style corn

1 (16-ounce) can whole kernel corn,
   drained

2 pounds crawfish tails

1 quart half-and-half

1 (11-ounce) can tomatoes with
   green chiles

1 potato, chopped

1 teaspoon salt

black pepper to taste

cayenne pepper to taste

Whisk the oil and flour in a heavy saucepan until blended. Cook over medium-low heat until the roux is the color of light brown peanut butter, stirring constantly. Add the onion, bell pepper and garlic and cook for 3 to 5 minutes, stirring constantly. Add the corn and crawfish tails and mix well.

Cook for 3 minutes, stirring frequently. Stir in the half-and-half, tomatoes with green chiles, potato and salt and cook over medium heat until the chowder begins to thicken and the potato is tender, stirring occasionally. Season to taste with black pepper and cayenne pepper and ladle into soup bowls. Serves 10 to 12.

Three-Mushroom Soup

6 ounces button mushrooms, sliced

6 ounce shiitake mushrooms, sliced

6 ounces portobello mushrooms,
  sliced

1 onion, finely chopped

6 tablespoons butter, melted

1/4 cup all-purpose flour

3 cups chicken broth (page 261)

2 cups half-and-half

1/2 cup dry sherry

1 teaspoon salt

1/4 teaspoon angostura bitters

1/8 teaspoon white pepper

Sauté the mushrooms and onion in the butter in a heavy saucepan over low heat until tender. Add the flour and stir until combined. Cook for 1 minute, stirring constantly. Add the broth gradually, stirring constantly.

Cook over medium heat until thickened and bubbly, stirring constantly. Reduce the heat to low and stir in the half-and-half, sherry, salt, angostura bitters and white pepper. Cook just until heated through, stirring frequently. Ladle into bowls and serve immediately. Makes 1 1/2 quarts.

Thick-as-Fog Pea Soup

1 (16-ounce) package dried green
  split peas

2 quarts water

2 (14-ounce) cans chicken broth

3 or 4 red potatoes, peeled and
  chopped

2 or 3 onions, chopped

2 or 3 carrots, peeled and chopped

1 ham bone

1/4 teaspoon dried tarragon

1/4 teaspoon dried thyme

1/4 teaspoon ground celery seeds

2 cups chopped cooked ham

salt and pepper to taste

Sort and rinse the peas. Combine the peas, water and broth in a Dutch oven or stockpot and bring to a boil. Cook, covered, for 5 minutes. Add the potatoes, onions, carrots, ham bone, tarragon, thyme and celery seeds and return to a boil. Reduce the heat.

Simmer, covered, for 1 1/2 to 2 1/2 hours or until the peas are tender and the soup has thickened, stirring occasionally. Discard the ham bone and stir in the chopped ham. Season to taste with salt and pepper and simmer for 15 to 20 minutes longer. Ladle into soup bowls and serve with hot crusty French bread. Serves 6.

Butternut Squash Bisque with Lobster Dumplings

Chef Stephen Pyles

5 slices bacon, chopped

2 butternut squash, peeled, seeded and coarsely chopped

1/2 cup packed brown sugar

2 teaspoons chopped fresh Italian parsley

2 teaspoons chopped fresh chives

salt and pepper to taste

4 cups lobster stock, heated

2 cups heavy cream

1/2 cup (1 stick) butter

Lobster Dumplings

Preheat the oven to 500 degrees. Cook the bacon in a Dutch oven over medium heat for 5 minutes. Stir in the squash, brown sugar, parsley and chives and season to taste with salt and pepper. Bake, covered with foil, for 30 minutes. Remove the foil and bake for 15 minutes longer.

Heat the heavy cream in a saucepan until reduced by 1/2. Process the squash mixture, lobster stock and heavy cream 1/2 at a time in a blender until puréed. Pour the purée into a saucepan and add the butter. Season to taste with salt and simmer just until heated through, stirring occasionally. Ladle into soup bowls and serve with the Lobster Dumplings. Serves 6 to 8.

1 tablespoon olive oil

3 garlic cloves, minced

1 shallot, minced

1/3 cup cremini mushrooms, chopped

1 (8-ounce) lobster, steamed, meat removed and chopped

2 teaspoons unsalted butter

1 teaspoon chopped fresh Italian parsley

1 teaspoon chopped fresh chives

salt and pepper to taste

1 egg

1 tablespoon water

16 won ton wrappers

2 tablespoons olive oil

chicken stock, lobster stock or water

LOBSTER DUMPLINGS

Heat 1 tablespoon olive oil in a saucepan over medium heat just until smoking. Add the garlic and shallot and cook until tender. Stir in the mushrooms and cook just until the mushrooms are light brown, stirring frequently. Add the lobster meat and cook until heated through, stirring frequently. Stir in the butter, parsley and chives and season to taste with salt and pepper. Spoon the lobster filling onto a baking sheet and chill, covered, in the refrigerator.

Whisk the egg and water in a small bowl until blended. Spoon 1 tablespoon of the lobster filling on half of 1 won ton wrapper. Brush the outer 1/8 inch edge of the wrapper with the egg wash and fold over to cover the filling, pressing the edges to seal. Repeat the process with the remaining won ton wrappers, lobster filling and egg wash.

Heat 2 tablespoons olive oil in a large skillet over medium heat just until smoking. Add the dumplings, shaking the pan to prevent sticking. Cook for 2 minutes or until light brown. Add enough stock to the skillet to measure 1/2 inch and steam, covered, for 3 to 5 minutes or until heated through.

Cream of Poblano with Crostini

3 poblano chiles, cut into halves

1/2 cup chopped onion

1/4 cup chopped carrots

2 tablespoons clarified butter

2 tablespoons all-purpose flour

4 cups chicken stock

3/4 cup heavy cream

1 tablespoon chopped fresh cilantro

salt to taste

8 tortilla chips

4 slices Monterey Jack cheese

Discard the seeds from the poblano chiles using plastic gloves. Sauté the poblano chiles, onion and carrots in the clarified butter in a small saucepan for 5 minutes. Stir in the flour and cook over low heat for 5 minutes, stirring constantly. Whisk in the stock and simmer for 30 minutes or to the desired consistency, stirring occasionally.

Process the poblano chile mixture in a blender until puréed. Return the purée to the saucepan and continue to simmer, stirring occasionally. Stir in the heavy cream and cilantro and season to taste with salt.

Ladle the soup into ovenproof bowls and top each serving with 2 tortilla chips and 1 slice of cheese. Arrange the bowls on a baking sheet and broil until the cheese melts. Serve immediately. Serves 4.

The poblano chile, originating in Pueblo, Mexico, has long been a favorite in Dallas homes. These heart-shaped, thick-skinned dark green chiles appeal to all Mexican food lovers because they are not too spicy and they taste like an old staple, the bell pepper. Along with chili, poblanos are used for chiles rellenos. Simply stuff with cheese, beans, beef, or picadillo and bake.

Fire and Ice Tomato Soup
with Dainty BLTs

1 small onion, minced

¼ cup (½ stick) butter

8 ripe tomatoes, sliced

1 cup dry white wine

1 tablespoon chopped fresh dill weed

4 cups milk

2 cups heavy cream

2 (8-ounce) cans tomato sauce

salt and pepper to taste

Dainty BLTs (page 77)

fresh chives

Sauté the onion in the butter in a stockpot until tender. Add the tomatoes, wine and dill weed and cook for 15 minutes, stirring occasionally. Stir in the milk, heavy cream, tomato sauce, salt and pepper.

Simmer for 1 hour, stirring occasionally; do not allow to boil. Serve hot or chilled with Dainty BLTs. Garnish the soup with fresh chives. You may add chicken stock or bouillon for more flavor. Serves 4.

Photograph for this recipe on page 58.

Tomatillo Gazpacho with Lobster

1 yellow bell pepper, finely chopped

1 red bell pepper, finely chopped

1 green bell pepper, finely chopped

1/2 cup finely chopped red onion

1 green jalapeño chile, seeded and finely chopped

2 cups chopped ripe tomatoes

1 (24-ounce) can vegetable juice cocktail

1 cup quartered husked tomatillos

4 garlic cloves

juice of 1 lemon and 1 lime

2 teaspoons kosher salt

1 teaspoon black pepper

1 teaspoon ground cumin

1/2 teaspoon red pepper flakes, or to taste

1 cucumber, seeded and chopped

3 tablespoons chopped fresh cilantro

2 tablespoons olive oil

1 (1- to 2-pound) lobster, steamed, meat removed and chopped

Avocado Crème Fraîche

Place equal portions of the bell peppers, onion, jalapeño chile and tomatoes in 2 separate bowls. Pour the contents of 1 bowl into a food processor and add the vegetable juice cocktail, tomatillos, garlic, lemon juice, lime juice, salt, black pepper, cumin and red pepper flakes. Process until puréed.

Pour the purée into a large bowl and add the ingredients of the remaining bowl along with the cucumber, cilantro and olive oil. Chill, covered, in the refrigerator.

To serve, divide the lobster meat evenly among 8 soup bowls. Spoon the gazpacho over the lobster and top with a dollop of the Avocado Crème Fraîche. Serves 8.

AVOCADO CRÈME FRAÎCHE

1 ripe avocado, cut into halves

1/2 cup crème fraîche (page 109) or sour cream

1 garlic clove, minced

1 tablespoon fresh lemon juice

salt to taste

Cut the avocado into halves and remove the pit. Scoop the pulp into a bowl and mash. Stir in the crème fraîche, garlic and lemon juice and season to taste with salt. Chill, covered, in the refrigerator.

Fresh Herb Tortilla Soup

2 pounds boneless skinless chicken
  breasts, chopped

1 yellow onion (Texas 1011), chopped

1 or 2 jalapeño chiles, chopped

2 garlic cloves, minced

1$\frac{1}{2}$ tablespoons vegetable oil

1 (14-ounce) can tomatoes

1 (10-ounce) can beef broth

1 (10-ounce) can chicken broth

1 (10-ounce) can tomato soup

1$\frac{1}{2}$ soup cans water

1 (5-ounce) can tomatoes with green
  onions

1 avocado, chopped

2 bay leaves

1 tablespoon Tabasco sauce

2 teaspoons lemon pepper

2 teaspoons Worcestershire sauce

1 teaspoon ground cumin

1 teaspoon chili powder

1 teaspoon salt

6 corn tortillas, cut into $\frac{1}{2} \times 2$-inch
  rectangles

4 ounces Cheddar cheese or Colby
  Jack cheese, shredded

Sauté the chicken, onion, jalapeño chiles and garlic in the oil in a stockpot until the chicken is cooked through and the onion is tender. Add the undrained tomatoes, beef broth, chicken broth, soup, water, undrained tomatoes with green onions and avocado. Stir in the bay leaves, Tabasco sauce, lemon pepper, Worcestershire sauce, cumin, chili powder and salt.

Simmer for 50 minutes, stirring occasionally. Discard the bay leaves and stir in the tortillas. Simmer for 10 minutes longer, stirring occasionally. Ladle into soup bowls and sprinkle with the cheese. If you prefer crispy tortilla strips, refer to the sidebar below for preparation. Sprinkle the crisp strips over the soup along with the cheese. Serves 6 to 8.

*Top Fresh Herb Tortilla Soup with **Fried Tortilla Strips.** Cut the desired amount of corn tortillas into $\frac{1}{2} \times 2$-inch rectangles and fry in batches in hot oil in a deep skillet until crispy. Drain and sprinkle over the soup.*

Turkey and Wild Rice Cream Soup

6 tablespoons butter

1/4 cup all-purpose flour

2 cups half-and-half

3 cups turkey or chicken broth

1 1/2 cups cooked wild rice

1 cup chopped cooked turkey

1/2 cup chopped onion

1/2 cup sliced celery

salt and pepper to taste

Heat the butter in a large saucepan. Add the flour and stir until blended. Cook for 2 minutes, stirring constantly; do not allow to brown. Add the half-and-half and 1 cup of the broth gradually, whisking constantly until blended. Bring to a boil and cook for several minutes, stirring frequently.

Add the remaining 2 cups broth, wild rice, turkey, onion and celery to the half-and-half mixture and mix well. Season to taste with salt and pepper and simmer for 30 minutes, stirring occasionally. Ladle into soup bowls. Serves 8.

Turnip Greens Soup

2 (32-ounce) cans chicken broth

1 ham hock or chicken kielbasa

2 slices bacon

1/3 cup chopped onion

2 ribs celery, chopped

1/2 cup water

3 tablespoons all-purpose flour

2 (10-ounce) packages frozen
   turnip greens

1/3 cup heavy cream

2 tablespoons cider vinegar

1 tablespoon hot sauce

1 teaspoon pepper

Bring the broth and ham hock to a boil in a large saucepan and reduce the heat. Simmer, partially covered, for 30 minutes. Cook the bacon in a skillet until brown and crisp. Drain, reserving the pan drippings. Crumble the bacon.

Sauté the onion and celery in the reserved pan drippings for 5 minutes and stir in the bacon. Mix the water and flour in a small bowl until blended. Add the flour mixture, bacon mixture and turnip greens to the warm broth and mix well.

Simmer, covered, for 1 hour, stirring occasionally. Remove the ham hock and cut the meat from the bone, discarding the bone. Return the ham to the saucepan. Stir in the heavy cream, vinegar, hot sauce and pepper and simmer just until heated through, stirring occasionally. Ladle into soup bowls. Makes 15 cups.

Hot Asparagus Sandwiches

1 bunch asparagus, trimmed and
   cooked al dente
6 ounces cream cheese, softened
2 hard-cooked eggs, sieved
   (page 262)
1 teaspoon seasoned salt
1 teaspoon Dijon mustard
extra-thin sliced bread, crusts
   trimmed
melted butter
grated Parmesan cheese

Combine the asparagus, cream cheese, eggs, seasoned salt and Dijon mustard in a food processor and pulse 3 times; do not purée. The mixture should have texture. Spread the asparagus mixture on 1/2 of the bread slices and top each with another bread slice.

Cut the sandwiches diagonally into halves. Dip in melted butter and coat with cheese. Freeze until firm. Just before serving, arrange the frozen sandwiches on a baking sheet and broil on both sides. Serve immediately.

You may prepare in advance and store in the freezer. For variety, serve without broiling or split the asparagus spears vertically and arrange over the cream cheese mixture. Makes 12 (2- to 3-sandwich) servings.

These variations on the traditional tea sandwich are a perfect dish for baby and wedding showers. Serve them with scones, clotted cream, preserves, and your favorite teas as a light snack in the afternoon. Often called high tea, this formal treat is best known as afternoon tea and was first served by duchesses in nineteenth-century England. As dinner was usually served at 8 p.m., afternoon tea provided ladies with both a snack and an opportunity to socialize.

Dainty BLTs

1¹/₂ pounds thick-slice hickory-
    smoked peppered bacon
3 cups water
4 ounces sun-dried tomatoes
1 cup mayonnaise
kosher salt and freshly ground pepper
24 thin slices firm white sandwich
    bread or rye bread, crusts trimmed
6 ounces mâche or other baby lettuce
    (about 2 cups)

Preheat the oven to 375 degrees. Arrange the bacon in a single layer on 2 baking sheets with sides; do not allow the slices to touch. Place 1 of the baking sheets on the center oven rack and bake for 10 minutes. Drain and bake for 10 minutes longer. Drain the bacon on paper towels, let stand until cool and crumble. Repeat the process with the remaining bacon.

Bring the water almost to a boil in a small saucepan. Remove from the heat and add the sun-dried tomatoes. Soak for 20 minutes and drain. Pat the sun-dried tomatoes dry with paper towels and finely chop. Mix the sun-dried tomatoes and mayonnaise in a bowl and season to taste with salt and pepper.

Spread 1 side of each bread slice with some of the mayonnaise mixture. Generously sprinkle ¹/₂ of the bread slices with the bacon and top with the lettuce. Sprinkle with pepper and top with the remaining bread slices mayonnaise side down. Slice the sandwiches diagonally into halves and serve immediately. Makes 2 dozen sandwiches.

Photograph for this recipe on page 58.

Chicken à la Crescents

¹/₃ cup crushed herb-seasoned
    stuffing mix
¹/₄ cup chopped walnuts or pecans
3 ounces cream cheese, softened
2 tablespoons butter, melted
lemon pepper to taste
1 cup chopped cooked chicken
1 (8-count) can crescent rolls
2 tablespoons butter, melted

Preheat the oven to 375 degrees. Mix the stuffing mix and walnuts in a bowl. Combine the cream cheese, 2 tablespoons butter and lemon pepper in a bowl and mix well. Stir in the chicken.

Separate the roll dough into 8 triangles. Place a heaping tablespoon of the chicken mixture at the wide end of each triangle and roll to enclose the filling, pinching the edges to seal. Dip the crescents in 2 tablespoons butter and coat with the stuffing mixture.

Arrange the crescents on an ungreased baking sheet and bake for 15 to 20 minutes or until brown. Serve immediately or serve cold if desired. For variety, drizzle the crescents with chicken gravy. Makes 8 crescents.

Smoked Turkey Tea Sandwiches

12 thin slices firm white sandwich
    bread, crusts trimmed
Arugula Mayonnaise
10 ounces smoked turkey,
    thinly sliced

1/2 cup mayonnaise
1 cup packed coarsely chopped
    arugula leaves
1 tablespoon minced shallots
1/2 teaspoon grated lemon zest
salt and pepper to taste

Spread 1 side of each bread slice equally with the Arugula Mayonnaise. Layer 1/2 of the bread slices with equal portions of the turkey and top with the remaining bread slices mayonnaise side down. Press lightly to adhere. Cut each sandwich diagonally into quarters. Makes 2 dozen sandwiches.

ARUGULA MAYONNAISE

Combine the mayonnaise, arugula, shallots and lemon zest in a bowl and mix well. Season to taste with salt and pepper.

Turkey Ham Rolls

2 (8- to 12-count) packages small
   dinner rolls
8 ounces thinly sliced deli turkey
8 ounces thinly sliced deli ham
6 ounces thinly sliced Swiss cheese
1/2 cup (1 stick) butter, melted
1 1/2 tablespoons poppy seeds
1 1/2 tablespoons onion flakes
1 1/2 tablespoons prepared mustard
1/2 teaspoon Worcestershire sauce

Preheat the oven to 350 degrees. Split each package of rolls horizontally into 2 layers and arrange the bottom layers on a baking sheet. Layer the turkey, ham and cheese over the bottom roll layer and top with the remaining roll layer.

Mix the butter, poppy seeds, onion flakes, prepared mustard and Worcestershire sauce in a bowl and spoon over the tops of the rolls. Bake for 15 minutes. Separate into individual rolls and serve hot.

If you prefer, use just turkey or ham and not a combination of the two. Double or triple the recipe for a larger crowd. Makes 16 to 24 rolls.

Smoked Salmon Tea Sandwiches

24 thin slices white or wheat bread

4 ounces Ginger-Cilantro Lime Butter

8 ounces smoked salmon,
thinly sliced

lettuce leaves

Spread 1 side of each bread slice generously with some of the Ginger-Cilantro Lime Butter. Arrange 1 slice of salmon on $1/2$ of the bread slices and top with the remaining bread slices butter side down. Cut the sandwiches into rounds using a 2-inch cutter. Serve on a platter lined with lettuce. Makes 2 dozen sandwiches.

$1/2$ cup (1 stick) unsalted butter,
softened

$1/4$ cup cream cheese, softened

3 tablespoons chopped fresh cilantro

1 tablespoon grated fresh ginger

1 tablespoon fresh lime juice

1 teaspoon kosher salt

GINGER-CILANTRO LIME BUTTER

Combine the butter, cream cheese, cilantro, ginger, lime juice and salt in a food processor and pulse for 30 seconds or just until combined. Shape the butter mixture into a $1^1/2\times10$-inch log on a sheet of baking parchment or waxed paper. Chill until serving time.

Citrus Crab Salad Tea Sandwiches

12 ounces fresh lump crab meat,
   drained and shells removed
2 tablespoons mayonnaise
2 tablespoons grated lemon zest
2 tablespoons fresh lemon juice
4 scallions (white and green parts),
   thinly sliced
kosher salt and freshly ground
   pepper to taste
24 thin slices white bread
1/4 cup mayonnaise
4 ounces red leaf lettuce or baby
   spinach leaves

Combine the crab meat, 2 tablespoons mayonnaise, lemon zest, lemon juice and scallions in a bowl and mix gently. Season to taste with salt and pepper.

Spread 1 side of each of the bread slices with 1/4 cup mayonnaise. Layer each slice with lettuce and spread the crab meat mixture over 1/2 of the slices. Top with the remaining bread slices lettuce side down. Trim the crusts and cut each sandwich diagonally into halves. Makes 2 dozen sandwiches.

Open-Faced
Corned Beef Bagels

1 (3-pound) corned beef
freshly ground pepper to taste
1 garlic clove, minced
olive oil
2 cups water
3/4 cup dark or stout beer
2 tablespoons butter
1 head cabbage, shredded
12 bagels, split into halves
pizza or spaghetti sauce
shredded fontina cheese,
   crumbled goat cheese or
   grated Parmesan cheese

Preheat the oven to 250 degrees. Rub the brisket with pepper and the garlic. Sear the brisket on all sides in olive oil in a Dutch oven. Remove the brisket to a platter, reserving the pan drippings. Deglaze the pan with the water. Add the beer and butter and stir to combine. Add the cabbage and bring to a boil, stirring occasionally. Reduce the heat and simmer, covered, for 5 to 10 minutes, stirring occasionally.

Arrange the brisket over the cabbage. Roast, covered, for 4 hours or until the brisket is tender. Maintain the oven temperature. Remove the corned beef to a platter and slice.

Spread the cut sides of the bagels with pizza sauce and layer with the warm corned beef. Sprinkle with cheese and arrange the bagels on a baking sheet cheese side up. Bake until the cheese melts. Use miniature bagels if desired or just serve the corned beef with a good horseradish mustard. This brisket is usually prepared as a main dish and the leftovers are used to make these delicious sandwiches. Bake the brisket and cabbage 1 day in advance and use the leftover brisket to prepare these sandwiches. Makes 2 dozen open-face sandwiches from leftovers, or 3 to 4 dozen sandwiches if the brisket is specifically prepared for this recipe.

Grilled Honey Cilantro Chicken Sandwiches

2 tablespoons vegetable oil

2 tablespoons honey

juice of 1 lime

1/2 bunch fresh cilantro, trimmed
   and chopped

1 teaspoon ground cumin

4 boneless skinless chicken breasts

Cajun seasoning to taste

butter, softened

4 to 6 hamburger buns

lettuce

sliced fresh tomatoes

thinly sliced red onion

Combine the oil, honey, lime juice, cilantro and cumin in a sealable plastic bag. Rub the chicken with Cajun seasoning and add the chicken to the bag. Seal tightly and turn to coat. Marinate in the refrigerator for 30 to 60 minutes, turning occasionally.

Preheat the grill. Grill the chicken until a meat thermometer inserted in the thickest part of the chicken registers 170 degrees, turning occasionally. Several minutes before the end of the grilling process spread butter on the cut sides of the buns and lightly grill. Slice the chicken or serve whole on the grilled buns topped with lettuce, tomatoes and red onion. Makes 4 to 6 sandwiches.

Salads

THE DISH ON DALLAS

Fresh ingredients are no problem in the Dallas area. The Dallas Farmers Market is one of the largest open-air markets in the country and welcomes more than five million visitors a year. The market began in the late 1800s when rural farmers came to the city to sell their fresh fruits and vegetables, as well as chickens and pigs, directly to customers.

Arugula and Parmesan Salad recipe on page 96.

Layered Avocado Salad

2 large avocados, chopped

8 green onions, chopped

2 garlic cloves, minced

2/3 cup grapeseed oil or oil of choice

1/3 cup red wine vinegar

1/4 cup (1 ounce) grated
  Parmesan cheese

2 tablespoons grated Romano cheese

1 tablespoon Dijon mustard

2 teaspoons salt

1 teaspoon pepper

2 heads romaine, trimmed and torn

Combine the avocados, green onions and garlic in a bowl and mix gently. Whisk the grapeseed oil, vinegar, Parmesan cheese, Romano cheese, Dijon mustard, salt and pepper in a bowl until incorporated.

Add the dressing to the avocado mixture and toss to coat. Layer the romaine over the avocado mixture; do not toss. Chill, covered, for 6 to 8 hours and toss just before serving. Serves 6 to 8.

Mixed Greens with Pears and Raspberry Vinaigrette

16 ounces mixed salad greens, or
   2 small heads red leaf lettuce, torn
1 pear or apple, sliced
4 ounces blue cheese, crumbled
$^1/_2$ cup chopped pecans, toasted
   (page 268)
Raspberry Vinaigrette

Toss the salad greens, pear, blue cheese and pecans in a salad bowl. Add the Raspberry Vinaigrette and mix until coated. Serves 6 to 10.

RASPBERRY VINAIGRETTE

$^1/_2$ cup canola oil
$^1/_4$ cup raspberry vinegar
$^1/_4$ cup chopped dried cranberries
1 teaspoon sugar

Whisk the canola oil, vinegar, cranberries and sugar in a bowl until the oil is incorporated. Store in the refrigerator.

Prepare **Sweet and Spicy Pecans** by mixing 3 tablespoons light corn syrup, $1^1/_2$ tablespoons sugar, $^3/_4$ teaspoon salt, $^1/_4$ heaping teaspoon freshly ground black pepper and $^1/_8$ teaspoon cayenne pepper in a bowl. Add $1^1/_2$ cups pecan pieces and toss to coat. Spread the pecan mixture on a baking sheet sprayed with nonstick cooking spray and bake at 325 degrees for 5 minutes. Stir to coat the pecans with the spice mixture and bake for 10 minutes longer or until golden brown and bubbly. Immediately spread the pecans on a sheet of foil and separate the pecans with a fork. Let stand until cool.

Grapefruit with Red Leaf Lettuce

1 head red leaf lettuce, trimmed

2 grapefruit

18 ripe olives, pitted

1/4 cup sliced pickled beets

1/4 cup minced red onion

pomegranate seeds (when in season)

Mustard Vinaigrette

Tear the large lettuce leaves if needed and place in a salad bowl. Peel and section the grapefruit, carefully removing all of the white membrane surrounding the sections and any seeds. Add the grapefruit sections, olives, pickled beets, onion and pomegranate seeds to the salad bowl and toss to mix. Add the Mustard Vinaigrette and mix until coated. Serve with chicken or fish. Serves 4.

MUSTARD VINAIGRETTE

2 tablespoons strong-flavor mustard

1 teaspoon cider vinegar

1 teaspoon sugar

salt and white pepper to taste

1/4 cup extra-virgin olive oil

Whisk the mustard, vinegar, sugar, salt and white pepper in a bowl. Add the olive oil gradually, whisking constantly until incorporated.

Spicy Noodle Salad

1 (16-ounce) package
   angel hair pasta
2 tablespoons vegetable oil
2 carrots, grated
1 bunch green onions, chopped
Asian Dressing

Cook the pasta in boiling water in a saucepan for 8 minutes; drain. Toss the pasta with the oil in a bowl. Add the carrots, green onions and chilled Asian Dressing to the pasta and mix well. For variety, add chopped cooked chicken breasts or other vegetables such as sugar snap peas. Serves 8.

ASIAN DRESSING

1/3 cup soy sauce
1/4 cup white wine vinegar
2 tablespoons red chili sauce
2 tablespoons sugar
2 tablespoons sesame oil
2 tablespoons finely chopped or
   grated fresh ginger
4 garlic cloves, minced
1 to 2 teaspoons dried chile flakes
freshly ground black pepper to taste
1/4 cup vegetable oil

Whisk the soy sauce, vinegar, chili sauce, sugar, sesame oil, ginger, garlic, chile flakes and black pepper in a bowl until combined. Add the vegetable oil gradually, whisking constantly until incorporated. Chill, covered, in the refrigerator for up to 1 week.

Sliced Sirloin Salad with Blue Cheese Dressing

The Capital Grille

1 (10-ounce) sirloin steak

seasoned salt to taste

4 asparagus spears

4 ounces mesclun salad mix

Blue Cheese Dressing

crumbled Roquefort cheese to taste

Preheat the grill. Sprinkle the steak with seasoned salt and grill to the desired degree of doneness, turning once or twice. Grill the asparagus until light brown. Cut the steak diagonally into 6 or 7 equal slices.

Toss the salad mix with the desired amount of the Blue Cheese Dressing and mound on a serving plate. Arrange the asparagus over the salad mix and the steak slices across the bottom of the plate, slightly propped on the salad. Sprinkle with cheese and serve immediately. Serves 1.

BLUE CHEESE DRESSING

8 anchovy fillets

1/4 cup cider vinegar

2 tablespoons Dijon mustard

1/4 cup egg whites

1 tablespoon granulated garlic

1 tablespoon cafe-grind pepper

juice of 1 lemon

1/2 gallon blended vegetable oil

1/2 cup sifted grated Romano cheese

1/2 cup sifted grated
   Parmesan cheese

8 ounces Roquefort cheese, crumbled

Process the anchovy fillets, vinegar and Dijon mustard in a blender until the mixture is puréed and the consistency of a paste. Combine the anchovy purée, egg whites, garlic, pepper and lemon juice in a stainless mixing bowl and beat until the egg whites are frothy.

Add the oil to the egg white mixture gradually, beating constantly until incorporated. Add the Romano cheese and Parmesan cheese gradually, beating constantly. Stir in the Roquefort cheese. If you are concerned about using raw eggs, use eggs pasteurized in their shells, which are sold at some specialty food stores, or use an equivalent amount of pasteurized egg substitute.

Chicken Salad with Peanut Dressing

Peanut Dressing

1 pound boneless skinless chicken breasts

6 cups chopped romaine

2 cups chopped sliced red cabbage

1 cup grated carrots

1/4 cup chopped fresh cilantro

chopped peanuts

1/4 cup peanut butter

1/3 cup rice wine vinegar

2 tablespoons vegetable oil

2 tablespoons sesame oil

1 tablespoon soy sauce

2 tablespoons sugar

3/4 tablespoon chopped peanuts

1 teaspoon minced garlic

1/2 teaspoon minced fresh ginger

Pour 1/2 of the Peanut Dressing over the chicken in a shallow dish and turn to coat. Marinate, covered, in the refrigerator for 2 hours, turning occasionally. Preheat the grill. Grill the chicken until cooked through, turning once or twice.

Toss the romaine, cabbage, carrots and cilantro with the remaining Peanut Dressing in a bowl and spoon onto a serving platter. Slice the chicken and arrange over the top of the salad. Sprinkle with chopped peanuts. Serves 4 to 6.

PEANUT DRESSING

Spoon the peanut butter into a small bowl. Add the vinegar, vegetable oil, sesame oil and soy sauce gradually, whisking constantly until blended. Add the sugar, peanuts, garlic and ginger and whisk until mixed.

Chicken Salad

**4 chicken breasts, poached
   (page 263)**
³/₄ cup chopped celery (about 3 ribs)
¹/₂ cup chopped onion
**2 tablespoons chopped fresh
   Italian parsley**
1 cup mayonnaise
1 tablespoon heavy cream
¹/₂ teaspoon garlic powder
¹/₂ teaspoon salt
¹/₂ teaspoon freshly ground pepper

Chop the chicken, discarding the skin and bones. The chopped chicken should measure 4 cups. Combine the chicken, celery, onion and parsley in a bowl and mix well. Stir in the mayonnaise, heavy cream, garlic powder, salt and pepper. Taste and adjust the seasonings if desired. Store, covered, in the refrigerator. Makes 4 sandwiches, or 12 tea sandwiches.

¹/₂ cup sliced almonds
¹/₂ cup dried currants
2 teaspoons Madras curry powder

CURRIED CHICKEN SALAD

Prepare the Chicken Salad as directed above, omitting the parsley. Toast the almonds in a small skillet over medium heat until golden brown, stirring constantly. Spread the almonds on a sheet of waxed paper to cool. Stir the almonds, currants and curry powder into the Chicken Salad. Serve on a slightly sweeter bread, such as croissants. Or hollow out a round bread loaf, fill with the salad and cut into wedges.

SOUTHWEST CHICKEN SALAD

1 cup rinsed drained black beans
¹/₂ cup finely chopped red bell pepper
**1 tablespoon minced seeded
   jalapeño chiles**
1 teaspoon ground cumin

Prepare the Chicken Salad as directed above, omitting the parsley. Stir in the beans, bell pepper, jalapeño chiles and cumin. Chill, covered, for several hours to allow the flavors to marry. Spoon the salad into avocado halves or serve on a bed of lettuce topped with Fried Tortilla Strips on page 72.

Southwestern Crab Cake Salad

1 pound backfin lump crab meat,
   drained
1 1/2 tablespoons chopped fresh
   parsley
1 egg, beaten
2 tablespoons mayonnaise
1 1/2 tablespoons Worcestershire
   sauce
1/2 teaspoon dry mustard
1/4 teaspoon salt
1/8 teaspoon pepper
1/16 teaspoon (heaping) dried sage
1/16 teaspoon (heaping) dried thyme
1/2 cup (about) cracker meal
vegetable oil for frying
1 head romaine, chopped
1/4 cup crumbled Mexican queso
   blanco or shredded Parmesan
   cheese
Cilantro Cream

Remove the shells from the crab meat, being careful to leave the crab meat in large pieces. Combine the crab meat, parsley, egg, mayonnaise, Worcestershire sauce, dry mustard, salt, pepper, sage and thyme in a bowl and mix gently. Add just enough of the cracker meal to hold the mixture together. Shape the crab meat mixture into patties. Chill the patties between sheets of waxed paper for about 1 hour.

Preheat the oven to 200 degrees. Pour enough oil into a deep skillet to measure 1/2 inch and heat until hot. Fry the crab cakes in batches in the hot oil until dark golden brown on both sides, turning once. Drain on paper towels and arrange on a baking sheet. Keep warm in the oven.

Arrange the crab cakes on the chopped romaine on serving plates and sprinkle with the cheese. Serve with the Cilantro Cream. Makes 6 servings as salad course, or 4 servings as main course.

94

CILANTRO CREAM

1 bunch cilantro, stems removed
3 tablespoons sour cream
3 tablespoons mayonnaise
3 tablespoons chopped green chiles
1 (or more) jalapeño chile
salt and pepper to taste

Combine the cilantro, sour cream, mayonnaise, green chiles, jalapeño chile, salt and pepper in a blender or food processor and process until blended. Store, covered, in the refrigerator.

Arugula and Roast Beet Salad

4 fresh beets

1/2 cup olive oil

1/4 cup balsamic vinegar

1 tablespoon Dijon mustard

1 tablespoon chopped fresh tarragon

1 garlic clove, minced

1 teaspoon fresh lemon juice

1 teaspoon sugar

coarse sea salt and pepper to taste

1 bunch arugula, trimmed

4 ounces goat cheese, crumbled
   (optional)

Preheat the oven to 450 degrees. Rinse the beets and trim off the tops and bottoms. Wrap each beet in foil and arrange on a baking sheet. Roast for 45 minutes. Cool, peel and cut into quarters.

Whisk the olive oil, vinegar, Dijon mustard, tarragon and garlic in a bowl. Stir in the lemon juice, sugar, salt and pepper. Arrange the arugula in a salad bowl and top with the beets. Drizzle with the dressing and toss lightly. Sprinkle with the goat cheese and serve immediately. Serves 4 to 6.

95

Arugula, a common salad ingredient, has many uses: sautéed and served as a side dish; stuffed in meat or poultry; and used as an herb for soups. Fresh leaves are bright green in color and free of spots and bruises. Store in a sealable plastic bag in the refrigerator for up to two days.

Arugula and Parmesan Salad

3 large bunches arugula

4 ounces pancetta, chopped and crisp-cooked

1/2 cup thinly sliced fennel

Lemon Vinaigrette

4 ounces Parmesan cheese

Remove the roots of the arugula if needed. Rinse the arugula in a sink filled with cold water. Spin-dry the leaves and place in a large bowl. Add the pancetta, fennel and just enough of the Lemon Vinaigrette to moisten and toss.

Arrange equal portions of the arugula salad on each of 6 salad plates. Using a very sharp knife or vegetable peeler, shave the cheese into large shards and place over the top of each salad. Serves 6.

LEMON VINAIGRETTE

1/2 cup olive oil

1/4 cup fresh lemon juice

1/2 teaspoon kosher salt

1/4 teaspoon freshly ground pepper

Whisk the olive oil, lemon juice, salt and pepper in a bowl until the olive oil is incorporated.

Photograph for this recipe on page 84.

Layered Black Bean Salad

2 (15-ounce) cans black beans,
   drained and rinsed

2 tablespoons vegetable oil

2 tablespoons white wine vinegar

$1/2$ teaspoon salt

$1/2$ cup shredded iceberg lettuce

$1/2$ cup chopped red onion

$1^1/_2$ cups chopped seeded tomatoes

1 cup cooked fresh or frozen corn

$1/2$ cup chopped green bell pepper

1 avocado, chopped

1 cup (4 ounces) shredded Monterey
   Jack cheese

4 slices bacon, crisp-cooked and
   crumbled

Jalapeño Dressing

Mix the beans, oil, vinegar and salt in a bowl and marinate, covered, in the refrigerator for up to 1 day, stirring occasionally. Layer the lettuce, marinated beans, onion, tomatoes, corn, bell pepper, avocado, cheese and bacon in a salad bowl. Add the Jalapeño Dressing and toss to coat or serve the salad with the dressing on the side. Serves 4.

JALAPEÑO DRESSING

$1/2$ cup packed chopped fresh cilantro

3 pickled jalapeño chiles, seeded

$1/3$ cup vegetable oil

$1/3$ cup olive oil

$1/4$ cup white wine vinegar

1 teaspoon salt

Process the cilantro, jalapeño chiles, vegetable oil, olive oil, vinegar and salt in a food processor until blended. Chill, covered, until serving time.

Margarita Coleslaw

1 (10-ounce) can frozen margarita
  mix, thawed
1/4 cup canola oil
2 teaspoons seasoned salt
2 teaspoons garlic powder
1 teaspoon celery seeds
12 cups shredded red cabbage
leaves of 1 bunch cilantro, chopped
3 green onions, sliced
1 large Fuji apple, chopped
1 large firm pear, chopped
6 ounces dried cherry-flavor
  cranberries

Whisk the margarita mix, canola oil, seasoned salt, garlic powder and celery seeds in a bowl. Chill, covered, in the refrigerator.

Combine the cabbage, cilantro, green onions, apple, pear and cranberries in a bowl and mix well. Add the desired amount of the dressing and toss to coat. Serve immediately. Serves 8.

Spring Salad with English Peas

1 package coleslaw mix or
  shredded cabbage
2 bunches green onions, chopped
1 cup chopped celery
1 cup chopped green bell pepper
1 cup mayonnaise
1 cup sour cream
1 (10-ounce) package frozen English
  peas, slightly thawed
1/2 cup (2 ounces) grated Parmesan
  cheese or shredded Swiss cheese
salt and pepper to taste

Rinse and drain the coleslaw mix. Layer the coleslaw mix, green onions, celery and bell pepper in a glass salad bowl. Mix the mayonnaise and sour cream in a bowl and spread over the prepared layers, sealing to the edge. Prepare to this point early in the day and store, covered, in the refrigerator. Just before serving, top with the peas and sprinkle with the cheese, salt and pepper. Serves 12 to 14.

Corn Bread Salad

1 recipe Iron Skillet Corn Bread
   (page 228)
1 envelope buttermilk ranch salad
   dressing mix
6 slices bacon
1 small head romaine, trimmed and
   shredded
2 large tomatoes, chopped
1 (15-ounce) can black beans,
   drained and rinsed
1 (15-ounce) can whole kernel corn,
   drained
$1/4$ cup chopped red bell pepper
$1/4$ cup chopped green bell pepper
1 (8-ounce) package shredded
   Mexican four-cheese blend
5 green onions, chopped
1 large avocado, chopped

Prepare and bake the corn bread. Cool slightly and crumble. Prepare the salad dressing using the package directions. Cook the bacon in a skillet until crisp and drain on paper towels. Crumble the bacon.

Layer the corn bread, romaine, tomatoes, beans, corn, bell peppers, cheese and dressing $1/2$ at a time in a large salad bowl. Chill, covered, for 2 hours or longer. Sprinkle with the bacon, green onions and avocado just before serving. Serves 10 to 12.

Oven-Roasted Four-Potato Salad

1 pound sweet potatoes, peeled and
  cut into 1-inch pieces
1 pound gold potatoes, peeled and
  cut into 1-inch pieces
1 pound red new potatoes, peeled
  and cut into 1-inch pieces
1 pound purple potatoes, peeled and
  cut into 1-inch pieces
3 tablespoons olive oil
1/2 teaspoon salt
freshly ground black pepper to taste
cayenne pepper to taste
1/2 cup mayonnaise
1/4 cup fresh lemon juice
1/4 cup chopped scallions
1 tablespoon Dijon mustard
1 teaspoon celery seeds
salt to taste

Preheat the oven to 450 degrees. Toss the sweet potatoes, gold potatoes, red potatoes and purple potatoes with the olive oil, 1/2 teaspoon salt, black pepper and cayenne pepper in a bowl.

Arrange the potatoes in a single layer on several baking sheets and roast for 20 to 30 minutes or until tender, brown and crispy, turning occasionally. Let stand until cool.

Whisk the mayonnaise, lemon juice, scallions, Dijon mustard and celery seeds in a bowl. Add the potatoes and toss gently to coat. Season to taste with salt and black pepper. Serve at room temperature. Serves 8.

Spinach and Pear Salad with Rosemary Vinaigrette

4 cups fresh baby spinach leaves

4 teaspoons coarsely chopped
  pecans, toasted (page 268)

Rosemary Vinaigrette

2 ripe pears, thinly sliced

1/4 cup crumbled blue cheese or
  Gorgonzola cheese

Toss the spinach and pecans in a salad bowl. Add just enough of the Rosemary Vinaigrette to coat and toss gently. Divide the spinach mixture evenly among 4 salad plates and top evenly with the pears and cheese. Serves 4.

1/2 cup olive oil

2 tablespoons red wine vinegar

2 tablespoons rice vinegar

1 1/2 tablespoons minced shallots

1 1/2 teaspoons chopped fresh
  rosemary

ROSEMARY VINAIGRETTE

Combine the olive oil, wine vinegar, rice vinegar, shallots and rosemary in a jar with a tight-fitting lid and seal tightly. Shake to mix.

Instead of Rosemary Vinaigrette, drizzle the Spinach and Pear Salad with **Cranberry Dressing.** Whisk 1/2 cup canola oil, 1/4 cup raspberry vinegar, 1/4 cup chopped dried cranberries and 1 teaspoon sugar until the canola oil is incorporated.

Crispy Goat Cheese on Vine-Ripened Tomatoes

11 ounces fresh goat cheese

2 eggs, beaten

1/2 cup fine fresh bread crumbs

6 vine-ripened tomatoes

2 tablespoons olive oil

1 bunch watercress,
   large stems removed

1 bunch arugula, stems removed

1/4 cup fresh basil, julienned

3 tablespoons chopped fresh chives

3 tablespoons chopped fresh
   Italian parsley

1/4 cup olive oil

2 tablespoons balsamic vinegar

salt and pepper to taste

6 fresh basil leaves

Shape the cheese into 1-inch discs. Dip in the eggs and coat with the bread crumbs, pressing lightly. Place the coated cheese discs on a plate lined with waxed paper and chill. Slice off the top of the tomatoes and remove the core if it is too thick, reserving the tops. Cut a small slice from the bottom of each tomato to form a flat base.

Heat 2 tablespoons olive oil in a large nonstick skillet over medium-high heat. Cook the cheese in the hot oil for 1 minute per side or until golden brown. Remove the cheese to a platter using a slotted spoon, reserving the pan drippings. Reduce the heat to medium and add the tomatoes to the reserved pan drippings. Cook for 3 to 5 minutes.

Toss the watercress, arugula, 1/4 cup basil, the chives and parsley in a bowl. Drizzle with a mixture of 1/4 cup olive oil and the vinegar and toss to coat. Season to taste with salt and pepper.

Divide the watercress mixture evenly among 6 salad plates and arrange 1 tomato on each plate. Top with the hot cheese discs. Return the reserved tomato tops to the tomatoes and garnish each top with 1 basil leaf to represent the stem. Sprinkle with salt and pepper to taste and serve immediately. Makes a great first course as well as a salad. Serves 6.

Stacked Tomato Salad

4 or 5 red and yellow tomatoes, cut
    into $1/4$- to $1/2$-inch slices
3 stalks whole hearts of palm,
    julienned
$1/3$ cup crumbled blue cheese
2 tablespoons drained capers
3 tablespoons olive oil
1 tablespoon balsamic vinegar
kosher salt and freshly ground
    pepper to taste
kalamata olives (optional)
caper berries (optional)
$1/2$ cup coarsely chopped fresh basil

Stack the tomatoes evenly, alternating colors, on 4 salad plates. Top with the julienned hearts of palm and sprinkle with the cheese and capers. Whisk the olive oil and vinegar in a bowl.

Just before serving, sprinkle the tomato stacks with salt and pepper and generously garnish with olives and caper berries. Sprinkle with the basil and drizzle with the olive oil mixture. Serve immediately. Serves 4.

For **Baked Hazelnuts,** spread $1/2$ cup hazelnuts in a single layer on an ungreased baking sheet and bake at 350 degrees for 15 minutes or until the skins split. Place the hazelnuts in a colander and rub briskly with a tea towel to remove the skins, discarding the skins. Coarsely chop the hazelnuts or grind in a nut grinder. Store in an airtight container in the refrigerator for up to 9 months or freeze for up to 2 years. Bring to room temperature before using.

Verde Vegetable Salad

4 cups fresh broccoli florets

4 cups (2-inch pieces) fresh
   asparagus spears

1 cup haricots verts

salt to taste

1 (15-ounce) can water-pack
   artichokes hearts, drained

1 red bell pepper, julienned

1/2 cucumber, sliced

Verde Dressing

Blanch the broccoli, asparagus and beans in boiling salted water in a saucepan for 4 minutes or until tender-crisp. Drain and spoon the vegetables into a large serving bowl. Add the artichokes, bell pepper, cucumber and Verde Dressing and toss gently. Chill, covered, in the refrigerator for 8 to 10 hours. Chilling enhances the flavor of the salad. Serves 12.

VERDE DRESSING

1 cup mayonnaise

3/4 cup chopped fresh parsley

1/2 cup finely chopped onion

1/2 cup half-and-half

2 tablespoons fresh lemon juice

2 tablespoons garlic vinegar

2 tablespoons anchovy paste

Combine the mayonnaise, parsley, onion, half-and-half, lemon juice, vinegar and anchovy paste in a bowl and mix well.

Buttermilk Ranch Dressing

1¹/2 cups buttermilk

1 cup mayonnaise

1¹/2 tablespoons cider vinegar

1 teaspoon freshly ground pepper

1¹/2 teaspoons chopped fresh chives

1 teaspoon chopped fresh parsley

1/2 teaspoon garlic powder

1/4 teaspoon salt

Whisk the buttermilk, mayonnaise and vinegar in a bowl until blended. Stir in the pepper, chives, parsley, garlic powder and salt. Taste and adjust the seasonings if needed. Store, covered, in the refrigerator for up to 3 days. Toss with your favorite salad greens. Makes 2¹/2 cups.

1/3 cup minced seeded peeled cucumber

1 teaspoon chopped fresh dill weed

1/2 teaspoon celery salt

CUCUMBER RANCH DRESSING

Prepare the Buttermilk Ranch Dressing as directed above, omitting the herbs and adding the cucumber, dill weed and celery salt. Store and serve as directed above.

2 tablespoons chopped seeded peeled roasted jalapeño chiles (page 265)

1¹/2 teaspoons chopped fresh cilantro

1/4 teaspoon cayenne pepper

SPICY JALAPEÑO RANCH DRESSING

Process the jalapeño chiles and cilantro in a food processor until blended. Prepare the Buttermilk Ranch Dressing as directed above, omitting the herbs and adding the jalapeño chile mixture and cayenne pepper. Store and serve as directed above.

Best-Ever Blue Cheese Dressing

**12 ounces Roquefort cheese or
   blue cheese**

8 ounces cream cheese, softened

1¹/₂ cups sour cream

1¹/₂ cups mayonnaise

1 tablespoon fresh lemon juice

2 teaspoons wine vinegar

1¹/₂ teaspoons Durkee sauce

2 large heads garlic, crushed

¹/₂ teaspoon Worcestershire sauce

¹/₈ teaspoon white pepper

¹/₈ teaspoon dry mustard

¹/₈ teaspoon Tabasco sauce

Crumble the Roquefort cheese into a bowl. Add the cream cheese, sour cream and mayonnaise and mix until blended. Stir in the lemon juice, vinegar, Durkee sauce, garlic, Worcestershire sauce, white pepper, dry mustard and Tabasco sauce. Chill, covered, for 24 hours or longer for the best flavor. Makes 5 cups.

Celery Seed Dressing

1/2 cup vegetable oil

1/4 cup white vinegar

5 tablespoons sugar

1 teaspoon salt

1/2 teaspoon dry mustard

1/2 teaspoon celery seeds

2 garlic cloves, minced

Combine the oil, vinegar, sugar, salt, dry mustard, celery seeds and garlic in a blender and process until combined. Chill, covered, for 8 to 10 hours for enhanced flavor. Drizzle the dressing over mixed salad greens and sprinkle with blue cheese. Makes 3/4 cup.

109

To make your own **Crème Fraîche,** mix 1/2 cup whipping cream and 1 tablespoon buttermilk in a bowl. Let stand, covered, at room temperature for 8 hours. Store, covered, in the refrigerator for up to 10 days.

Sides

THE DISH ON DALLAS

Dallas/Fort Worth is rich in diverse cultures and ethnic influences with more than fifty languages spoken by area residents. This translates directly to our local cuisine and cooking styles, with more than seventy-five international restaurants in the area.

Grilled Sweet Corn on the Cob recipe on page 124.

Brussels Sprouts a Tejas

2 teaspoons butter

1 cup chopped onion

4 garlic cloves, thinly sliced

8 cups fresh brussels sprouts,
   cut into halves and thinly sliced
   (about 1$^{1}/_{2}$ pounds)

$^{1}/_{2}$ cup fat-free less-sodium
   chicken broth

1$^{1}/_{2}$ tablespoons sugar

$^{1}/_{2}$ teaspoon salt

8 teaspoons coarsely chopped
   pecans, toasted (page 268)

Heat the butter in a large nonstick skillet over medium-high heat.
Add the onion and garlic to the butter and sauté for 4 minutes or until
light brown. Stir in the brussels sprouts and sauté for 2 minutes longer.

Add the broth and sugar to the brussels sprouts mixture and cook for
5 minutes or until the liquid evaporates, stirring frequently. Stir in the
salt. Spoon the brussels sprouts into a serving bowl and sprinkle with
the pecans. Serves 8.

Throughout the South, many people eat black-eyed peas on
New Year's Day hoping they will bring good luck and prosperity. In
Texas, cabbage is sometimes served with the black-eyed peas.
Black-eyed peas are symbolic of good luck, and cabbage is
symbolic of money.

Carrots with Shallot Rings

2 pounds carrots, peeled

salt to taste

1/4 cup (1/2 stick) butter

4 large shallots, cut into thin slices
and separated into rings

1/4 cup honey

2 tablespoons Dijon mustard

juice of 1/2 lime

1 teaspoon kosher salt, or to taste

Cut the carrots diagonally into 1-inch slices. Combine the carrots with enough water to cover in a saucepan and season to taste with salt. Cook for 10 to 15 minutes or until tender; drain.

Heat the butter in a medium skillet over medium-high heat and add the shallots. Cook for 3 minutes or until they begin to brown, stirring frequently. Stir in the honey, Dijon mustard and carrots. Drizzle with the lime juice and sprinkle with 1 teaspoon salt. Serves 8.

Asparagus with Fresh Parmesan Cheese

1 pound fresh white or green
   asparagus spears
2 teaspoons unsalted butter
1 tablespoon extra-virgin olive oil
1/4 cup vermouth
1/2 cup (2 ounces) freshly grated
   Parmesan cheese
sea salt to taste

Snap off the woody ends of the asparagus spears. Steam the asparagus for 3 minutes or until tender-crisp. Immediately plunge the asparagus into a bowl of ice water to stop the cooking process and preserve the bright green color. Cool and remove to a thick tea towel to drain.

Heat the butter and olive oil in a large skillet over medium heat and stir in the vermouth. Add the asparagus and sauté for 2 to 3 minutes or until heated through. Remove the asparagus to a serving platter and sprinkle with the cheese and salt. Serve immediately. Serves 4.

Traditional Green Beans

3 pounds green beans (haricots verts or small young green beans), trimmed
8 ounces (1/4-inch-thick) slices bacon
1/2 cup chopped shallots
2 garlic cloves, chopped
1/4 cup sherry wine vinegar
3 tablespoons Dijon mustard
1 teaspoon dry mustard
1/2 cup olive oil
salt and pepper to taste
2 cups (8 ounces) crumbled soft fresh goat cheese, chilled
1/2 cup dried cherries or cranberries

Steam the beans until tender-crisp. Immediately rinse with cold water to stop the cooking process. Pat dry and chill. You may prepare up to 1 day in advance. Wrap the beans in paper towels and place in a sealable plastic bag. Bring to room temperature before proceeding with the recipe.

Cook the bacon in a skillet until crisp. Remove the bacon to paper towels to drain, reserving the pan drippings. Crumble the bacon. Add the shallots and garlic to the reserved pan drippings and sauté over medium heat for 1 minute or until the shallots are tender. Mix in the vinegar, Dijon mustard and dry mustard and stir to release any browned bits from the bottom of the skillet. Whisk in the olive oil and season to taste with salt and pepper.

Toss the beans with the warm dressing in a salad bowl and sprinkle with the bacon, cheese and cherries. If desired, let the dressing come to room temperature and toss with the chilled beans. Serves 8 to 10.

Green Beans and Tomatoes in White Wine

1 pound fresh green beans

1/2 onion, thinly sliced

1 garlic clove, minced

2 tablespoons olive oil

1/4 cup dry white wine

2 large vine-ripe tomatoes, chopped

1 tablespoon fresh lemon juice

pepper to taste

Trim the ends of the beans and rinse under cold water. Pour enough water into a saucepan to cover the beans and bring to a boil over high heat. Add the beans to the boiling water and reduce the heat. Simmer for 8 to 10 minutes or until tender. Drain and immediately plunge the beans into a bowl of ice water to stop the cooking process and preserve the bright green color; drain.

Sauté the onion and garlic in the olive oil in a saucepan over medium heat for 3 to 4 minutes or until the onion is tender. Stir in the wine and tomatoes and simmer over medium-low heat for 20 minutes, stirring occasionally. Add the beans and cook for 3 minutes or until heated through, stirring occasionally. Remove from the heat and drizzle with the lemon juice and season to taste with pepper. Serves 4.

Sesame Long Beans

1½ pounds Chinese long beans,
    trimmed and cut into 3- or
    4-inch pieces
1½ tablespoons sesame oil
3 tablespoons soy sauce
1½ tablespoons rice vinegar
1½ tablespoons brown sugar
¼ teaspoon freshly ground pepper
2 tablespoons sesame seeds, toasted
    (page 268)

Combine the beans with enough water to generously cover in a large saucepan and cook for 3 minutes or until tender-crisp. Drain and immediately plunge the beans into a bowl of ice water to stop the cooking process; drain. You may prepare up to 1 day in advance. Wrap the beans in paper towels and place in a sealable plastic bag and store in the refrigerator.

Heat the sesame oil in a large wok or nonstick skillet over high heat. Add the beans and stir-fry for 2 minutes or until heated through. Mix in the soy sauce, vinegar, brown sugar and pepper and stir-fry for 2 minutes or until the sauce reduces slightly and loosely coats the beans. Add the sesame seeds and toss to coat.

Spoon the beans into a bowl and serve immediately. You may substitute green beans or French-style green beans for the Chinese long beans. Serves 4 to 6.

Asparagus with Champagne Vinaigrette

6 tablespoons minced shallots

1/2 cup extra-virgin olive oil

1 1/2 cups finely chopped mushrooms

1/2 cup chicken stock

1/2 cup Champagne vinegar

1 tablespoon whole grain mustard

2 tablespoons chopped fresh herbs
   (dill weed, chervil, parsley,
   tarragon and/or basil)

salt and freshly ground pepper
   to taste

2 pounds asparagus spears

Cook the shallots in 1 tablespoon of the olive oil in a saucepan for 3 to 4 minutes, stirring frequently. Stir in the mushrooms and cook for 3 to 4 minutes or until the mushrooms have rendered their liquid and the liquid has evaporated, stirring frequently. Add the stock and simmer until reduced by 1/2, stirring occasionally. Stir in the vinegar.

Bring the vinaigrette to a boil and gradually add the remaining olive oil, whisking constantly. Remove from the heat and stir in the mustard and fresh herbs and season to taste with salt and pepper. Cover to keep warm.

Snap off the woody ends of the asparagus spears. Using a vegetable peeler, strip off the outer layer of each asparagus spear from just below the tip to the end of the spear. Gather the asparagus into 3 or 4 bundles and tie each bundle securely with kitchen twine.

Bring a saucepan filled with salted water to a boil and add the asparagus with the tips facing up. Boil for 6 to 8 minutes and drain. Snip the twine and arrange the asparagus on a heated platter. Drizzle with the desired amount of the warm vinaigrette and pass the remaining vinaigrette. Serves 8.

119

Follow these simple guidelines when storing and using fresh herbs. Always wrap fresh herbs loosely in damp paper towels and place in a sealable plastic bag filled with air. Herbs will keep up to five days in the refrigerator. To revive limp herbs, trim one-half inch from the stem and place the cut stem in a glass of water for a couple of hours. Fresh herbs should be added to a dish at the end of preparation, as heat will kill their flavor.

Rosemary Broccoli

Florets of 1¹/₂ to 2 pounds fresh
   broccoli
2 tablespoons butter
1 tablespoon peanut oil or olive oil
6 (2- to 3-inch-long) sprigs of
   rosemary
¹/₄ cup seasoned bread crumbs,
   crushed croutons or crushed
   butter crackers
salt and pepper to taste

Steam the broccoli over boiling water for 5 minutes or until tender. Plunge the broccoli into a bowl of ice water to stop the cooking process and preserve the bright green color. Drain and pat dry. You may prepare to this point up to 1 day in advance and store, covered, in the refrigerator. Bring to room temperature before proceeding with the recipe.

Heat a skillet over medium heat. Combine the butter, peanut oil, broccoli and rosemary in the skillet and sauté for 2 to 3 minutes. Add the bread crumbs and toss to coat. Season to taste with salt and pepper.

Leaving the rosemary sprigs whole imparts a big flavor burst without leaving rosemary needles stuck in the broccoli. Serve the broccoli with the rosemary left in as a garnish. Serves 4 to 6.

Cointreau Carrots

1¹/₂ pounds baby carrots, julienned

7 tablespoons unsalted butter

2 tablespoons brown sugar

1 teaspoon grated orange zest

¹/₄ cup Cointreau

chopped fresh parsley

Sauté the carrots in 3 tablespoons of the butter in a skillet just until tender-crisp. Remove the carrots to a bowl using a slotted spoon and cover to keep warm, reserving the pan drippings.

Heat the remaining 4 tablespoons butter with the reserved pan drippings and stir in the brown sugar. Cook over low heat until the brown sugar dissolves, stirring frequently. Stir in the orange zest and cook for 1 to 2 minutes to extract the oil, stirring occasionally. Add the liqueur and whisk until mixed. Add the carrots and toss gently until coated. Spoon the carrots into a serving bowl and sprinkle with parsley. Serve immediately. Serves 8.

Julienned vegetables are also known as matchsticks. The ideal length is about two inches, which allows an easy fit when eating. A sharp nonserrated knife will be the best tool for this job.

Baked Chiles Rellenos

1 (28-ounce) can whole tomatoes,
   drained
1 (14-ounce) can whole tomatoes,
   drained
1 large onion, chopped
bacon drippings
2 teaspoons pollo de galena
   (chicken bouillon powder)
1 teaspoon ground cumin
1 teaspoon dried oregano
1 teaspoon dried thyme
1 bay leaf
minced garlic to taste
salt and pepper to taste
2 (27-ounce) cans whole green
   chiles, drained (do not use diced
   green chiles)
1 cup (4 ounces) (or more) shredded
   Monterey Jack cheese
1 cup (4 ounces) (or more) shredded
   Cheddar cheese

Process the tomatoes in a blender until smooth. Sauté the onion in bacon drippings in a large saucepan until tender. Add the blended tomatoes, bouillon powder, cumin, oregano, thyme, bay leaf, garlic, salt and pepper to the saucepan and mix well. Cook over low heat until the mixture forms a thick paste, stirring occasionally. This process could take up to 2 hours. Discard the bay leaf.

Preheat the oven to 375 degrees. Arrange 1/2 of the green chiles back to back in a baking dish. Layer with 1/2 of the tomato mixture, 1/2 of the Monterey Jack cheese and 1/2 of the Cheddar cheese. Top with the remaining green chiles back to back, remaining tomato mixture, remaining Monterey Jack cheese and remaining Cheddar cheese. Bake for 20 minutes or until bubbly. Serves 12.

Green Chile Casserole

1/2 cup chopped onion

1/2 cup (1 stick) butter

4 cups cooked rice

2 cups sour cream

1 cup cream-style cottage cheese

1 teaspoon salt

1/4 teaspoon pepper

2 (4-ounce) cans diced green chiles, drained

2 cups (8 ounces) shredded sharp Cheddar cheese

Preheat the oven to 350 degrees. Sauté the onion in the butter in a large skillet until tender. Remove from the heat and stir in the rice, sour cream, cottage cheese, salt and pepper.

Layer the rice mixture, green chiles and Cheddar cheese 1/2 at a time in a shallow baking dish. Bake for 25 minutes or until brown and bubbly. You may assemble in advance and store, covered, in the refrigerator. Bake just before serving. Serves 12.

Grilled Sweet Corn on the Cob

8 ears of unhusked corn

Jalapeño Lime Butter (page 125)

Pull the corn husks back, leaving the husks attached at the base of the cobs. Remove the silk and reposition the husks to cover the corn. Soak the ears of corn in a large container of chilled water for 1 to 2 hours; drain.

Preheat the grill to low to medium. Pull back the corn husks and generously coat the corn kernels with Jalapeño Lime Butter. Reposition the husks and secure with kitchen twine. Grill for 20 to 25 minutes, turning 4 or 5 times. Remove the twine, pull back the husks, coat with additional Jalapeño Lime Butter and serve immediately. Serves 8.

Photograph for this recipe on page 110.

When choosing and storing corn, always buy the freshest corn possible. Check the local farmer's markets. Choose corn with grass-green dewy husks, soft dry-tipped silk, and plump, even kernels. Inspect kernels by peeling back some of the husk. When pierced, kernels should spurt cloudy juice. The stem should be moist, not chalky or yellowed. Avoid anything that is shriveled past the very tip. Tough skin indicates over-ripeness. Corn can be stored in a sealable plastic bag in the refrigerator for up to two days. Corn freezes well on or off the cob. For best results, corn should be blanched for two to three minutes before freezing.

Chive Butter

**¹/₂ cup (1 stick) unsalted butter,
    softened**
1 tablespoon minced fresh chives
¹/₁₆ teaspoon salt

Using a mixer fitted with a whisk attachment, blend the butter in a mixing bowl for 30 seconds or until smooth. Add the herbs and salt and beat until well distributed.

Fill an 8-ounce ramekin with the butter mixture and cover with waxed paper or shape the butter mixture into a log and cover with waxed paper or plastic wrap and secure the ends. Chill for 2 hours or longer. The butter may be prepared 2 to 3 days in advance and stored, covered, in the refrigerator or frozen for up to 2 months. Makes ¹/₂ cup.

DIJON AND PEPPERCORN BUTTER

**1 teaspoon brine-pack green
    peppercorns**
1 tablespoon Dijon mustard

Crush the peppercorns on a cutting board using the back of a wooden spoon. Prepare the Chive Butter, omitting the chives. Add the peppercorns and Dijon mustard to the butter mixture and mix. Store as directed above.

JALAPEÑO LIME BUTTER

**1 jalapeño chile, roasted, peeled and
    seeded (page 265)**
1 teaspoon minced garlic
1 teaspoon grated lime zest

Process the jalapeño chile and garlic in a food processor until minced. Prepare the Chive Butter, omitting the chives. Add the jalapeño chile mixture and lime zest to the butter mixture and mix. Store as directed above.

*C*ompound butters are easy to prepare and add a special touch to everyday foods. Try them on meat, fish, vegetables, pasta, or your favorite artisan bread. Create endless varieties by adding one or more of the following: fresh herbs, fruit juices, alcohol, nuts, puréed fruit, and/or citrus zest. Consider substituting cream cheese for the butter.

Corn Soufflé

¼ cup (½ stick) butter

¼ cup all-purpose flour

1½ tablespoons sugar

2 teaspoons salt

1¾ cups milk

3 cups fresh or frozen corn kernels,
  chopped or whole

3 eggs, beaten until frothy

Preheat the oven to 350 degrees. Heat the butter in a saucepan and stir in the flour, sugar and salt until blended. Cook until bubbly, stirring constantly. Add the milk and cook until thickened, stirring constantly. Stir in the corn and eggs.

Spoon the corn mixture into a buttered 2-quart soufflé dish and place the soufflé dish in a larger baking pan. Add enough hot water to the baking pan to reach halfway up the side of the soufflé dish. Bake for 45 to 60 minutes or until light brown. Chopped corn makes for a smoother consistency. Serves 8.

Dried beans are not only a good source of protein, but are one of the best fiber sources. To prepare, first sort through the beans and discard any pebbles. Cover the beans with water and discard any beans that rise to the surface. Drain and cover with fresh water if soaking. To speed the soaking process, bring the beans to a boil and boil for 2 minutes. Remove from the heat and let stand, covered, for 1 hour; drain. Cook the beans in 3 parts liquid to 1 part beans. Always cook the beans at a simmer to keep the beans in their jackets. Salting the beans prior to the end of the cooking process will cause the beans to toughen.

Creamed Summer Corn

10 ears of fresh corn, boiled until
   tender
1 cup heavy cream
1 cup milk
1 to 2 tablespoons sugar
1 teaspoon kosher salt
1/2 teaspoon pepper
1/2 teaspoon granulated garlic
1/2 teaspoon dried thyme
1/2 cup (1 stick) salted butter
1 tablespoon all-purpose flour

Cut the tops off the corn kernels into a stockpot using a sharp knife. Add the heavy cream, milk, sugar, salt, pepper, garlic and thyme and mix well. Bring to a boil gradually, stirring frequently. Reduce the heat and simmer for 3 minutes, stirring occasionally.

Bring the butter to a boil in a saucepan and reduce the heat to simmer. Add the flour and cook until blended, stirring constantly. Stir the butter mixture into the corn mixture and simmer for 3 minutes, stirring frequently. Serve warm. Serves 8.

Marinated Cucumbers

4 large cucumbers, thinly sliced

1 large onion, thinly sliced

1¹/₂ cups sugar

1 cup apple cider vinegar

1 tablespoon salt

1¹/₂ teaspoons celery seeds

1¹/₂ teaspoons mustard seeds

1 teaspoon turmeric

Toss the cucumbers and onion in a large bowl. Whisk the sugar, vinegar, salt, celery seeds, mustard seeds and turmeric in a bowl until mixed. Pour the vinegar mixture over the cucumber mixture and stir gently.

Spoon the cucumber mixture in an airtight refrigerator container and store in the refrigerator for up to 1 week. Serves 6 to 8.

Boursin Potatoes

5 ounces boursin cheese

2 cups heavy cream

3 pounds unpeeled red potatoes

Preheat the oven to 375 degrees. Combine the cheese and heavy cream in a medium saucepan and cook until blended, stirring frequently. Thinly slice the potatoes.

Layer the potatoes and cheese mixture alternately in a shallow baking dish until all of the ingredients are used, ending with the cheese mixture. Bake for 35 to 45 minutes or until light brown and bubbly. Serves 6.

When selecting potatoes, choose firm potatoes and avoid those with green spots and sprouted eyes. Store in a dark cool environment, preferably in a hanging mesh bag. Stored at 70 degrees, potatoes will keep about ten days; at 50 degrees, they will keep approximately six weeks. Do not store potatoes in the refrigerator. Potatoes should be stored away from onions and shallots to prevent sprouting. Potatoes should not be cleaned until ready to use. To clean, scrub potatoes under cool running water with a stiff brush, taking care not to break the skin. If a potato sprouts, cut out each eye and the green spots.

The Best Mashed Potatoes

**4 pounds Yukon gold potatoes, peeled
    and cut into 1- or 2-inch pieces**
1 tablespoon salt
1 cup milk
1/2 cup heavy cream
1/2 cup (1 stick) butter, softened
salt and pepper to taste
chopped green onions

Place the potatoes and 1 tablespoon salt in a large stockpot and cover with cold water. Bring to a boil over high heat. Reduce the heat to medium-low and cook for 15 to 20 minutes or until tender.

Heat the milk and heavy cream in a small saucepan over low heat. Drain the potatoes and mash in a large bowl with the warm milk mixture. Stir in the butter and season to taste with salt and pepper.

Depending on the desired texture, mash the potatoes accordingly. For a creamy whipped texture, beat the potatoes in a mixing bowl at medium speed until smooth or force the potatoes through a potato ricer and stir in the warm milk mixture, butter, salt and pepper. For a rustic texture, use a hand masher. Garnish with green onions. Serves 12 to 15.

MASHED POTATOES WITH ROASTED GARLIC

**1 head garlic (about 10 cloves),
    roasted (below)**
fresh chives

Prepare the potatoes as directed above. Add the roasted garlic cloves while warming the milk and heavy cream. Drain the potatoes and mash with the warm milk mixture and butter as directed above for a creamy texture. Season to taste and garnish with chives.

COWBOY MASHED POTATOES

12 ounces baby carrots
6 garlic cloves
**2 fresh jalapeño chiles, seeded and
    sliced**
**3 cups (12 ounces) shredded Cheddar
    cheese**
2 (11-ounce) cans corn, drained
1/2 cup sour cream
1 thin slice jalapeño chile

Combine the carrots, garlic and 2 jalapeño chiles with the potatoes as directed above and boil until tender; drain. Mash the potato mixture with a hand masher for a more rustic texture, adding the cheese, corn and sour cream along with the warm milk mixture and butter as directed above. Season to taste and garnish with 1 jalapeño chile slice.

*T here are two basic techniques for **Roasted Garlic,** peeled or unpeeled. We prefer the peeled technique, which calls for more work up front, but is less messy in the end. Peel the garlic cloves by trimming the base of each clove and peeling back the papery outer layers. Arrange the cloves in a small ovenproof baking dish and drizzle with just enough olive oil to cover. Roast, covered with foil, at 375 degrees for 45 minutes or until golden brown. The aroma will tell you when to check the garlic. Let stand until room temperature before using.*

Southwestern Squash

5 yellow squash, peeled and sliced

1 tablespoon minced onion

1/2 teaspoon salt

1/4 cup (1/2 stick) butter

3/4 (11-ounce) can tomatoes with
   green chiles

1 cup (4 ounces) shredded sharp
   Cheddar cheese

2 tablespoons butter, melted

1/3 cup butter cracker crumbs

Preheat the oven to 350 degrees. Sauté the squash, onion and salt in 1/4 cup butter in a skillet until tender; drain. Stir in the tomatoes with green chiles and cheese.

Spoon the squash mixture into a buttered 1 1/2-quart baking dish and drizzle with 2 tablespoons melted butter. Sprinkle with the cracker crumbs and bake for 30 minutes or until bubbly. Serves 4 to 6.

Purchase okra that is bright green, less than four inches in length, and with few black age spots. Short term, store okra in the refrigerator in a brown paper bag. Long term, chop the okra into 1/2-inch slices and freeze in water. For **Fried Okra,** lightly coat the sliced okra with a mixture of egg and milk. Toss the coated slices in fresh cornmeal and fry in 375-degree oil. Drain on paper towels, season to taste, and serve immediately. For **Sautéed Okra,** fry 4 slices of bacon in a skillet until golden brown. Remove the bacon, reserving the pan drippings. Crumble the bacon. Add the okra to the reserved pan drippings and sauté until the okra is light brown. Season to taste and remove the okra to a serving platter using a slotted spoon. Toss the okra with the crumbled bacon and red pepper flakes and serve immediately.

Squash Pickles

6 cups thinly sliced yellow squash

6 cups thinly sliced zucchini

6 cups sliced onions

2 cups sliced bell peppers

1/2 cup pickling salt

4 cups sugar

4 cups vinegar

2 teaspoons celery seeds

2 teaspoons mustard seeds

1 teaspoon ground ginger

1 (7-ounce) jar pimentos

8 small jalapeño chiles

8 garlic cloves

Mix the squash, zucchini, onions, bell peppers and pickling salt in a bowl. Cover the squash mixture with ice cubes from 2 ice trays. Let stand, covered, for 2 hours; drain.

Combine the sugar, vinegar, celery seeds, mustard seeds, ginger and pimentos in a stockpot and mix well. Cook until of a syrupy consistency, stirring frequently. Bring to a rolling boil and stir in the squash mixture. Return to a boil and remove from the heat.

Place 2 jalapeño chiles and 2 garlic cloves in each of 4 sterilized pint jars. Pack the jars with the squash mixture using a slotted spoon. Add the hot syrup, leaving a 1/2-inch headspace; seal with 2-piece lids. Process in a boiling water bath for 5 minutes. Makes 4 pint jars.

Water Bath for Canning: Fill a boiling water-bath canner 2/3 full of water. Thirty minutes before filling jars, bring to a boil. Use new lids and canning jars free of nicks and cracks. Wash, rinse, and air-dry the jars. Fifteen minutes before filling, place the jars, funnel, and a 1/2-cup metal measure in the canner rack and boil for 15 minutes. Fill jars using the sterilized funnel and sterilized metal measure, leaving a 1/2-inch headspace and wiping the rims if necessary. Center lids on jars and screw on bands until finger-tight. Return the jars to the canner. Cover, return to a boil and boil for 10 minutes. Cool the jars on a rack for 24 hours. The lids should curve downward. Store in a cool, dry, dark environment for up to 1 year.

Water Bath for Baking: Place the filled pan in a larger pan that reaches at least 3/4 of the way up the side of the filled pan. Add boiling water to the larger pan until it reaches halfway up the side of the filled pan. To keep water from seeping into springform pans, wrap the outside of the springform pan with 1 or 2 layers of foil, ensuring that the pan is covered past the height the water will reach.

Twice-Baked Blue Cheese Sweet Potatoes

4 sweet potatoes

1/4 cup (1/2 stick) butter, softened

1/4 cup sour cream

1/2 cup crumbled blue cheese

Jalapeño Maple Cream

Preheat the oven to 400 degrees. Arrange the sweet potatoes on a baking sheet and bake for 45 minutes or until tender. Cut the sweet potatoes lengthwise into halves and scoop out the pulp. Reduce the oven temperature to 350 degrees.

Combine the pulp, butter and sour cream in a bowl and mix well. Mound the pulp mixture in the potato shells and arrange on a baking sheet. Bake for 5 minutes and sprinkle with the blue cheese. Serve with Maple Jalapeño Cream. Serves 8.

MAPLE JALAPEÑO CREAM

1/2 cup sour cream or plain yogurt

1 tablespoon maple syrup

2 teaspoons minced seeded jalapeño chile

1 teaspoon fresh lime juice

salt to taste

Tabasco sauce to taste

Combine the sour cream, maple syrup, jalapeño chile and lime juice in a bowl and mix well. Season to taste with salt and Tabasco sauce.

134

Sweet potatoes are not actually potatoes. Rather, they are a member of the morning glory family, ranging in color from orange to red. The most popular variety of sweet potato is the Red Garnet.

Mushroom-Stuffed Tomatoes

8 firm ripe tomatoes

8 cups sliced mushrooms

1/2 cup (1 stick) butter

1 cup sour cream

3 ounces Roquefort cheese, crumbled

2 tablespoons dry sherry

4 teaspoons all-purpose flour

1 teaspoon chopped fresh parsley

1/4 teaspoon ground dried oregano

salt and pepper to taste

paprika

Preheat the oven to 375 degrees. Cut a slice from the top of each tomato and scoop out the pulp. Invert the tomatoes on a wire rack and drain. Sauté the mushrooms in the butter in a skillet until tender and drain. Combine the sour cream, cheese, sherry, flour, parsley and oregano in a saucepan and mix well.

Cook over low heat until smooth and thickened, stirring occasionally. Add the mushrooms, salt and pepper and mix well. Spoon the mushroom mixture into the tomato shells and arrange the stuffed tomatoes in a shallow baking pan. Sprinkle with paprika and bake for 5 to 10 minutes or until heated through. Serves 8.

Here are a few tips for mashing potatoes. If fluffy potatoes are desired, choose russet baking potatoes. If opting for creamy mashed potatoes, choose boiling potatoes. Use a potato ricer or a food mill to make smooth mashed potatoes. Use an old-fashioned potato masher or a fork for coarser, lumpier mashed potatoes. Do not use a food processor to mash potatoes.

Tamarind Vegetables

2 sweet potatoes, coarsely chopped

1 red onion, cut into eighths

1 eggplant, coarsely chopped

1 red bell pepper, chopped

2/3 cup coarsely chopped fresh cilantro leaves

1/3 cup coarsely chopped fresh mint leaves

2 tablespoons tamarind paste or tamarind concentrate

2 tablespoons vegetable oil

2 tablespoons honey

2 garlic cloves, minced

2 stalks lemon grass, peeled and chopped

2 teaspoons grated fresh ginger

1/2 teaspoon salt

1/4 teaspoon pepper

Preheat the oven to 400 degrees. Toss the sweet potatoes, onion, eggplant and bell pepper in a large bowl. Combine the cilantro, mint, tamarind paste, oil, honey, garlic, lemon grass, ginger, salt and pepper in a bowl and mix well. Add the cilantro mixture to the sweet potato mixture and toss to coat.

Spoon the sweet potato mixture into a 9×13-inch baking pan and bake, covered with foil, for 45 minutes or until the sweet potatoes are tender. Remove the foil and broil for 3 to 5 minutes. Serve hot or at room temperature. Serves 6 to 8.

Follow these guidelines when freezing fresh herbs: Blanch herb leaves by placing in boiling water for fifteen minutes. Remove the leaves from the water with a slotted spoon and immediately plunge in ice water to stop the cooking process. Drain and pat dry with paper towels. Arrange the leaves in a single layer on a baking sheet and freeze. Once frozen, remove to a sealable freezer bag and store in the freezer for future use.

Spicy Veggie Couscous

6 cups chicken broth

1/2 cup (1 stick) butter

1 cup chopped onion

1 cup chopped zucchini

1 cup shredded carrots

2 teaspoons ground coriander

1 teaspoon ground cumin

3 cups couscous

salt and pepper to taste

1 cup sliced almonds, toasted
   (page 268)

Bring the broth to a boil in a medium saucepan. Reduce the heat to low and cover to keep warm. Heat the butter in a large heavy saucepan over medium heat. Stir in the onion, zucchini and carrots and sauté for 8 to 10 minutes or until tender. Mix in the coriander and cumin and stir in the couscous.

Add the hot broth to the couscous mixture and mix well. Remove from the heat and let stand, covered, for 10 to 15 minutes or until the broth is absorbed. Fluff the couscous with a fork and season to taste with salt and pepper. Spoon into a serving bowl and sprinkle with the almonds. Serve as a side dish with beef or chicken or topped with stewed lamb. Serves 4 to 6.

137

Roast vegetables in a heavy pan to prevent burning. Spread the vegetables in a single layer to ensure even roasting. To ease cleanup, use a nonstick pan or line a baking pan with foil coated with nonstick baking spray. For Roasted Plum Tomatoes, cut the tomatoes into halves and remove the seeds. Arrange the tomatoes cut side up on a baking sheet lined with baking parchment. Drizzle with olive oil and sprinkle with fresh herbs as desired. Roast at 400 degrees for 5 minutes. Reduce the heat to 325 degrees and roast for 1 3/4 hours longer. For Roasted Zucchini, cut the zucchini into 1-inch rounds and toss with olive oil, salt, and pepper. Roast at 450 degrees for 15 minutes, turning occasionally.

Polenta with Roasted Vegetables

2 cups chicken broth

1 cup yellow cornmeal

1/4 cup (1/2 stick) butter

1/2 cup chopped green onions

1/4 cup chopped fresh parsley

1 garlic clove, minced

1/4 cup sun-dried tomatoes, chopped

salt and pepper to taste

Roasted Vegetables

Bring the broth to a boil in a large saucepan over medium-high heat. Reduce the heat to medium and gradually add the cornmeal, whisking constantly. Cook until the polenta is thick and smooth, stirring frequently. Remove from the heat and stir in the butter, green onions, parsley, garlic, sun-dried tomatoes, salt and pepper.

Cook over low heat for 1 minute, stirring constantly. Pour the polenta into a greased 4×8-inch loaf pan and let stand until cool. Chill until firm. Invert the polenta onto a hard surface and cut into twelve 1/2-inch-thick slices.

Heat a large skillet sprayed with nonstick cooking spray over medium-high heat. Add the polenta slices to the hot skillet and cook until brown on both sides, turning once. Serve the polenta topped with the Roasted Vegetables. Serves 12.

ROASTED VEGETABLES

1 eggplant, peeled

1 red bell pepper

1 orange bell pepper

1 yellow bell pepper

olive oil

salt and pepper to taste

1/4 cup olive oil

2 tablespoons balsamic vinegar

1 tablespoon honey

1/4 teaspoon salt

1/8 teaspoon pepper

1/16 teaspoon dried thyme

Preheat the oven to 400 degrees. Line a baking sheet with foil and coat with nonstick cooking spray. Cut the eggplant and each bell pepper into 16 long strips. Arrange the eggplant and bell peppers in a single layer on the prepared baking sheet and brush with olive oil. Season with salt and pepper to taste and roast for 20 minutes.

Whisk 1/4 cup olive oil, the vinegar, honey, 1/4 teaspoon salt, 1/8 teaspoon pepper and thyme in a bowl until the olive oil is incorporated. Pour over the roasted vegetables in a bowl and toss to coat.

Classic Risotto

6 cups chicken stock (page 261)
1 tablespoon butter
1 tablespoon olive oil
1/2 cup finely chopped onion
freshly ground pepper to taste
2 cups arborio rice
1/2 cup dry white wine
1 tablespoon butter
1/4 cup (1 ounce) freshly grated
   Parmesan cheese
1 tablespoon chopped fresh parsley

Bring the stock to a simmer in a saucepan over low heat and cover to keep warm. Heat a deep skillet over medium heat. Combine 1 tablespoon butter and the olive oil in the skillet. Add the onion and sauté until tender. Season to taste with pepper. Stir in the rice until coated.

Cook for 1 to 2 minutes, stirring frequently. Add the wine and cook until most of the liquid is absorbed, stirring frequently. Reduce the heat to low and add about 1/2 cup of the warm stock. Cook until the stock is absorbed, stirring constantly. Add the remaining stock 1/2 cup at a time and cook until the stock is absorbed after each addition, stirring constantly. This process should take approximately 20 minutes. Stir in 1 tablespoon butter. Spoon the risotto into a serving bowl and sprinkle with the cheese and parsley. Serves 6 to 8.

RISOTTO WITH WILD MUSHROOM RAGU

1 to 2 tablespoons olive oil
3/4 cup chopped shallots
4 or 5 garlic cloves, minced
5 cups assorted mushrooms
1/2 cup bourbon
salt and pepper to taste

Prepare the Classic Risotto. Heat the olive oil in a skillet and add the shallots and garlic. Sauté for 1 minute. Stir in the mushrooms and cook over medium heat until tender and all the liquid has evaporated, stirring frequently. Stir in the bourbon and season to taste with salt and pepper. Stir the mushroom mixture into the risotto and spoon into a serving bowl. Sprinkle with the cheese, if desired, and the parsley.

RISOTTO WITH ROASTED SOUTHWESTERN CHILES AND CORN

1 cup fresh corn kernels, or
   1 (11-ounce) can corn, drained
3 tablespoons olive oil
salt and pepper to taste
1/2 cup (2 ounces) shredded
   Pepper Jack cheese
1/2 cup chopped roasted poblano
   chiles (page 265)
3 canned chipotle chiles, seeded
   and chopped
fresh cilantro leaves

Prepare the Classic Risotto, omitting the Parmesan cheese and parsley. Preheat the oven to 400 degrees. Spread the corn on a baking sheet, drizzle with the olive oil and sprinkle with salt and pepper, stirring to coat. Roast for 15 minutes or until golden brown, stirring once or twice. Stir the roasted corn, cheese, poblano chiles and chipotle chiles into the risotto. Spoon the risotto into a serving bowl and sprinkle with cilantro.

To add flavor to rice or potatoes, cook in a mixture of one-half water and one-half chicken or vegetable broth. If using a low-sodium broth, cook the rice entirely in broth instead of a mixture of broth and water.

Main Dishes

THE DISH ON DALLAS

Many people imagine the Texas landscape sprinkled with oil pumps and expansive cattle ranches. This mystique has a strong influence on visitors' desire for a sensational steak when they come to town. From elegant fine dining to hole-in-the-wall steakhouses, they are not disappointed. A typical Dallas steakhouse sells between five hundred to seven hundred pounds of prime beef a week.

Rosemary Pesto Lamb with Wild Rice Spinach Timbales recipe on page 147.

Mushroom-Crusted Beef Tenderloin with Balsamic Jus

Dallacites love a great steak and an excellent bottle of wine. The Capital Grille serves both.

Balsamic Jus
8 large shiitake mushroom caps
1/2 cup dried morel mushrooms
6 (10-ounce) center-cut
    filets mignons
salt and pepper to taste
2 tablespoons clarified butter

Prepare the Balsamic Jus. Preheat the oven to 350 degrees. Process the shiitake mushrooms and dried mushrooms in a food processor until finely minced. Season the filets with salt and pepper and press each side of the filets in the mushroom mixture to coat.

Heat the clarified butter in a large sauté pan over medium-high heat. Sear the filets in batches in the hot butter for 5 minutes on each side. Arrange the filets on a baking sheet and bake to the desired degree of doneness. Bake for approximately 3 minutes for medium-rare, depending on the thickness. Remove the filets to heated serving plates and drizzle with the Balsamic Jus. Serves 6.

BALSAMIC JUS

1 1/4 cups red wine
6 large button mushrooms, chopped
1 large onion, chopped
6 cups veal stock
1/4 cup balsamic vinegar
coarse salt to taste
freshly ground pepper to taste

Combine the wine, button mushrooms and onion in a saucepan and simmer over medium heat for 15 minutes or until the most of the wine has evaporated. Stir in the stock and increase the heat to high. Bring to a boil and reduce the heat to low.

Simmer for 1 1/2 hours or until the mixture is reduced to 2 cups, stirring occasionally. Stir in the vinegar and simmer for 2 minutes longer. Strain the sauce into a bowl and season to taste with salt and pepper.

Beef Tenderloin with Mustard Cream Sauce

1 (3- to 4-pound) beef tenderloin,
   at room temperature
1 tablespoon olive oil
salt and pepper to taste
Mustard Cream Sauce

Preheat the oven to 425 degrees. Rub the tenderloin with the olive oil and sprinkle with salt and pepper. Arrange the tenderloin in a baking pan and bake for 30 minutes or to the desired degree of doneness. Remove the tenderloin to a serving platter and slice as desired. Serve with the Mustard Cream Sauce. Serves 8 to 10.

3 tablespoons coarse grain mustard
2 egg yolks
2 to 3 tablespoons fresh lemon juice
1 green onion, chopped
1/4 teaspoon minced fresh marjoram
3/4 cup olive oil
1/4 cup vegetable oil
1/4 to 1/2 cup whipping cream,
   lightly whipped

MUSTARD CREAM SAUCE

Combine the mustard, egg yolks, lemon juice, green onion and marjoram in a food processor and process until pale yellow in color and creamy in texture. Add the olive oil and vegetable oil gradually, processing constantly until thickened. Fold the whipped cream into the sauce just before serving.

If you are concerned about using raw egg yolks, use eggs pasteurized in their shells, which are sold at some specialty food stores, or use an equivalent amount of pasteurized egg substitute.

Beer-Marinated Steaks with Peppercorn Sauce

6 (12-ounce) top loin (New York strip)
  or rib-eye steaks
1 (12-ounce) bottle dark beer
1/2 cup packed dark brown sugar
5 tablespoons fresh lime juice
2 tablespoons Worcestershire sauce
2 tablespoons whole grain mustard
2 tablespoons olive oil
1 tablespoon minced fresh ginger
1/2 teaspoon hot pepper sauce
Peppercorn Sauce

Arrange the steaks in a single layer in a glass dish or place in a sealable plastic bag. Whisk the beer, brown sugar, lime juice, Worcestershire sauce, whole grain mustard, olive oil, ginger and hot pepper sauce in a bowl until the olive oil is incorporated and pour over the steaks, turning to coat. Marinate, covered, in the refrigerator for 8 to 10 hours, turning occasionally.

Preheat the grill to medium-high. Remove the steaks and discard the marinade. Grill the steaks for 4 minutes per side for medium-rare or to the desired degree of doneness. Drizzle some of the warm Peppercorn Sauce over each steak.

You may substitute one 2- to 3-pound beef tenderloin for the steaks. Brown the tenderloin in a skillet in a small amount of olive oil over medium-high heat. Bake in a preheated 350-degree oven for 35 minutes or to the desired degree of doneness. Let the tenderloin rest for 10 minutes and slice as desired. Serve with the warm Peppercorn Sauce. Serves 6.

PEPPERCORN SAUCE

1/2 cup white wine
1 shallot, finely chopped
1 to 11/2 tablespoons coarsely
  crushed four-peppercorn mix
13/4 cups chicken stock
13/4 cups beef stock
1/2 cup heavy cream

Bring the wine, shallot and crushed peppercorns to a boil in a heavy saucepan and reduce the heat. Simmer for 5 minutes or until the mixture is reduced by 1/2, stirring occasionally. Stir in the chicken stock and beef stock and return to a boil.

Boil for 25 minutes or until the mixture is reduced to 2 cups, stirring occasionally. Add the heavy cream and cook for 6 minutes or until the sauce coats the back of a spoon, stirring occasionally. You may prepare 2 to 10 hours in advance and store, covered, in the refrigerator. Reheat gently over low heat before serving.

Marinated Flank Steak

1¹/2 pounds beef flank steak
3 tablespoons vegetable oil
¹/4 cup soy sauce
¹/4 cup pineapple juice
¹/4 cup packed brown sugar
3 green onions, chopped
2 tablespoons minced fresh cilantro
2 tablespoons minced fresh ginger
1 garlic clove, minced
1 teaspoon red pepper flakes

Place the steak in a sealable plastic bag. Mix the oil, soy sauce, pineapple juice, brown sugar, green onions, cilantro, ginger, garlic and red pepper flakes in a bowl and pour over the steak. Seal tightly and turn to coat. Marinate in the refrigerator for 4 to 10 hours, turning occasionally.

Preheat the grill to medium-high. Remove the steak and discard the marinade. Grill the steak for 6 to 8 minutes per side for medium-rare or to the desired degree of doneness. Remove the steak to a platter and tent with foil. Let rest for 5 minutes. Thinly slice the steak against the grain, reserving any juices. Drizzle some of the reserved juices over each serving. Serves 4.

FLANK STEAK WITH WINE AND SHALLOTS

1¹/2 pounds beef flank steak
2 tablespoons soy sauce
1 teaspoon dried thyme
Freshly ground pepper to taste
2 cups bordeaux
1 cup chopped shallots
¹/2 cup (1 stick) butter
2 tablespoons chopped fresh parsley

Preheat the grill to medium-high. Brush both sides of the steak with the soy sauce and sprinkle with the thyme and pepper. Grill the steak as directed above, tent and allow to rest.

Bring the wine and shallots to a boil in a saucepan. Reduce the heat and simmer for 10 minutes or until the mixture is reduced by ¹/2, stirring frequently. Remove from the heat and whisk in the butter until melted. Stir in the parsley. Thinly slice the steak against the grain and ladle some of the sauce over each serving.

CHILI FLANK STEAK

1¹/2 pounds beef flank steak
¹/2 cup vegetable oil
2¹/2 tablespoons white wine vinegar
1¹/2 teaspoons chili seasoning
1 teaspoon salt
¹/2 teaspoon garlic powder
¹/4 teaspoon onion powder

Place the steak in a sealable plastic bag. Mix the oil, vinegar, chili seasoning, salt, garlic powder and onion powder in a bowl and pour over the steak. Seal tightly and marinate in the refrigerator for 4 to 10 hours, turning occasionally.

Preheat the grill. Remove the steak and discard the marinade. Grill the steak as directed above, tent and allow to rest. Thinly slice the steak against the grain and serve immediately.

Do-Ahead Brisket

1 (6-pound) beef brisket, trimmed
garlic to taste
pepper to taste
1 (10-ounce) bottle Worcestershire
   sauce
3 tablespoons liquid smoke
1 cup ketchup
3/4 cup packed brown sugar
1/3 cup Worcestershire sauce
1 tablespoon fresh lemon juice

Season the brisket with garlic and pepper and place in a large baking pan. Mix 10 ounces Worcestershire sauce and the liquid smoke in a bowl and pour over the brisket, turning to coat. Marinate, covered, in the refrigerator for 8 to 10 hours, turning occasionally.

Preheat the oven to 450 degrees. Bake the brisket, uncovered, for 30 minutes. Reduce the oven temperature to 225 degrees and bake, covered, for 1 hour per pound. Drain, reserving the pan juices. Chill, wrapped in foil, for 8 to 10 hours.

Preheat the oven to 350 degrees. Slice the brisket against the grain and arrange in a baking pan. Mix 2 cups of the reserved pan juices, the ketchup, brown sugar, 1/3 cup Worcestershire sauce and the lemon juice in a bowl and pour over the brisket. Bake, covered, for 45 minutes or until heated through. Serves 6 to 8.

Veal Stroganoff

1 1/2 pounds veal
2 to 3 tablespoons butter
8 ounces mushrooms
1 tablespoon minced onion
1 tablespoon all-purpose flour
1 cup sour cream
6 tablespoons veal or beef stock
1 teaspoon salt
1/8 teaspoon pepper

Preheat the oven to 250 degrees. Brown the veal in the butter in a skillet. Remove the veal to a baking dish, reserving the pan drippings. Lightly sauté the mushrooms and onion in the reserved pan drippings. Remove from the heat and add the flour, stirring constantly until incorporated. Stir in the sour cream, stock, salt and pepper.

Spoon the mushroom mixture over the veal and bake, covered, for 1 1/2 hours. Serve with buttered egg noodles. Serves 6.

Rosemary Pesto Lamb with Wild Rice Spinach Timbales

2 large portobello mushrooms

2 racks of lamb with 7 to 8 bones, cut between each bone

salt and pepper to taste

2 tablespoons olive oil

Rosemary Pesto

Wild Rice Spinach Timbales

Fava Beans

3 to 4 tablespoons chopped fresh Italian parsley

Preheat the oven to 200 degrees. Cut the mushrooms into 1/4-inch pieces and scrape out the dark gills from the bottom side. Scrape the bones of the lamb down to the chop area and season to taste with salt and pepper. Heat a large skillet over high heat and add the olive oil. Sear the chops in the hot oil for 3 to 4 minutes. Turn and spread the top of each chop with 1 tablespoon of the Rosemary Pesto. Cook for 1 to 2 minutes; the chops should be medium-rare. Remove the chops to an ovenproof platter and keep warm in the oven, reserving the pan drippings. Add the mushrooms and remaining Rosemary Pesto to the reserved pan drippings and mix well. Cook for 5 minutes or until the mushrooms begin to brown and wilt slightly. Unmold the timbales in the center of a serving platter. Stack the lamb chops vertically against the rice and spoon the mushroom mixture over the top. Garnish the outer edge of the platter with the Fava Beans and sprinkle with the parsley. Serves 6.

ROSEMARY PESTO

1/2 cup fresh rosemary, stemmed

1/2 cup pine nuts

4 large garlic cloves

1 tablespoon olive oil

Combine the rosemary, pine nuts, garlic and olive oil in a food processor and pulse until finely chopped.

WILD RICE SPINACH TIMBALES

2 cups long grain and wild rice mix

2 carrots, grated

1 bunch green onions, trimmed and chopped

1 bunch fresh spinach, trimmed

salt to taste

butter

Preheat the oven to 200 degrees. Cook the rice using the package directions and stir in the carrots and green onions. Blanch the spinach in boiling salted water in a saucepan for 30 seconds. Immediately remove the spinach with a slotted spoon and dip in a bowl of ice water to stop the cooking process. Drain on paper towels. Coat 6 ramekins with butter and line with the spinach leaves, overlapping each leaf and allowing enough overhang to cover the filling. Fill each spinach-lined ramekin with 1/6 of the rice mixture and fold the spinach leaves over to completely cover. Cover with foil that has been coated with nonstick cooking spray and keep warm in the oven.

FAVA BEANS

1 tablespoon salt

fava beans, shelled

olive oil

Bring a saucepan of water to a boil and add the salt and beans. Cook for 3 to 5 minutes or to the desired crispness. Drain and cool slightly. Peel off the white interior skin of the beans by pinching the beans at one end. Toss the beans with a small amount of olive oil in a bowl.

Photograph for this recipe on page 140.

Pork with Cherry Cream Sauce

2 (8- to 10-ounce) pork tenderloins
salt and pepper to taste
1/4 cup (1/2 stick) butter or *extra min/side* vegetable oil
Cherry Sauce
Blue Cheese Sauce

Cut the tenderloins into medallions and season with salt and pepper. Heat the butter in a large skillet over medium heat. Sauté the pork in the butter for 3 minutes on 1 side and 2 minutes on the remaining side. Remove the pork to a platter using a slotted spoon, reserving 1 tablespoon of the pan drippings.

Spoon equal portions of the warm Cherry Sauce onto each of 4 to 6 serving plates. Top evenly with pork and drizzle with the warm Blue Cheese Sauce. Serve immediately. Serves 4 to 6.

CHERRY SAUCE

2 tablespoons minced shallots
2 garlic cloves, minced
1 tablespoon pan drippings
1/2 cup dried cherries
1 tablespoon sugar
1/2 cup dry red wine
1/2 cup port
1 1/3 cups demi-glace
1/2 cup dried cherries
1 teaspoon chopped fresh basil
2 tablespoons butter, softened

Cook the shallots and garlic in the pan drippings for 20 seconds. Stir in 1/2 cup cherries and the sugar and cook for 1 minute longer, stirring frequently. Deglaze the skillet with the red wine and port. *not careful/ not enough liquid left*

Cook over high heat until the cherry mixture is reduced by 3/4, stirring frequently. Process the cherry mixture in a blender until puréed. Pour the purée through a fine strainer into a clean skillet, discarding the solids, and add the demi-glace and 1/2 cup cherries. Simmer for 3 to 5 minutes, stirring occasionally. Whisk in the basil and butter. Remove from the heat and cover to keep warm.

BLUE CHEESE SAUCE

1 cup heavy cream
1/2 cup pine nuts, toasted (page 268)
2 ounces blue cheese

Combine the heavy cream and pine nuts in a saucepan. Cook over high heat until the mixture is reduced by 1/3, stirring occasionally. Remove from the heat and whisk in the blue cheese until blended. Cover to keep warm.

Dallas Chalupas

1 (16-ounce) package dried
   pinto beans
1 (2^1/$_2$- to 2^3/$_4$-pound) pork butt,
   trimmed
3 garlic cloves, minced
3 tablespoons chili powder
1 tablespoon dried oregano
1 tablespoon ground cumin
1 tablespoon plus 2 teaspoons salt
2 bay leaves
corn chips
shredded Cheddar cheese
chopped green onions
chopped tomatoes
shredded iceberg lettuce
chopped avocados
hot sauce
sour cream

Sort and rinse the beans. Generously cover the beans with water in a bowl and let stand for 8 to 10 hours; drain and rinse. Combine the beans and pork in a slow cooker or large Dutch oven. Add enough water to cover the beans and ^{3}/$_4$ of the pork. Stir in the garlic, chili powder, oregano, cumin, salt and bay leaves. Cook, covered, on Low for 6 to 8 hours, stirring occasionally.

Remove the pork to a platter and cool slightly. Remove the meat from the bones and shred. Return the pork to the slow cooker and cook for 20 minutes or to the desired consistency, adding water as needed. Discard the bay leaves. Spoon the bean mixture over corn chips in bowls. Serve with shredded cheese, chopped green onions, chopped tomatoes, shredded lettuce, chopped avocados, hot sauce and/or sour cream. Serves 6 to 8.

The French way of carving a leg of lamb is to cut horizontal slices. That way, those who like well-done lamb can be served the first slices and those who prefer it rare can have the slices near the bone, which are always more rare. With a very sharp carving knife, remove a few thin slices lengthwise, slicing from the underside of the lamb. Turn the leg over so that the meatier side faces up. Using a large fork to steady the roast, carve fairly thin horizontal slices from one end of the roast to the other. Keep slicing until you hit the bone. Be sure to remove all the meaty pieces, particularly around the knucklebone.

Creole Chops

Caroline Rose Hunt, co-founder of Lady Primrose's Royal Bathing & Skin Luxuries and Lady Primrose's Shopping English Countryside, is also the woman behind Rosewood Hotels & Resorts, which operates and manages fourteen properties throughout the world. Ms. Hunt was named one of the Most Powerful Women in the Travel Industry by Travel Agent Magazine *in 1999, one of America's 100 Most Influential Women in 1983, and one of the Fifty Most Powerful Women in the United States by* Ladies Home Journal *in 1990. She is a Sustainer in the Junior League of Dallas and has contributed one of her favorite recipes that was served in her restaurant.*

5 tomatoes, chopped
1 (15-ounce) can beef bouillon
1 (15-ounce) can tomato sauce
1 onion, chopped
¹/₂ cup apple cider vinegar
1 tablespoon minced garlic
1 tablespoon crushed red pepper
minced fresh basil or dried basil
  to taste
8 pork or venison chops
vegetable oil

Combine the tomatoes, bouillon, tomato sauce, onion, vinegar, garlic, red pepper and basil in a saucepan and mix well. Simmer for 20 minutes, stirring occasionally.

Preheat the oven to 325 degrees. Brown the pork chops on both sides in a small amount of oil in a skillet. Remove the chops to a baking dish and pour the tomato mixture over the top. Bake, covered, until the pork chops are cooked through. Serves 8.

Grilled Pork Chops

3 tablespoons hoisin sauce
1 tablespoon hot mustard
1 tablespoon chopped shallot
1 tablespoon minced garlic
1 tablespoon chopped fresh ginger
1 tablespoon chopped fresh
   jalapeño chile
1 tablespoon chopped scallion
1 tablespoon chopped fresh cilantro
4 pork chops, butterflied
salt and pepper to taste

Preheat the grill. Process the hoisin sauce, mustard, shallot, garlic, ginger, jalapeño chile, scallion and cilantro in a blender until puréed and of a sauce consistency.

Season the pork chops with salt and pepper. Grill for 10 minutes and turn. Liberally baste the pork chops with the sauce and grill for 10 minutes longer or until cooked through. Serves 4.

Tangy Texas Ribs

4 slabs pork baby back ribs

1 tablespoon garlic powder

1 teaspoon cayenne pepper

1/2 cup soy sauce

1/2 cup packed brown sugar

Remove the thin membrane on the ribs' lower side. Mix the garlic powder and cayenne pepper in a bowl and rub over the surface of the ribs. Wrap the ribs with 2 layers of foil and chill for 8 to 10 hours.

Preheat the oven to 300 degrees. Arrange the foil-wrapped ribs on a baking sheet and bake for 2 hours. Preheat a gas grill to medium-high. Remove the ribs from the foil and baste with a mixture of the soy sauce and brown sugar.

Arrange the ribs on the grill rack and grill, covered, over indirect heat for 30 minutes. Uncover and grill for 30 minutes longer, basting every 10 minutes with the soy sauce mixture. If using hardwood charcoal, grill over indirect heat for 45 to 60 minutes, turning and basting frequently. Serves 4 to 6.

Deep-in-the-Heart-of-Texas Backyard Barbecue Chicken

A Dallas icon for twenty-five years, The Mansion on Turtle Creek is a destination for people who appreciate the finer things in life…five-star dining, service, and luxury accommodations. Famous chef Dean Fearing brings his take on Dallas to the world with a twist on Southwestern flavors.

1 (3- to 4-pound) chicken

1 tablespoon vegetable oil

salt and black pepper to taste

dried thyme to taste

crushed red bell pepper flakes to taste

3 cups smoky bacon barbecue sauce

Peach Jalapeño Chutney

Rinse the chicken under running water and cut into quarters. Pat the chicken dry and brush with the oil and season with salt, black pepper, thyme and bell pepper flakes.

Start with a clean grill, making sure old ashes are discarded and grates are brushed clean. Add wood charcoal and ignite. When the charcoal has burned to white ash, arrange the chicken quarters skin side down on the grill rack. The process now is to render as much grease as possible from the skin without burning the skin or causing the grease to flare up on the fire and burn the skin. Take your time and be attentive to the chicken. Add water-soaked hickory chips a small handful at a time to the edge of the fire. This will start the smoking process. Seal in the smoke with a lid or the cover of the grill. Grill for 8 to 10 minutes, remembering to keep a close eye on the chicken and turning when the fat is rendered. If the smoke dies down, add another handful of hickory chips.

Grill and smoke the chicken for about 15 minutes or until cooked through, making sure the chicken is cooking evenly on both sides. Baste heavily with the barbecue sauce and turn frequently to prevent burning. Remove from the grill and serve with the Peach Jalapeño Chutney. Serves 4.

PEACH JALAPEÑO CHUTNEY

5 ripe peaches, peeled

1 tablespoon finely chopped fresh ginger

1 tablespoon sugar

2 teaspoons fresh lemon juice

1 teaspoon ground cinnamon

Coarsely chop 3 of the peaches. Process the remaining peaches in a blender until puréed. Pour the purée into a saucepan and stir in the ginger, sugar, lemon juice and cinnamon. Cook over medium heat for 5 to 6 minutes or until reduced and thickened, stirring frequently. Stir in the reserved chopped peaches and cook for 3 minutes longer or until heated through, stirring occasionally.

Chicken and Dumplings

Dale Wooton, Garden Cafe

3 carrots

1 roasting chicken or fryer parts

2 onions, coarsely chopped

2 ribs celery

2 bay leaves

pepper to taste

2 cups all-purpose flour

$1/16$ teaspoon salt

1 egg

Cut the carrots into halves lengthwise and cut each half into $1/2$-inch pieces. Combine the carrots, chicken, onions, celery, bay leaves and pepper in a stockpot with enough water to cover. Simmer until the chicken is tender. Remove the chicken to a platter using a slotted spoon, reserving the stock. Drain the stock and skim the excess fat, discarding the solids. Chop the chicken, discarding the skin and bones.

Mix the flour and salt in a bowl. Add the egg and enough cold water until the mixture is the consistency of bread dough. Roll the dough into balls the size of marbles and pinch flat. Arrange on a flour-coated tray.

Return the chicken to the stock and skim off any excess fat. Add the dumplings and simmer until tender, stirring occasionally. For a thicker consistency, add a mixture of 1 cup water and 2 tablespoons cornstarch. For a richer flavor, add 1 or 2 chicken bouillon cubes. Serves 4 to 6.

155

9-15-11
Easy! Great. Marinated in slow cooker. Used smoked paprika- pretty strong try regular next time + add vessies to bottom

*S**low-Cooker Sticky Chicken** is the answer to a homemade dinner with very little effort. Mix 4 teaspoons salt, 2 teaspoons paprika,1 teaspoon cayenne pepper, 1 teaspoon onion powder, 1 teaspoon dried thyme, 1 teaspoon white pepper, $1/2$ teaspoon garlic powder and $1/2$ teaspoon black pepper in a bowl. Remove the giblets from 1 large roasting chicken and discard. Rinse the chicken inside and out and pat dry with paper towels. Rub the spice mixture evenly over the inside cavity and outside surface. Place the chicken in a sealable plastic bag, seal tightly, and marinate in the refrigerator for 8 to 10 hours. Place the chicken in a slow cooker; do not add any liquid. Cook on Low for 8 to 10 hours or until tender.*

Crispy Oven-Fried Chicken

3 quarts water

1/2 cup kosher salt

1/2 cup sugar

1 (2 1/2- to 3-pound) chicken, cut up

3 cups cornflakes, crushed

1/2 cup (2 ounces) grated Parmesan
   cheese

1 teaspoon salt

1/4 teaspoon garlic powder

1/4 teaspoon pepper

1/2 cup (1 stick) butter, melted

Mix the water, salt and sugar in a large bowl until dissolved and add the chicken to the brining solution. Soak for 45 minutes and drain. Rinse and pat dry with paper towels. Chill the chicken in the refrigerator for up to 1 day.

Preheat the oven to 400 degrees. Toss the cornflakes, cheese, salt, garlic powder and pepper in a sealable plastic bag. Dip the chicken in the butter and add to the cornflake mixture. Seal the bag tightly and shake until the chicken is coated. Arrange the chicken in a single layer on a baking sheet and bake for 40 to 45 minutes or until cooked through and crispy. Serves 4.

Basil-Stuffed Chicken with Caper Sauce

6 slices bacon

2 cups chopped fresh basil

1 small garlic clove

1/4 cup extra-virgin olive oil

1/2 teaspoon fresh lemon juice

salt to taste

4 boneless skinless chicken breasts,
   cut into halves vertically

freshly ground pepper to taste

1 cup all-purpose flour

2 eggs, lightly beaten

1 cup bread crumbs

Caper Sauce

Preheat the oven to 375 degrees. Cook the bacon in a skillet until brown and crisp; drain. Crumble the bacon and process with the basil and garlic in a food processor until a paste forms. Add the olive oil gradually, processing constantly until incorporated. Spoon into a bowl and mix in the lemon juice. Season to taste with salt.

Make a horizontal slit in the side of each breast portion to form a pocket. Stuff 1 tablespoon of the basil mixture in each pocket and sprinkle the surface of the chicken with salt and pepper.

Coat the chicken with the flour and dip in the eggs. Coat with the bread crumbs and arrange in a single layer in a greased baking dish. Bake for 20 to 30 minutes or until the chicken is cooked through. Drizzle with the Caper Sauce. Serves 4.

CAPER SAUCE

1 cup low-salt chicken broth

1/2 cup white wine

2 tablespoons drained capers

3 tablespoons unsalted butter

Combine the broth and wine in a heavy saucepan. Bring just to a boil over medium-high heat and cook until the mixture is reduced by 1/4, stirring occasionally. Stir in the capers and simmer. Remove from the heat and add the butter, stirring until thickened.

Grilled Barbecued Chicken Salad Pizza

1 envelope dry yeast

1 teaspoon honey

3/4 cup warm (105 to 115 degrees)
    water

2 3/4 cups all-purpose flour

1 teaspoon salt

2 tablespoons olive oil plus extra
    for brushing

1/2 cup barbecue sauce

1 small red onion, thinly sliced

1 cup drained cooked black beans

1 cup whole kernel corn

2 chicken breasts with rib meat,
    grilled and shredded

2 cups (8 ounces) shredded
    Cheddar cheese

2 cups (8 ounces) shredded Monterey
    Jack cheese

1/2 head iceberg lettuce, shredded

2 cups shredded peeled jicama

2 cups chopped tomatoes

blue cheese or ranch salad dressing

Best-Ever Blue Cheese Dressing
    (page 108) or ranch salad dressing

Dissolve the yeast and honey in 1/2 cup of the warm water. Mix the flour and salt in a mixing bowl and add the remaining 1/4 cup water, the yeast mixture and 2 tablespoons olive oil. Beat with an electric mixer fitted with a dough hook at low speed for 6 to 7 minutes, scraping the bowl occasionally. Knead once or twice on a lightly floured hard surface. Remove the dough to a bowl and let rise, covered with a damp tea towel, for 30 minutes.

Divide the dough into 4 equal portions and roll each portion into a ball. Let rise, covered with a damp tea towel, for 20 minutes. The dough may be covered with plastic wrap for up to 1 day.

Preheat the grill to high. Roll each dough ball into a 7- or 8-inch round on a lightly floured surface and brush lightly with olive oil. Grill the rounds for 7 to 8 minutes or until brown and turn. Brush each round with some of the barbecue sauce and top each with equal portions of the onion, beans, corn, chicken, Cheddar cheese and Monterey Jack cheese.

Grill, covered, until the cheese melts. Remove the pizzas from the grill. Toss the lettuce, jicama and tomatoes in a bowl with the desired amount of dressing. Cut the pizzas into wedges and top with the lettuce mixture. Serve immediately.

If preferred, you may bake the pizzas in the oven. Preheat the oven and a pizza stone to 525 degrees. Dust the hot pizza stone with cornmeal and arrange the pizzas on the stone. Or, bake on a 10×15-inch baking sheet with sides dusted with cornmeal for 15 to 20 minutes. Serves 6.

Chicken with Charred Tomato Chutney

1 cup plain yogurt

3 tablespoons finely chopped fresh
   cilantro leaves

1 tablespoon hot curry paste, or
   2 tablespoons mild curry paste

juice of 1 lemon

2 pounds boneless skinless chicken
   breasts, cut into 1¼-inch pieces

1 package flatbread

Charred Tomato Chutney

Preheat a grill pan or indoor electric grill to high. Combine the yogurt, cilantro, curry paste and lemon juice in a shallow dish and mix well. Add the chicken and turn to coat evenly. Thread the chicken on metal skewers and grill for 5 to 6 minutes per side or until the chicken is charred at the edges and cooked through.

Remove the chicken to a platter and grill the flatbread until blistered and heated through. Slide the chicken off the skewers onto a serving platter. Pile the chicken onto the flatbread and top with the Charred Tomato Chutney. Serves 4.

CHARRED TOMATO CHUTNEY

3 plum tomatoes

½ cup tomato sauce or purée

1 teaspoon mustard seeds

1 teaspoon coriander seeds

½ teaspoon crushed red pepper
   flakes

coarse salt to taste

Heat a small heavy skillet over high heat until very hot. Place the whole tomatoes in the hot skillet and pan-roast the tomatoes until charred on all sides, turning frequently. Place the tomatoes and tomato sauce in a food processor.

Heat the same skillet over high heat until hot. Combine the mustard seeds, coriander seeds and red pepper flakes in the skillet and toast until the seeds pop, stirring frequently. Add the toasted mustard seed mixture and a few pinches of salt to the food processor and pulse until of a chunky consistency.

Green and White Chicken Enchiladas

1 (3½-pound) chicken, cut up

sliced carrots

sliced parsnips

¼ cup (½ stick) butter

¼ cup all-purpose flour

3 cups sour cream

2 cups heavy cream

¼ cup grated onion

1 tablespoon salt

pepper to taste

1 pound fresh spinach, trimmed

¼ cup (½ stick) butter

12 corn tortillas

8 ounces Monterey Jack cheese,
   shredded

pickled jalapeño chiles

Combine the chicken, carrots, parsnips and your favorite seasonings with enough water to cover in a stockpot. Cook until the chicken is tender. Drain, discarding the carrots and parsnips and reserving 1½ cups of the broth and the chicken. Strain the reserved broth through cheesecloth. Chop the chicken, discarding the skin and bones.

Preheat the oven to 350 degrees. Heat ¼ cup butter in a saucepan and stir in the flour. Cook until blended and bubbly, stirring constantly. Stir in the reserved 1½ cups broth and simmer until thickened, stirring constantly. Mix in the sour cream, heavy cream, onion, salt and pepper. Increase the heat to high and bring to a boil. Reduce the heat to low and cover to keep warm. Lightly sauté the spinach in ¼ cup butter in a skillet.

Dip the tortillas 1 at a time in the sour cream mixture to soften. Spoon equal portions of the chicken and spinach down the center of each tortilla and sprinkle with some of the cheese. Roll the tortillas to enclose the filling and arrange seam side down in a baking dish. Spoon the remaining sour cream mixture over the enchiladas. Top with pickled jalapeño chiles and sprinkle with the remaining cheese. Bake for 30 minutes. You may substitute canned broth for the homemade broth. Makes 12 enchiladas.

Tomatillo Chicken Enchiladas

1/3 cup half-and-half

6 ounces cream cheese, softened

2 cups shredded cooked chicken

3/4 cup finely chopped onion

1/2 teaspoon salt

vegetable oil

12 (8-inch) corn tortillas

Tomatillo Sauce

3/4 cup (3 ounces) shredded
   Cheddar cheese

3/4 cup (3 ounces) shredded
   Monterey Jack cheese

shredded lettuce

chopped tomatoes

olives

sour cream

24 tomatillos, husked

4 to 6 serrano chiles, stemmed
   and seeded (leave some seeds
   to add spice)

3 cups chicken broth

2 tablespoons cornstarch

2 tablespoons chopped fresh cilantro

1 teaspoon salt

Preheat the oven to 350 degrees. Beat the half-and-half and cream cheese in a mixing bowl until smooth and fluffy. Add the chicken, onion and salt and mix until combined. Heat a small amount of oil in a skillet until hot. Dip the tortillas in the hot oil to soften, or microwave the tortillas in a buttered microwave-safe dish.

Spread a thin layer of the Tomatillo Sauce in a 9×13-inch baking dish. Spread a thin layer of the Tomatillo Sauce on each tortilla. Spoon about 1/4 cup of the chicken mixture down the center of each tortilla and roll to enclose the filling.

Arrange the enchiladas seam side down in the prepared baking dish. Spoon the remaining Tomatillo Sauce over the top and cover with foil. Bake for 20 minutes and remove the foil. Sprinkle with the Cheddar cheese and Monterey Jack cheese and bake for 5 minutes longer or until the cheese melts. Serve with shredded lettuce, chopped tomatoes, olives and sour cream. Makes 12 enchiladas.

TOMATILLO SAUCE

Bring the tomatillos, serrano chiles and broth to a boil in a saucepan and boil for 7 to 10 minutes. Dissolve the cornstarch in a small amount of cold water in a bowl and add to the boiling tomatillo mixture along with the cilantro and salt and mix well. Boil for 5 minutes longer, stirring occasionally. Remove from the heat and cool slightly. Process in a blender or food processor until puréed.

Salmon with Horseradish

1/2 cup (1 stick) butter, softened

1/2 cup bread crumbs

4 ounces horseradish

2 tablespoons chopped fresh parsley

2 teaspoons fresh lemon juice

2 1/4 pounds salmon fillets

olive oil

salt and pepper to taste

Preheat the oven to 400 degrees. Process the butter, bread crumbs, horseradish, parsley and lemon juice in a food processor until blended. Brush the salmon with olive oil and sprinkle with salt and pepper. Arrange the fillets in a single layer on a baking sheet.

Bake for 8 to 10 minutes or until the salmon flakes easily. Spread the horseradish butter over the top of the salmon and broil for 2 minutes or until golden brown. Serves 6.

Caramelized Grouper

1 grapefruit

1 lime

1 lemon

1 orange

1 cup Citrus Simple Syrup (page 260)

2 slices bacon, chopped

1 red onion, chopped

4 grouper fillets or similar fish

olive oil

all-purpose flour

2 eggs, lightly beaten

1 (6-ounce) can French-fried onions

Zest the grapefruit, lime, lemon and orange and add the zest to the Citrus Simple Syrup in a bowl. Squeeze the juice from $1/2$ of each fruit into the syrup mixture and mix well. Cook the bacon in a skillet until brown and crisp. Remove the bacon to a platter using a slotted spoon, reserving the pan dripping.

Cook the red onion in the reserved pan drippings until caramelized, stirring frequently. Stir in the syrup mixture and bacon and simmer over medium heat until thickened, reduced and of a sauce consistency, stirring frequently. You may prepare to this point up to 5 days in advance and store, covered, in the refrigerator. Reheat before serving.

Preheat the broiler. Sear the fillets on both sides in olive oil in a skillet. Coat the fillets with flour and dip in the eggs. Cover the coated fillets with the fried onions and arrange in a single layer on a baking sheet. Broil for about 5 minutes per $1/2$ inch thickness or until the fillets flake easily. Serve with the sauce and garnish with any remaining fried onions and slices of the leftover fruit. Serves 4.

Baja Fish Tacos

With locations city-wide, Blue Mesa's unique design, architecture, and atmosphere match the distinctive Southwestern flavors offered in the restaurant. Owners Jim and Liz Baron introduced the delicious blue margarita, a house specialty that can be prepared with over fifty types of tequila.

1 cup all-purpose flour

2 teaspoons each salt, garlic powder, dry mustard and dried oregano

1/2 teaspoon pepper

1 cup beer

1 pound mahi mahi

all-purpose flour

vegetable oil for deep-frying

16 (6-inch) corn tortillas, heated

Ancho Mayonnaise

Grilled Jicama Slaw

Mix 1 cup flour, the salt, garlic powder, dry mustard, oregano and pepper in a bowl. Add the beer and stir until the batter is smooth. Cut the fish into 2-inch strips and coat with additional flour, shaking off the excess. Dip the fish in the batter and deep-fry in the oil in a skillet for 2 to 3 minutes or until light brown. Drain on paper towels.

Stack the tortillas 2 high for each taco and spread the top of each stack with Ancho Mayonnaise. Top each with equal portions of the fried fish and Grilled Jicama Slaw. Serves 4.

ANCHO MAYONNAISE

1 cup mayonnaise

1 or 2 ancho chiles, roasted and chopped (page 265)

Combine the mayonnaise and ancho chiles in a bowl and mix well.

GRILLED JICAMA SLAW

5 corn tortillas, cut into julienne strips

vegetable oil for frying

1 cup (1/4-inch) sliced peeled jicama

1/2 cup each julienned red, yellow and green bell pepper

1 cup finely shredded red cabbage

1 cup finely shredded green cabbage

3/4 cup canola oil

1/2 cup fresh lime juice

1/4 cup finely chopped fresh cilantro

1 large garlic clove, minced

1 shallot, minced

1 teaspoon salt

2 tablespoons grated cotija cheese or Parmesan cheese

Preheat the grill. Fry the tortilla chips in oil in a skillet until brown and crisp and drain on paper towels. Grill the jicama for 3 minutes or until the jicama has grill marks and is slightly softened. Cool and cut into julienne strips.

Toss the jicama, bell peppers, cabbage and tortilla strips in a bowl. Whisk the canola oil, lime juice, cilantro, garlic, shallot and salt in a bowl until the canola oil is incorporated and pour over the jicama mixture. Sprinkle with the cheese and mix well.

Pecan-Crusted Salmon

2 tablespoons Dijon mustard

2 tablespoons butter, melted

4 teaspoons honey

1/4 cup fresh bread crumbs

1/4 cup finely chopped pecans

2 teaspoons chopped fresh parsley

4 (4- to 6-ounce) salmon fillets

salt and pepper to taste

Preheat the oven to 450 degrees. Combine the Dijon mustard, butter and honey in a bowl and mix well. Toss the bread crumbs, pecans and parsley in a shallow dish. Season the salmon with salt and pepper and arrange in a single layer on a greased baking sheet.

Brush the fillets with the mustard mixture and pat some of the bread crumb mixture over the top of each fillet. Bake for 10 minutes or until the salmon just begins to flake easily. You may prepare in advance and store, covered, in the refrigerator. Bake just before serving. Serves 4.

You need a sturdy cut of fish for poaching. Thin, flimsy fillets are apt to disintegrate in the poaching liquid. A steak cut from a larger fish, such as halibut, cod, or salmon, works well.

Polenta-Crusted Sea Bass

4 (4-ounce) sea bass fillets
1/2 cup buttermilk
1 tablespoon extra-virgin olive oil
salt and pepper to taste
1/2 cup polenta mix or cornmeal
Corn Salsa
sprigs of fresh cilantro (optional)

Arrange the fillets in a single layer in a shallow dish. Pour the buttermilk over the fillets, turning to coat. Marinate, covered, for 8 to 10 hours.

Preheat the oven to 350 degrees. Heat the olive oil in an ovenproof skillet. Remove the fillets from the buttermilk and season to taste with salt and pepper. Coat both sides of the fillets with polenta mix, pressing gently, and add to the hot oil. Cook for 2 minutes and turn. Cook for 1 minute longer.

Bake for 15 minutes or until the fillets flake easily. Arrange 1 fillet on each of 4 serving plates. Spoon some of the Corn Salsa around each fillet and top with a sprig of cilantro. Serves 4.

CORN SALSA

1 1/2 cups corn kernels
1 tablespoon fresh lime juice
1/4 teaspoon salt
1/4 teaspoon freshly ground
   black pepper
2 tomatillos, husked, blanched and
   chopped (1/3 cup)
8 ounces tomatoes, chopped (3/4 cup)
1 small jalapeño chile, seeded and
   finely chopped
1/2 small cucumber, chopped
1/2 small red bell pepper, chopped
2 tablespoons chopped fresh
   cilantro leaves

Preheat the broiler. Spread the corn kernels on a baking sheet sprayed with nonstick cooking spray. Broil until roasted, stirring occasionally. Mix the lime juice and salt in a bowl until the salt dissolves. Stir in the black pepper. Add the corn, tomatillos, tomatoes, jalapeño chile, cucumber, bell pepper and cilantro and mix well. Let stand at room temperature until serving time.

Miso-Marinated Sea Bass

¹/₂ cup mirin (sweet Japanese rice wine)
¹/₂ cup white miso
¹/₂ cup sake
¹/₄ cup sugar
4 (6-ounce) sea bass fillets, 1 inch thick

Combine the mirin, miso, sake and sugar in a shallow dish and mix well. Add the fillets and turn to coat. Marinate, covered, in the refrigerator for 2 to 4 hours, turning occasionally.

Reposition the top oven rack 6 inches from the top and preheat the oven to 450 degrees. Arrange the fillets on a greased baking sheet and place the baking sheet on the top oven rack. Bake for 6 minutes. Broil for 2 minutes, watching carefully. The fillets should be caramel in color on top but opal in the center. Serves 4.

Sautéed Sole
with Chardonnay Sauce

$1/2$ cup all-purpose flour

salt and pepper to taste

$1^1/_2$ pounds sole fillets

$3/_4$ tablespoon butter

1 cup chardonnay

1 tablespoon crushed shallots

1 garlic clove, finely chopped

$1/_4$ cup heavy cream

$1/_2$ teaspoon sugar

$1/_8$ teaspoon salt

$1/_{16}$ teaspoon cayenne pepper

4 to 6 tablespoons butter

Mix the flour, salt and pepper and coat the fillets with the flour mixture. Lightly sauté in $3/_4$ tablespoon butter in a skillet until the fillets flake easily. Remove the fillets to a plate and cover to keep warm, reserving the pan drippings.

Add the wine to the reserved pan drippings and deglaze. Bring to a boil and boil for 1 minute. Stir in the shallots and garlic and cook until the mixture is reduced by $1/_2$, stirring frequently. Add the heavy cream, sugar, salt and cayenne pepper and mix well.

Simmer over low heat until thickened, stirring frequently. Whisk in 4 to 6 tablespoons butter 1 tablespoon at a time and cook until blended and of the desired consistency. Spoon the sauce over the fillets and serve immediately. Serves 3 to 4.

Baked Lobster with Crab Meat Stuffing

Famous in the artsy Deep Ellum neighborhood, Daddy Jacks serves seafood with Italian sizzle. Owner and chef Salvatore Gisellu brings his native Sardinian style to Texas.

2 gallons water

1 carrot, chopped

1 onion, chopped

1 rib celery, chopped

juice of 1 lemon

1 tablespoon salt

2 bay leaves

crushed peppercorns

2 whole live Maine lobsters

1 pound Crab Meat Stuffing

1/2 cup Lemon Butter Sauce
    (page 171)

Celeriac Slaw (page 171)

Bring the water, carrot, onion, celery, lemon juice, salt, bay leaves and peppercorns to a boil in a stockpot. Add the lobsters and return to a boil. Boil for 3 to 5 minutes. Drain and cool for several minutes.

Preheat the oven to 350 degrees. Using a chef's knife, split the lobsters down the middle into halves, crush the claws and remove all the meat. Discard the liver (green portion). Fill the lobster shells with the lobster meat and top with the Crab Meat Stuffing. Place the stuffed lobster shells on a baking sheet and bake for 8 to 12 minutes. Arrange 1 stuffed lobster half on each of 4 serving plates and drizzle with the Lemon Butter Sauce. Serve with the Celeriac Slaw. Serves 4.

1 tablespoon butter

1/2 cup chopped yellow onion

1/2 cup chopped celery

1 tablespoon chopped green onions

1 teaspoon chopped fresh tarragon

salt and pepper to taste

1/2 cup butter cracker crumbs

8 ounces fresh special white
    crab meat

CRAB MEAT STUFFING

Heat the butter in a sauté pan and stir in the yellow onion, celery and green onions. Sweat for 3 to 4 minutes or until the vegetables are tender. Stir in the tarragon and season to taste with salt and pepper. Spoon the onion mixture into a bowl and mix in the cracker crumbs and crab meat. Add additional melted butter if needed for a moister consistency.

LEMON BUTTER SAUCE

1 cup dry white wine

1 tablespoon chopped shallots

2 cups heavy cream

juice of 1 lemon

1/2 cup (1 stick) butter

salt and white pepper to taste

Combine the wine and shallots in a saucepan and cook until the mixture is reduced by 3/4. Stir in the heavy cream and cook until the mixture is reduced by 1/2, stirring frequently. Strain the sauce, discarding the shallots, and return the sauce to the saucepan. Add the lemon juice and butter and cook until incorporated and thickened, stirring frequently. Season to taste with salt and white pepper.

CELERIAC SLAW

1/2 cup vegetable oil

1 egg yolk

1 tablespoon whole grain mustard

1 tablespoon sherry vinegar

1 teaspoon honey

salt and pepper to taste

2 pounds celeriac, julienned

1/2 cup chopped fresh chives

1 tablespoon chopped bell pepper

Whisk the oil, egg yolk, whole grain mustard, vinegar, honey, salt and pepper in a bowl until the oil is incorporated. Add the celeriac, chives and bell pepper to the dressing and toss until coated. If you are concerned about using raw egg yolks, use eggs pasteurized in their shells, which are sold at some specialty food stores, or use an equivalent amount of pasteurized egg substitute. Serves 4.

Crawfish Pie

1 recipe Perfect Pie Pastry (page 271)
1 pound crawfish tails
3 cups chopped onion
2 ribs celery, finely chopped
2 tablespoons vegetable oil
1/2 cup (1 stick) butter
1/4 cup chopped green onions
2 garlic cloves, chopped
1/2 cup milk
1/2 cup seasoned bread crumbs
1/4 cup tomato sauce
1 egg, beaten
1/4 cup chopped fresh parsley
1 tablespoon salt
1/2 teaspoon pepper

Preheat the oven to 350 degrees. Fit 1 of the pastries into a 9-inch pie plate. Chop 1/3 of the crawfish tails, leaving the remaining ones whole. Sauté the onion and celery in the oil in a skillet until tender. Stir in the butter, green onions and garlic and sauté for 2 minutes longer. Reduce the heat to low and cook for 10 minutes, stirring occasionally. Remove from the heat and stir in the crawfish tails, milk, bread crumbs, tomato sauce, egg, parsley, salt and pepper.

Spoon the crawfish mixture into the pastry-lined pie plate and top with the remaining pastry, crimping the edge and cutting vents. Bake for 1 1/2 hours or until the crust is golden brown. Serves 4 to 6.

Grilled Shrimp with Spicy Garlic Paste

1 large garlic clove, minced
1 teaspoon salt
1 teaspoon paprika
1/2 teaspoon cayenne pepper
2 tablespoons olive oil
2 teaspoons fresh lemon juice
2 pounds shrimp in shells, brined
lemon wedges

Preheat the grill or broiler. Mix the garlic with the salt in a bowl and stir in the paprika and cayenne pepper. Add the olive oil and lemon juice to the garlic mixture and stir until the consistency of a thin paste. Add the shrimp and toss until evenly coated. You may chill at this point for up to 1 hour.

Thread the shrimp onto skewers if desired and grill or broil for 2 to 3 minutes per side or until the shells turn bright pink, turning once. Serve hot or at room temperature with lemon wedges. Serves 2.

Shrimp with White Wine and Dill Sauce

3 tablespoons margarine or butter

3 tablespoons all-purpose flour

1^1/$_2$ cups half-and-half

^{3}/$_4$ teaspoon dried dill weed

^{1}/$_2$ teaspoon salt

2 tablespoons margarine or butter

1 tablespoon chopped onion

^{3}/$_4$ cup white wine

2 teaspoons fresh lemon juice

1 pound shrimp, peeled and deveined

hot cooked angel hair pasta or
   fettuccini

Heat 3 tablespoons margarine in a medium saucepan. Add the flour gradually, stirring constantly until blended. Cook until of a paste consistency, stirring constantly. Add the half-and-half gradually, stirring constantly. Stir in the dill weed and salt and simmer over medium-low heat until thickened and of a sauce consistency, stirring frequently. Remove from the heat and cover to keep warm.

Heat 2 tablespoons margarine in a large saucepan over medium-high heat. Mix in the onion and cook for 3 to 4 minutes or until tender. Stir in the wine and lemon juice and bring to a boil. Add the shrimp and cook for 2 minutes on each side; do not overcook.

Add the dill sauce to the shrimp and mix well. Reduce the heat to low and simmer until thickened, stirring frequently. Spoon over hot cooked pasta on a serving platter. Serves 2 to 4.

173

Gorgonzola and Pecan Tart

1 recipe Savory Tart Crust (page 272)
2 tablespoons olive oil
1 sweet onion, finely chopped
$1/2$ teaspoon coarse kosher salt
1 cup fresh or frozen cranberries
1 tablespoon sugar
$1^1/3$ cups finely chopped toasted
   pecans (page 268)
2 teaspoons minced fresh thyme
$1/2$ teaspoon dry mustard
$1/8$ teaspoon cayenne pepper
$3/4$ cup heavy cream
2 eggs
5 ounces Gorgonzola cheese,
   crumbled

Preheat the oven to 375 degrees. Prepare the Savory Tart Crust and fit into a tart pan. Line with foil or baking parchment and weight with pie weights or dried beans. Bake for 15 minutes. Cool slightly. Remove the pie weights. Maintain the oven temperature.

Heat the olive oil in a saucepan over medium heat. Add the onion and salt to the hot oil and cook for 10 to 15 minutes or until the onion is caramelized, stirring frequently. Stir in the cranberries and sugar and cook until the cranberries start to pop. Mix in the pecans, thyme, dry mustard and cayenne pepper and remove from the heat.

Whisk the heavy cream and eggs in a bowl until blended. Spoon the cranberry mixture into the baked crust and sprinkle with the cheese. Pour the egg mixture over the prepared layers and bake for 20 to 25 minutes or until set. Cool for 15 minutes before serving. Serve with mixed baby greens salad topped with candied pecans and drizzled with balsamic vinaigrette. You may substitute a commercially prepared tart shell for the homemade pastry. Serves 6.

Brie and Tomato Pasta

16 ounces fusilli
$2/3$ pound ripe Brie cheese, cubed
4 very ripe plum tomatoes, chopped
1 cup fresh basil leaves, julienned
$1/2$ to $2/3$ cup olive oil
2 or 3 garlic cloves, minced
salt and freshly cracked pepper to
   taste
freshly grated Parmesan cheese

Prepare the pasta using the package directions until al dente. Drain and cover to keep warm.

Combine the Brie cheese, tomatoes, basil, olive oil, garlic, salt and pepper in a bowl and mix well. Toss the cheese mixture with the hot pasta in a bowl. Serve with freshly grated Parmesan cheese. Serves 8.

Angry Pasta
for Manic Mondays

1/4 cup virgin olive oil

2 tablespoons minced garlic

1 pound Italian sweet sausage, casings removed and coarsely chopped

28 to 56 ounces canned Italian tomatoes

1/4 cup red wine

1 teaspoon sugar

1/2 teaspoon (or more) crushed red pepper

seasoned salt to taste

freshly ground black pepper to taste

1 (10-ounce) package frozen artichokes, thawed, or drained canned artichokes

1 tablespoon drained capers

1 tablespoon chopped fresh parsley

4 fresh basil leaves, torn

1/16 teaspoon (or more) dried oregano (optional)

16 ounces fidelini, capellini or linguini, cooked al dente and drained

freshly grated Parmesan cheese

Heat the olive oil in a large saucepan and add the garlic. Cook until almost golden brown and stir in the sausage. Cook until the sausage is brown, stirring frequently. Add the undrained tomatoes, wine, sugar, red pepper, seasoned salt and black pepper and mix well.

Cook over medium heat for 15 minutes, stirring and breaking up the tomatoes with a wooden spoon. Stir in the artichokes, capers, parsley, basil and oregano and simmer for 5 minutes. Stir and simmer for 1 hour longer, stirring occasionally. The longer the sauce simmers the better the flavor.

Spoon the sauce over the hot pasta on a serving platter and serve with freshly grated Parmesan cheese. You may prepare the sauce in advance and store, covered, in the refrigerator, or freeze for up to 3 months. Serves 8.

Desserts

THE DISH ON DALLAS

Dallas is known as a "shopper's Mecca." From haute couture to secondhand stores and from antique shops to discount outlets, Dallas has a bit of everything, including the first planned shopping center in the United States, Highland Park Village, built in 1931. All that shopping works up an appetite and is a great excuse to stop for coffee and dessert at one of the more than eight thousand eating and drinking establishments in the city.

Vanilla Crème Brûlée recipe on page 178.

Vanilla Crème Brûlée

4 cups heavy cream, chilled
2/3 cup granulated sugar
1/16 teaspoon salt
12 egg yolks
1 teaspoon vanilla extract
**1/4 cup turbinado sugar or large
    grain sugar**

Adjust the oven rack to the lower-middle position and preheat the oven to 300 degrees. Place a tea towel in the bottom of a large shallow baking dish and arrange twelve 4-ounce ramekins on the towel. Bring a large saucepan of water to a boil.

Combine 2 cups of the heavy cream, the granulated sugar and salt in a saucepan and scald over medium heat to about 155 degrees, stirring occasionally to dissolve the sugar. Remove from the heat and stir in the remaining 2 cups heavy cream. Whisk the eggs in a bowl until blended. Add the warm cream mixture to the egg yolks, whisking constantly until blended. Whisk in the vanilla.

Pour the cream mixture evenly into the ramekins and place the baking dish on the oven rack. Add enough boiling water to the baking dish to reach 2/3 of the way up the sides of the ramekins. Bake for 30 to 45 minutes or until the centers of the custards are set and an instant-read thermometer inserted in the center registers 180 degrees.

Remove the ramekins to a wire rack and cool to room temperature. Arrange the ramekins on a baking sheet, cover tightly with plastic wrap and chill until serving time. Just before serving, remove the plastic wrap and blot any condensation with paper towels. Sprinkle each with 1 teaspoon of the turbinado sugar and caramelize the sugar with a kitchen blowtorch or under the broiler, watching carefully to prevent scorching. Serve immediately. Serves 12.

Photograph for this recipe on page 176.

WHITE CHOCOLATE CRÈME BRÛLÉE

8 ounces white chocolate, chopped

Prepare the Vanilla Crème Brûlée as directed above, adding the white chocolate to the scalded cream mixture after removing it from the heat. Stir until the chocolate is blended and proceed as directed.

PRALINE CRÈME BRÛLÉE

1 1/2 teaspoons praline liqueur
12 pecan halves, toasted (page 268)

Prepare the Vanilla Crème Brûlée as directed above, substituting the liqueur for the vanilla. Garnish each custard by placing a toasted pecan half in the center of the warm caramelized sugar.

Lemon Cheesecake with Raspberry Sauce

1 Lemon Shortbread Crust (page 181)

2¹/₂ pounds cream cheese, softened

1³/₄ cups sugar

1 teaspoon grated lemon zest

¹/₄ teaspoon vanilla or lemon extract

3 tablespoons all-purpose flour

¹/₄ teaspoon salt

¹/₄ cup heavy cream

4 eggs

2 egg yolks

Raspberry Sauce

Prepare the Lemon Shortbread Crust and set aside. Increase the oven temperature to 425 degrees. Beat the cream cheese in a mixing bowl until smooth, scraping the bowl occasionally. Add the sugar, lemon zest and vanilla and beat until blended. Add the flour, salt, heavy cream, eggs and egg yolks 1 ingredient at a time, beating well after each addition.

Spoon the cream cheese filling into the baked crust and place on a baking sheet. Bake for 12 minutes and reduce the oven temperature to 300 degrees. Bake for 1 hour longer; the cheesecake will not be set. Remove to a wire rack to cool. Chill, covered, for 3 to 10 hours. Slice and serve with the Raspberry Sauce. Serves 10.

2¹/₂ cups fresh raspberries or frozen unsweetened raspberries, thawed

¹/₂ cup superfine sugar

¹/₄ cup framboise (optional)

RASPBERRY SAUCE

Process the raspberries, sugar and liqueur in a blender or food processor until puréed. Strain the sauce through a sieve into a bowl to remove the seeds if desired. Chill until serving time.

Pumpkin Cheesecake with Praline Sauce

1 Graham Cracker Cheesecake Crust (page 181)

24 ounces cream cheese, softened

1¹/₂ cups sugar

4 eggs

³/₄ cup canned solid pack pumpkin

1 tablespoon vanilla extract

¹/₂ teaspoon ground cinnamon

¹/₈ teaspoon ground nutmeg (optional)

Praline Sauce

Prepare the Graham Cracker Cheesecake Crust. Preheat the oven to 350 degrees. Beat the cream cheese and sugar in a mixing bowl until light and fluffy, scraping the bowl occasionally. Add the eggs and pumpkin and beat until smooth. Add the vanilla, cinnamon and nutmeg and beat until blended.

Spoon the cream cheese mixture into the prepared springform pan and bake for 1 hour or until the cheesecake is set. Turn off the oven and let the cheesecake stand in the oven with the door closed for 15 minutes. Remove to a wire rack to cool. Chill, covered, in the refrigerator until serving time. Serve with the Praline Sauce. Serves 10.

¹/₂ cup (1 stick) butter

1¹/₂ cups pecan pieces

2 cups packed brown sugar

¹/₂ cup corn syrup

1 cup sour cream

PRALINE SAUCE

Heat the butter in a saucepan over medium-high heat. Stir in the pecans and cook until light brown, stirring frequently. Mix in the brown sugar and cook until clear, stirring occasionally. Stir in the corn syrup and cook until thickened and of a sauce consistency, stirring frequently. Remove from the heat and stir in the sour cream.

Pour the sauce into clean canning jars and seal tightly. Store in the refrigerator for up to 3 weeks. The sauce may also be served over ice cream or pound cake.

Graham Cracker Cheesecake Crust

1¹/₄ cups graham cracker crumbs

3 tablespoons butter, melted

2 tablespoons sugar

¹/₂ teaspoon ground cinnamon

Combine the cracker crumbs, butter, sugar and cinnamon in a bowl and mix well. Press the crumb mixture over the bottom of a 9-inch springform pan. Chill for 15 minutes. You may substitute an equal amount of other cracker or cookie crumbs for the graham cracker crumbs. The possibilities are endless. Makes 1 (9-inch) crust.

2 cups all-purpose flour

¹/₂ cup sugar

2 teaspoons grated lemon zest

1 cup (2 sticks) butter, cubed

2 egg yolks, beaten

¹/₂ teaspoon vanilla or lemon extract

LEMON SHORTBREAD CRUST

Preheat the oven to 400 degrees. Mix the flour, sugar and lemon zest in a bowl and cut in the butter until crumbly. Add the egg yolks and vanilla and mix with a fork until the mixture forms a dough.

Divide the dough into 3 equal portions and pat 1 portion over the bottom of a 9-inch springform pan, wrapping the remaining portions in plastic wrap to prevent drying out. Remove the side of the pan and place the pan bottom on a baking sheet. Bake for 8 minutes. Remove to a wire rack to cool.

Increase the oven temperature to 425 degrees and reattach the side of the pan to the bottom. Pat the remaining dough over the side of the pan, at least 2 inches up from the bottom crust. Fill with your favorite cheesecake filling and bake. Makes 1 (9-inch) crust.

CHOCOLATE PECAN CRUST

1¹/₂ cups vanilla wafer crumbs

¹/₂ cup pecans, toasted and chopped (page 268)

¹/₃ cup (2 ounces) semisweet chocolate chips, chopped

3 tablespoons butter, melted

2 tablespoons sugar

¹/₄ teaspoon ground cinnamon

¹/₈ teaspoon salt

Preheat the oven to 300 degrees. Combine the cookie crumbs, pecans, chocolate chips, butter, sugar, cinnamon and salt in a bowl and mix well. Pat the crumb mixture over the bottom of a 9-inch springform pan and bake for 15 minutes. Remove to a wire rack to cool. Fill with your favorite cheesecake filling and bake. Makes 1 (9-inch) crust.

Blackberry Crisp

3/4 cup sugar

2 tablespoons all-purpose flour

4 to 5 cups fresh or frozen
  blackberries

Brown Sugar Topping

6 tablespoons butter, melted

whipped cream or cinnamon
  ice cream

Preheat the oven to 375 degrees. Combine the sugar and flour in a bowl and mix well. Sprinkle the sugar mixture over the blackberries in a bowl and toss gently to coat.

Spoon the coated berries into a greased 9-inch ceramic pie plate and sprinkle with the Brown Sugar Topping. Drizzle with the butter and bake for 45 minutes.

Serve warm with whipped cream or cinnamon ice cream. You may bake individual crisps in 6 to 8 small greased ramekins or soufflé dishes, reducing the baking time to 25 minutes. Serves 6 to 8.

1 cup all-purpose flour

1 cup packed brown sugar

1 teaspoon baking powder

1/2 teaspoon ground cinnamon

1/8 teaspoon salt

1 egg, beaten

BROWN SUGAR TOPPING

Combine the flour, brown sugar, baking powder, cinnamon and salt in a bowl and mix well. Make a well in the center of the flour mixture and add the egg to the well. Blend the egg into the dry ingredients and mix until crumbly.

Blueberry Buckle

1/2 cup granulated sugar

1/4 cup packed brown sugar

1/4 cup (1/2 stick) butter, softened

1 egg, lightly beaten

1/2 cup milk

1 teaspoon almond extract

2 cups all-purpose flour

2 teaspoons baking powder

1/2 teaspoon salt

2 cups fresh blueberries

Cinnamon Crumb Topping

ice cream

Preheat the oven to 375 degrees. Combine the granulated sugar, brown sugar, butter and egg in a bowl and mix well. Stir in the milk and flavoring. Sift the flour, baking powder and salt together and blend into the sugar mixture. Fold in the blueberries.

Spoon the blueberry mixture into a greased and floured 8- or 9-inch round baking dish and sprinkle with the Cinnamon Crumb Topping. Bake for 45 minutes; the topping should spring back when lightly touched. Serve warm with ice cream. Serves 6 to 8.

CINNAMON CRUMB TOPPING

1/2 cup sugar

1/3 cup all-purpose flour

1/2 teaspoon ground cinnamon

1/4 cup (1/2 stick) butter, softened

Combine the sugar, flour and cinnamon in a bowl and mix well. Cut in the butter until crumbly.

Rhubarb Crunch

1¹/₂ cups plus 3 tablespoons
all-purpose flour
1 cup sugar
¹/₂ teaspoon ground cinnamon
3¹/₂ cups chopped rhubarb
¹/₂ teaspoon almond extract
Oat and Brown Sugar Topping
whipped cream or ice cream

Preheat the oven to 375 degrees. Combine the flour, sugar and cinnamon in a bowl and mix well. Add the rhubarb and flavoring and stir until coated.

Spoon the rhubarb mixture into a 10-inch round baking dish and sprinkle with the Oat and Brown Sugar Topping. Bake for 40 minutes or until golden brown and bubbly. Serve warm with whipped cream or ice cream. Serves 6 to 8.

1 cup packed brown sugar
1 cup rolled oats
¹/₈ teaspoon salt
¹/₄ cup (¹/₂ stick) butter

OAT AND BROWN SUGAR TOPPING

Combine the brown sugar, oats and salt in a bowl and mix well. Cut in the butter until crumbly.

184

Peach Crisp with Toffee Pecan Topping

6 cups frozen sliced peaches or blackberries

3 tablespoons sugar

1 tablespoon fresh lime juice

Toffee Pecan Topping

ice cream

Preheat the oven to 350 degrees. Arrange six $1^1/4$-cup ramekins or custard cups on a baking sheet. Combine the peaches, sugar and lime juice in a bowl and mix gently. Spoon the peach mixture evenly into the ramekins and sprinkle with the Toffee Pecan Topping.

Bake for 40 minutes or until golden brown and bubbly. Cool for 10 minutes and serve warm with ice cream. The topping ingredients may be doubled, freezing the extra portion for future make-ahead convenience. Serves 6.

$3/4$ cup all-purpose flour

$1/3$ cup packed golden brown sugar

$1/4$ teaspoon salt

6 tablespoons unsalted butter, chilled and cubed

$3/4$ cup toffee bits

$1/2$ cup pecans, coarsely chopped

TOFFEE PECAN TOPPING

Combine the flour, brown sugar and salt in a bowl and mix well. Rub in the butter with fingertips until the mixture clumps together. Stir in the toffee bits and pecans.

Easy Mexican Flan

1 cup sugar

6 eggs

$1/2$ cup sugar

2 teaspoons vanilla extract

$1/3$ teaspoon salt

2 cups milk

2 cups half-and-half

$1/3$ cup brandy or brandy sauce
  (optional)

Place a deep 8- or 9-inch round baking dish in the oven and preheat the oven to 325 degrees. Heat 1 cup sugar in a heavy 2-quart skillet over medium heat until light brown and melted, stirring constantly. Pour the caramelized sugar into the heated baking dish and rotate the dish to evenly coat the bottom and side.

Whisk the eggs in a bowl until blended. Whisk in $1/2$ cup sugar, the vanilla and salt until combined. Heat the milk and half-and-half in a 2-quart saucepan until steaming. Stir a small amount of the hot milk mixture into the egg mixture. Gradually stir the egg mixture and brandy into the hot milk mixture and pour into the prepared baking dish.

Arrange the baking dish in a larger baking pan and add enough hot water to the larger pan to measure $1/2$ inch. Bake for 45 to 60 minutes or until a knife inserted in the center of the flan comes out clean. Remove to a wire rack to cool. Place a serving platter on top of the flan and invert. Serves 8.

Banana Pudding

1 (6-ounce) package vanilla instant
 pudding mix
3 cups milk
8 ounces cream cheese, softened
1 (14-ounce) can sweetened
 condensed milk
8 ounces frozen whipped topping,
 thawed
1 (12-ounce) package vanilla wafers
5 or 6 large ripe bananas, sliced

Prepare the pudding mix using the package directions with 3 cups milk. Beat the cream cheese and condensed milk in a mixing bowl until blended. Stir in the whipped topping and fold in the pudding.

Alternate layers of vanilla wafers, bananas and pudding mixture in a 9×13-inch dish or trifle bowl until all the ingredients are used, ending with the pudding mixture. Chill, covered, until serving time. You may substitute shortbread cookies for the vanilla wafers. Serve 8 to 10.

Texas comfort food at its best. Everyone has his or her favorite version, and here is one of ours. Few people know the banana plant is not a tree; it is actually the world's largest herb.

Bread Pudding with Whiskey Sauce

1 cup sugar

1/2 cup (1 stick) butter, softened

5 eggs, beaten

2 cups heavy cream

1/4 cup raisins

1 tablespoon vanilla extract

1/8 teaspoon ground cinnamon

12 slices fresh potato bread or
cinnamon raisin bread

Whiskey Sauce

Beat the sugar and butter in a mixing bowl until creamy, scraping the bowl occasionally. Add the eggs, heavy cream, raisins, vanilla and cinnamon and beat until mixed well. Pour the cream mixture into a 9×13-inch baking dish.

Preheat the oven to 350 degrees. Arrange the bread slices in a single layer over the egg mixture and let stand for 5 minutes to soak up some of the liquid. Turn the bread slices and let stand for 10 minutes longer. Carefully press the slices down into the egg mixture until almost covered, being careful not to tear the slices.

Place the baking dish in a larger baking pan and add enough water to the baking pan to come within 1/2 inch of the top of the baking dish. Bake, covered with foil, for 35 to 40 minutes and remove the foil. Bake for 10 minutes longer or until the top is brown and the custard is set but still soft, not firm. Spoon the pudding onto dessert plates. Pass the Whiskey Sauce separately. Serves 6.

WHISKEY SAUCE

1 cup sugar

1 cup heavy cream

1 tablespoon unsalted butter

1 cinnamon stick, or 1/8 teaspoon
ground cinnamon

1/4 cup water

1/2 teaspoon cornstarch

1 tablespoon bourbon

Mix the sugar, heavy cream, butter and cinnamon stick in a saucepan and bring to a boil, stirring occasionally. Mix the water and cornstarch in a bowl and add to the cream mixture.

Cook until clear and thickened, stirring constantly. Remove from the heat and stir in the bourbon. Discard the cinnamon stick.

Chocolate Soufflés with Crème Anglaise

unsalted butter for coating

sugar for coating

8 ounces semisweet chocolate or
  white chocolate, chopped

6 tablespoons unsalted butter

2 tablespoons brewed coffee
  or brandy

6 egg yolks, at room temperature,
  beaten

6 egg whites, at room temperature

1/4 teaspoon cream of tartar

1/2 cup sugar

Crème Anglaise or Chocolate Anglaise

Coat six 10-ounce ramekins with butter and sprinkle with sugar. Heat the chocolate and 6 tablespoons butter in a metal bowl over simmering water until smooth, stirring occasionally. Add the coffee and stir until blended. Cool for 10 minutes or until warm to the touch. Whisk in the egg yolks.

Beat the egg whites and cream of tartar in a mixing bowl until soft peaks form. Add 1/2 cup sugar gradually, beating constantly until stiff peaks form. Fold 1/2 of the egg whites into the chocolate mixture. Fold in the remaining egg whites. Spoon the batter into the prepared ramekins and cover with plastic wrap. Chill for 8 to 10 hours.

Preheat the oven to 375 degrees. Remove the plastic wrap from the ramekins and arrange on a baking sheet. Bake for 20 minutes. Serve with Crème Anglaise, Chocolate Anglaise or a raspberry/strawberry sauce. Serves 6.

CRÈME ANGLAISE

1 vanilla bean

2 cups half-and-half

6 egg yolks

1/2 cup sugar

2 teaspoons vanilla extract

Cut the vanilla bean lengthwise into halves and scrape out the seeds. Combine the vanilla bean, seeds and half-and-half in a saucepan and let stand for 10 to 15 minutes. Whisk the egg yolks and sugar in a heatproof bowl until thickened.

Heat the half-and-half mixture until hot to the touch. Whisk 1/2 of the hot half-and-half mixture into the egg yolk mixture. Stir in the remaining half-and-half mixture. Pour through a sieve into a saucepan, discarding the solids. Cook over low heat for 20 minutes or until thickened, stirring constantly. Remove from the heat and cool for 15 minutes. Stir in the vanilla extract. Crème Anglaise may be served warm or cold. To serve cold, place plastic wrap directly on the surface and chill in the refrigerator. You may prepare the Crème Anglaise several days in advance and store, covered, in the refrigerator. Reheat in the microwave before serving if desired.

CHOCOLATE ANGLAISE

4 to 6 ounces semisweet chocolate,
  grated

1 tablespoon Kahlúa

Prepare the Crème Anglaise as directed above, omitting the vanilla bean and adding the chocolate after the mixture is strained into the saucepan. Substitute the Kahlúa for the vanilla extract.

Warm Chocolate Molten with Chocolate Sauce

Samir Dhurandhar is the Executive Chef at Nick & Sam's, an Uptown steakhouse in the heart of Dallas. Samir is a graduate of the CIA and is the culinary genius behind Nick & Sam's.

1 cup ground toasted pistachios
  (page 268)
1¹/₂ pounds bittersweet chocolate,
  coarsely chopped
¹/₂ cup (1 stick) plus 2 tablespoons
  butter
1¹/₄ cups sugar
6 eggs
1¹/₄ cups cake flour
12 ounces vanilla ice cream
Chocolate Sauce
fresh berries

Preheat the oven to 350 degrees. Grease 6 individual ramekins or soufflé dishes and coat with the pistachios. Arrange the ramekins on a baking sheet. Heat the chocolate and butter in a double boiler over simmering water until blended, stirring occasionally. Remove from the heat.

Beat the sugar and eggs in a mixing bowl until pale yellow in color, scraping the bowl occasionally. Add the cake flour gradually, beating constantly until blended; do not overmix. Stir in the chocolate mixture.

Spoon the batter evenly into the prepared ramekins and bake for 11 minutes. Serve immediately with the ice cream, Chocolate Sauce and fresh berries. Serves 6.

¹/₄ cup light corn syrup
¹/₄ cup heavy cream
¹/₄ cup canola oil
1 pound bittersweet chocolate,
  chopped
¹/₄ cup heavy cream
¹/₂ cup milk

CHOCOLATE SAUCE

Combine the corn syrup, ¹/₄ cup heavy cream and canola oil in a saucepan and mix well. Bring to a boil and pour over the chocolate in a heatproof bowl. Stir until blended and whisk in ¹/₄ cup heavy cream and the milk.

Tiramisu

Since 1988, the Farris brothers, Francesco and Effisio, have represented their Sardinian heritage in Texas with Arcodoro & Pomodoro. Located in the heart of Uptown, the focus is Mediterranean delights, such as homemade pasta, wood-fired pizzas, steaks, and seafood.

4 egg yolks

1/2 cup sugar

2 tablespoons sweet Italian marsala

8 ounces mascarpone cheese, softened

4 egg whites, at room temperature

1/2 cup heavy whipping cream

3 cups Italian espresso, chilled

1/4 cup rum

1/4 cup Kahlúa

48 ladyfingers

bittersweet baking cocoa to taste

Whisk the egg yolks, sugar and wine in a bowl for 2 minutes and fold in the cheese. Beat the egg whites in a mixing bowl until stiff peaks form. Beat the heavy whipping cream in a mixing bowl until very stiff peaks form. Fold the egg whites and whipped cream into the cheese mixture with a spatula until the mixture has a soft, light and creamy texture. Mix the espresso, rum and Kahlúa in a bowl.

Arrange the ladyfingers 1/2 at a time on a large serving plate, brushing each layer lightly with the espresso mixture. Spread the mascarpone cheese mixture over the top. Chill, covered, for about 4 hours. Sprinkle with baking cocoa just before serving. If you are concerned about using raw eggs, use eggs pasteurized in their shells, which are sold at some specialty food stores, or use an equivalent amount of pasteurized egg substitute. Serves 6.

Grilled Peaches

1/4 cup (1/2 stick) unsalted butter

3 tablespoons amaretto or other almond liqueur

2 tablespoons sugar

1/4 teaspoon vanilla extract

4 large peaches

1 pint vanilla ice cream

Preheat the grill to medium. Combine the butter, liqueur, sugar and vanilla in a small saucepan. Cook over medium-high heat just until the mixture begins to boil, stirring constantly. Remove from the heat.

Cut the peaches into halves and remove the pits. Brush the surface of the peaches with the butter glaze. Grill over direct heat for 8 to 10 minutes or until brown in spots and heated through, turning and brushing with the glaze every 2 to 3 minutes. Serve warm with the ice cream. Serves 4 to 8.

193

Dallacites often grill 365 days a year. Some might even call it a religion, of sorts. Do not limit yourself to steaks and burgers. Most vegetables prepared in the kitchen can be tossed on the grill. And that goes for fruit as well. Be adventurous! Try sliced watermelon drizzled with honey, fresh pineapple dusted with sugar, or even bananas brushed with butter.

Fresh Cranberry Sorbet

1 pound fresh cranberries

4 cups water

1³/₄ cups sugar

1 teaspoon fresh lemon juice

Combine the cranberries and water in a medium saucepan and bring to a boil over high heat. Reduce the heat to low and simmer, covered, for 10 to 15 minutes or until the cranberries are soft enough to mash easily with a spoon. Stir in the sugar and lemon juice and simmer just until the sugar dissolves, stirring frequently. Remove from the heat.

Cool slightly and process the cranberry mixture in batches in a food processor or blender until puréed. Strain the purée into a freezer container. Freeze, covered, until firm. You may prepare to this point up to 1 week in advance. Two hours before serving, scoop the sorbet in batches into a food processor and pulse until puréed. Return the purée to the freezer container and freeze for 2 hours or until firm. Scoop the sorbet into dessert bowls or stemmed goblets. Serves 8.

ORANGE ROSEMARY SORBET

1¹/₂ cups water

1 cup sugar

zest of 1 orange

2 sprigs of fresh rosemary

1¹/₂ cups fresh orange juice, chilled

2 tablespoons fresh lemon juice

Combine the water, sugar and orange zest in a medium saucepan and mix well. Bring to a boil over high heat and boil until the sugar dissolves, stirring frequently. Reduce the heat to low and simmer, covered, for 5 minutes. Remove from the heat and stir in the rosemary. Let stand until cool.

Strain the rosemary syrup into a bowl, discarding the rosemary and orange zest. Chill, covered, for 30 minutes or longer. Stir in the orange juice and lemon juice and pour into an ice cream freezer container. Freeze using the manufacturer's directions until thick and fluffy. Spoon the sorbet into a freezer container and freeze until firm. Scoop the sorbet into dessert bowls or stemmed goblets. You may store the sorbet in the freezer for up to 2 weeks.

RUBY RED GRAPEFRUIT SORBET

2¹/₃ cups Ruby Red grapefruit juice

²/₃ cup sugar

2 cups Champagne, chilled

¹/₂ teaspoon grated grapefruit zest

Combine the grapefruit juice and sugar in a saucepan and mix well. Bring to a boil over medium-high heat, stirring occasionally. Reduce the heat to low and simmer, covered, for 5 minutes. Remove from the heat and cool for 10 minutes. Stir in the Champagne and grapefruit zest.

Pour the grapefruit mixture into a 9×13-inch dish and freeze, covered, for 2 to 3 hours or just until almost firm. Spoon the sorbet into a mixing bowl and beat at medium speed until slushy. Pour into a freezer container and freeze, covered, for 8 hours or longer. Scoop the sorbet into dessert bowls or stemmed goblets.

Photograph for this recipe on the cover.

Cinnamon Ice Cream

2 eggs

1¹/₂ cups half-and-half

1 cup sugar

1 cup heavy cream

2 teaspoons ground cinnamon

1 teaspoon vanilla extract

Whisk the eggs in a bowl until blended. Mix the half-and-half and sugar in a saucepan and cook over medium-low heat just until the mixture begins to simmer, stirring occasionally. Whisk ¹/₂ of the hot half-and-half mixture into the eggs; whisk quickly so the eggs do not scramble. Whisk the egg mixture and heavy cream into the hot half-and-half mixture.

Cook until the mixture is thick enough to coat the back of a metal spoon, stirring frequently. Remove from the heat and whisk in the cinnamon and vanilla. Set the saucepan in a bowl of ice water and let stand until cool, stirring occasionally.

Pour the custard into a stainless steel bowl and place the bowl in the freezer. Freeze for approximately 3 to 4 hours, mixing with a hand mixer or pulsing in a food processor every 30 to 45 minutes until the mixture is slushy frozen. Serve with one of the Apple Pies on pages 217, 218, 219 or 220. You may also use an ice cream freezer, although this ice cream takes a long time to freeze in an electric ice cream freezer. For best results, chill the custard until it is very cold before pouring into the freezer container. Makes 8 (¹/₂-cup) servings.

Kahlúa Brownie Torte

1 recipe Chocolate Brownies
   (page 212)

1¹/₂ cups whipping cream, chilled

¹/₃ cup packed light brown sugar

2 tablespoons Kahlúa

chocolate curls

3 English toffee candy bars, broken
   into small pieces

15 long-stemmed strawberries

Prepare the Chocolate Brownies and bake in two 9-inch cake pans for 20 to 25 minutes or until the layers test done. Cool in the pans for 5 minutes and remove to a wire rack to cool completely. Beat the whipping cream in a chilled mixing bowl until soft peaks form. Add the brown sugar and liqueur gradually, beating constantly until stiff but soft peaks form.

Spread 1 cup of the whipped cream mixture between the brownie layers. Frost the top with the remaining whipped cream mixture and sprinkle with the chocolate curls and crushed candy bars. Chill for 1 hour or longer before serving. Slice the torte and arrange on dessert plates. Garnish each serving with 1 strawberry. Serves 15.

Bavarian Layer Cake

3 egg whites, at room temperature

1 1/2 cups sugar

1 3/4 cups all-purpose flour

1 teaspoon salt

3/4 teaspoon baking soda

1 cup buttermilk

1/3 cup vegetable oil

3 egg yolks

2 ounces unsweetened chocolate, melted

Cream Cheese Frosting

1 ounce semisweet chocolate, grated

Preheat the oven to 350 degrees. Beat the egg whites in a mixing bowl until foamy. Add 1/2 cup of the sugar gradually, beating constantly until soft peaks form. Combine the remaining 1 cup sugar, the flour, salt and baking soda in a mixing bowl and mix well. Add 1/2 cup of the buttermilk and the oil and beat at high speed for 1 minute, scraping the sides as needed. Add the remaining 1/2 cup buttermilk, the egg yolks and unsweetened chocolate and beat until blended.

Fold the chocolate mixture into the meringue and spoon evenly into two greased and floured 9-inch cake pans. Bake for 30 to 35 minutes or until the layers test done. Cool in the pans for 5 minutes. Remove to a wire rack to cool completely.

Cut the layers horizontally into halves with a serrated knife. Spread the Cream Cheese Frosting between the layers and over the top. Sprinkle with the semisweet chocolate. Chill, covered, for 8 hours or longer before serving. Serves 12.

CREAM CHEESE FROSTING

8 ounces cream cheese, softened

2/3 cup packed brown sugar

1 teaspoon vanilla extract

1/8 teaspoon salt

1 1/2 cups whipping cream, chilled

Beat the cream cheese and brown sugar in a mixing bowl until creamy, scraping the bowl occasionally. Add the vanilla and salt and beat until blended. Beat the whipping cream in a mixing bowl until stiff peaks form. Blend the whipped cream into the cream cheese mixture and mix until of a spreading consistency.

Fall Spice Cake

3/4 cup golden raisins

1/4 cup bourbon

3/4 cup pecan halves (2 1/2 ounces)

1 cup cake flour

1 cup all-purpose flour

1 1/2 teaspoons baking soda

1/2 teaspoon salt

1/2 teaspoon ground nutmeg

1/2 teaspoon ground cinnamon

1/4 teaspoon ground cloves

1/8 teaspoon mace

2 cups sugar

1 cup vegetable oil

2 eggs

**2 large unpeeled Granny Smith
   apples, finely chopped (3 1/2 cups)**

Caramel Sauce

**butter pecan ice cream and/or
   whipped cream (optional)**

Soak the raisins in the bourbon in a bowl at room temperature for 2 to 10 hours; drain. Preheat the oven to 400 degrees. Spread the pecans in a single layer on a baking sheet and place the baking sheet on the middle oven rack. Toast for 5 minutes or until golden brown, stirring occasionally. Cool and coarsely chop. Reduce the oven temperature to 325 degrees.

Sift the cake flour, all-purpose flour, baking soda, salt, nutmeg, cinnamon, cloves and mace into a bowl and mix well. Beat the sugar and oil in a mixing bowl at medium speed for 5 minutes, scraping the bowl occasionally. Add the eggs 1 at a time, beating well after each addition. Add the flour mixture all at once and stir with a wooden spoon until incorporated; the batter will be very thick.

Fold the raisins, pecans and apples into the batter. Spoon the batter into a buttered and floured 10-inch springform pan and bake for 1 to 1 1/2 hours or until a knife inserted in the center comes out dry. Remove the pan to a wire rack and cool slightly. Remove the side of the pan and let stand until completely cool. Drizzle with the warm Caramel Sauce and serve with ice cream and/or whipped cream. Serves 10 to 12.

CARAMEL SAUCE

1 cup heavy cream

1 cup packed dark brown sugar

1/3 cup granulated sugar

1/4 cup maple syrup

1/4 cup light corn syrup

Combine the heavy cream, brown sugar, granulated sugar, maple syrup and corn syrup in a heavy saucepan and mix well. Cook over high heat until a candy thermometer registers 210 degrees. Cool for 20 minutes. You may prepare up to 3 days in advance and store, covered, in the refrigerator. Reheat over simmering water or in the microwave.

Quatro Leches

La Duni, a Latin brasserie with two locations, prepares Argentinean, Brazilian, Colombian, and Venezuelan dishes with an emphasis on sweet endings. An excellent example is the Quatro Leches cake which outdoes the traditional tres leches version. Espartaco and Dunia Borga, co-owners and chefs, oversee this delightful eating establishment.

unsalted butter for coating
3 cups all-purpose flour
1¹/₂ teaspoons baking powder
¹/₄ teaspoon salt
1 cup (2 sticks) unsalted butter
2 cups granulated sugar
4 eggs
1 teaspoon vanilla extract
1 cup milk
2¹/₄ cups Three Leches Sauce (page 199)
Caramelized Meringue (page 199)
Dulce de Leche (page 199)
³/₄ cup Arequipe Sauce (page 199)
confectioners' sugar to taste

Preheat the oven to 350 degrees. Line a buttered 8-inch cake pan with baking parchment. Sift the flour, baking powder and salt together. Beat the butter in a mixing bowl with an electric mixer fitted with a paddle attachment until light and fluffy, scraping the bowl occasionally. Add the granulated sugar gradually, beating constantly until incorporated. Add the eggs 1 at a time and beat at low speed until blended after each addition. Beat in the vanilla and ¹/₃ of the flour mixture until blended. Add the milk and remaining flour mixture ¹/₂ at a time, beating well after each addition. This process should take 1 minute or less; do not overmix.

Spoon the batter into the prepared pan and place the pan on the lower oven rack. Bake for 55 to 70 minutes or until the center springs back when lightly touched and the cake pulls from the side of the pan. Cool in the pan.

Invert the cake onto a cake board and remove the parchment paper. Cut the cake horizontally into 3 equal layers and pierce each layer in several places with a fork. Brush ³/₄ cup of the Three Leches Sauce on each layer and reassemble the layers on a cake plate.

Spread the Caramelized Meringue over the side and top of the cake, creating a ¹/₂-inch-thick layer and decorative peaks. Caramelize the meringue using a kitchen blowtorch until golden brown, watching carefully to prevent scorching. Drizzle with the Arequipe Sauce and dust with confectioners' sugar. Serves 12.

THREE LECHES SAUCE

2 cups evaporated milk

2 cups sweetened condensed milk

2 cups heavy cream

Whisk the evaporated milk, condensed milk and heavy cream in a bowl until blended. Chill, covered, in the refrigerator. Makes 6 cups.

CARAMELIZED MERINGUE

2 cups sugar

1/2 cup water

1 cup egg whites, at room temperature

1 tablespoon fresh lemon juice

1/2 teaspoon vanilla extract

Mix the sugar and water in a small saucepan. Cook to 240 degrees on a candy thermometer, soft-ball stage. Beat the egg whites in a mixing bowl until soft peaks form. Add the sugar syrup to the meringue gradually, beating constantly at medium speed until incorporated. Add the lemon juice and vanilla and beat at high speed until stiff peaks form. Serves 12.

DULCE DE LECHE

1 (14-ounce) can sweetened condensed milk

Pour the condensed milk into the top of a double boiler and place over boiling water. Simmer, covered, over low heat for 5 to 5 1/2 hours or until thickened and light caramel in color. Cool and chill, covered, in the refrigerator.

AREQUIPE SAUCE

1 cup Dulce de Leche

1/2 cup milk, heated

Whisk the Dulce de Leche and milk in a bowl until blended. Chill, covered, in the refrigerator.

Coconut Sour Cream Cake

1 (2-layer) package white cake mix
1 (15-ounce) can cream of coconut
1 cup sour cream
1/2 cup vegetable oil
3 eggs
Cream Cheese Frosting
1 (7-ounce) package flaked coconut

Preheat the oven to 350 degrees. Combine the cake mix, cream of coconut, sour cream, oil and eggs in a mixing bowl and beat until blended, scraping the bowl occasionally. Spoon the batter into a greased and floured 9×13-inch cake pan.

Bake for 45 to 55 minutes or until a wooden pick inserted in the center comes out clean. Cool in the pan on a wire rack. Spread the Cream Cheese Frosting over the top of the cake and sprinkle with the coconut. Store, covered, in the refrigerator. Serves 15.

CREAM CHEESE FROSTING

8 ounces cream cheese, softened
1 (16-ounce) package confectioners' sugar
1/2 cup (1 stick) butter, softened
1 teaspoon vanilla extract

Beat the cream cheese, confectioners' sugar and butter in a mixing bowl until smooth and of a spreading consistency, scraping the bowl occasionally. Add the vanilla and beat until blended.

Happy Hour Rum Cake

slivered almonds

5 eggs

1 (2-layer) package butter-flavor
   cake mix

1 (4-ounce) package French vanilla
   instant pudding mix

1/2 cup vegetable oil

1/2 cup water

1/3 to 1/2 cup light rum

Rum Glaze

Preheat the oven to 300 degrees. Grease and flour a bundt pan and sprinkle almonds over the bottom. Beat the eggs in a mixing bowl just until blended. Add the cake mix, pudding mix, oil, water and rum and beat until incorporated; do not overbeat.

Spoon the batter into the prepared pan and bake for 70 minutes. Pour the hot Rum Glaze over the cake in the pan, allowing the glaze to soak into the cake. Let stand until cool and invert onto a cake plate. Serves 16.

RUM GLAZE

1/2 cup (1 stick) butter

1 cup sugar

1/4 cup water

3 to 4 tablespoons light rum

Bring the butter, sugar and water to a boil in a saucepan. Boil for 5 minutes, stirring constantly. Stir in the rum.

Classic Chocolate Cake

2 cups sugar

1³/₄ cups all-purpose flour

³/₄ cup baking cocoa

1¹/₂ teaspoons baking soda

1¹/₂ teaspoons baking powder

1 teaspoon salt

1 cup milk

¹/₂ cup vegetable oil

2 eggs

2 teaspoons vanilla extract

1 cup boiling water

Chocolate Fudge Frosting

Preheat the oven to 350 degrees. Combine the sugar, flour, baking cocoa, baking soda, baking powder and salt in a mixing bowl and mix well. Add the milk, oil, eggs and vanilla and beat at medium speed for 2 minutes, scraping the bowl occasionally. Stir in the boiling water.

Spoon the batter into 3 greased and floured 8-inch cake pans or two greased and floured 9-inch cake pans. Bake for 20 to 23 minutes for 8-inch layers, 30 to 35 minutes for 9-inch layers, or until a wooden pick inserted in the centers comes out clean. Cool in the pans for 10 minutes. Invert onto a wire rack to cool completely.

Spread the Chocolate Fudge Frosting between the layers and over the top and side of the cake. For an added touch, swirl raspberry sauce or Crème Anglaise (page 189) on dessert plates and top with a slice of the cake. Garnish with fresh raspberries. Serves 12.

CHOCOLATE FUDGE FROSTING

1 cup (2 sticks) unsalted butter

4 cups sugar

1 cup milk

1 pound unsweetened chocolate, chopped

1 cup (2 sticks) unsalted butter

1 cup heavy cream

6 egg yolks, lightly beaten

Melt 1 cup butter in a medium saucepan and stir in the sugar and milk. Cook over medium heat to 232 degrees on a candy thermometer; do not stir. Stir in the chocolate and 1 cup butter.

Cook until the chocolate is almost melted, stirring frequently. Whisk in the heavy cream and egg yolks and remove from the heat. Continue to whisk until the chocolate is melted and the egg yolks are incorporated. Cool to room temperature.

Beat the frosting again before spreading over the cake. If you are concerned about using raw egg yolks, use eggs pasteurized in their shells, which are sold at some specialty food stores, or use an equivalent amount of pasteurized egg substitute.

Photograph for this recipe on facing page.

Perfect Pralines

1 cup granulated sugar
1/2 cup packed brown sugar
1/4 cup milk
1 tablespoon butter or margarine
1 cup pecan pieces
1 teaspoon vanilla extract

Combine the granulated sugar, brown sugar, milk, butter and pecans in a saucepan and mix well. Bring to a rolling boil and boil for 1 1/2 minutes. Remove from the heat and stir in the vanilla. Beat until creamy.

Drop by spoonfuls onto a foil-lined baking sheet and let stand until cool. Store in an airtight container. Double the recipe for a larger crowd. Makes 1 dozen pralines.

Pralines are a staple in Dallas Tex-Mex restaurants. These caramel-colored dollops of candy perfection are the ideal end to a spicy meal.

Blue Ribbon Toffee

1 cup (2 sticks) butter
1 cup sugar
1 cup blanched slivered almonds
1 (8-ounce) chocolate candy bar,
   chopped
1/2 cup chopped pecans

Combine the butter, sugar and almonds in a heavy skillet. Cook over medium-high heat to 234 to 240 degrees on a candy thermometer, soft-ball stage, stirring constantly. The candy mixture will be medium tan in color and will smoke slightly.

Pour onto a foil-lined baking sheet and spread evenly. Immediately sprinkle with the candy bar. Let stand for about 5 minutes or until the chocolate melts; spread evenly. Sprinkle with the pecans. Let stand for 8 to 10 hours and break into bite-size pieces. Store in an airtight container. Makes 2 dozen pieces.

Biscochitos

6 cups all-purpose flour

1 tablespoon baking powder

1 teaspoon salt

1 cup shortening

1 cup (2 sticks) butter, softened

1 1/2 cups sugar

2 eggs

1/3 cup (about) brandy

1 cup sugar

4 teaspoons ground cinnamon

Sift the flour, baking powder and salt together. Beat the shortening and butter in a mixing bowl until creamy, scraping the bowl occasionally. Add 1 1/2 cups sugar and beat until blended. Add the eggs and beat until blended. Beat in the flour mixture until smooth.

Add just enough brandy to the flour mixture to make a firm dough and mix well. Divide the dough into 4 equal portions and wrap each portion in plastic wrap. Chill for 30 minutes.

Preheat the oven to 350 degrees. Roll each dough portion fairly thin on a lightly floured surface. If the dough seems too dry, moisten your hands before handling each portion. Cut with the desired cookie cutters and arrange the cookies 2 inches apart on a nonstick cookie sheet.

Bake for 10 to 15 minutes or until light brown. Bake 17 minutes for more color. Coat the warm cookies with a mixture of 1 cup sugar and the cinnamon and cool on a wire rack. Store in an airtight container. Makes 2 to 3 dozen cookies.

Cowboy Cookies

1 cup all-purpose flour

1 teaspoon ground cinnamon

1/2 teaspoon baking soda

1/2 teaspoon salt

1 cup (2 sticks) unsalted butter,
  softened

1 cup packed brown sugar

2 tablespoons granulated sugar

2 eggs

1 1/2 teaspoons vanilla extract

2 1/2 cups old-fashioned oats

1 1/2 cups shredded sweetened
  coconut

12 ounces semisweet chocolate,
  chopped

3/4 cup pecans, toasted and chopped
  (page 268)

Preheat the oven to 375 degrees. Mix the flour, cinnamon, baking soda and salt together. Beat the butter, brown sugar and granulated sugar in a mixing bowl until light and fluffy, scraping the bowl occasionally. Add the eggs and beat until blended. Beat in the vanilla. Add the flour mixture and beat at low speed until blended, scraping the bowl occasionally. Stir in the oats, coconut, chocolate and pecans.

Drop by large spoonfuls 2 inches apart onto a lightly buttered cookie sheet. Pat the dough down until 1/2 inch thick and place the cookie sheet in the lower 1/3 of the oven.

Bake for 6 to 7 1/2 minutes and move the cookie sheet to the upper 1/3 of the oven. Bake for 6 to 7 1/2 minutes longer or until light brown. Cool on the cookie sheet for 2 minutes. Remove to a wire rack to cool completely. Store in an airtight container. Makes 2 1/2 dozen cookies.

Ginger Molasses Cookies

2¼ cups all-purpose flour
1½ teaspoons baking soda
1 teaspoon ground cinnamon
1 teaspoon ground ginger
½ teaspoon ground cloves
¼ teaspoon salt
1 cup packed brown sugar
¾ cup shortening
¼ cup molasses
1 egg
granulated sugar for coating

Mix the flour, baking soda, cinnamon, ginger, cloves and salt in a bowl. Beat the brown sugar, shortening, molasses and egg in a mixing bowl until creamy, scraping the bowl occasionally. Add the flour mixture and beat until blended. Chill, covered, in the refrigerator.

Preheat the oven to 350 degrees. Shape the dough into 1-inch balls and coat with granulated sugar. Arrange 2 inches apart on a nonstick cookie sheet and bake for 8 to 10 minutes or until crisp around the edges. Cool on the cookie sheet for 2 minutes. Remove to a wire rack to cool completely. Store in an airtight container. Makes 2 dozen cookies.

Oatmeal Wafer Crisps

4 cups quick-cooking oats
2 cups all-purpose flour
1 teaspoon baking soda
¼ teaspoon salt
2 cups (4 sticks) butter, softened
2 cups granulated sugar
1 egg
confectioners' sugar to taste

Preheat the oven to 350 degrees. Mix the oats, flour, baking soda and salt in a bowl. Cream the butter and granulated sugar in a mixing bowl until light and fluffy, scraping the bowl occasionally. Add the egg and beat until blended. Stir in the oats mixture.

Shape the dough into 1-inch balls and arrange 2 inches apart on an ungreased cookie sheet. Flatten with a fork dipped in ice water. Bake for 10 to 14 minutes or until light brown. Immediately remove the cookies to a wire rack and sprinkle with confectioners' sugar. Let stand until cool. Store in an airtight container. Makes about 6 dozen cookies.

The Love Cookie

1 cup (2 sticks) salted butter,
  softened
3/4 cup granulated sugar
3/4 cup packed brown sugar
1 teaspoon vanilla extract
1 egg
1 1/2 cups all-purpose flour
1 teaspoon baking soda
1 1/2 cups rolled oats
1 cup dried sweetened cranberries
1 cup (6 ounces) chocolate chips
1 cup toffee bits

Preheat the oven to 350 degrees. Cream the butter, granulated sugar, brown sugar, vanilla and egg in a mixing bowl until light and fluffy, scraping the bowl occasionally. Add a mixture of the flour and baking soda gradually, beating constantly until blended. Fold in the oats, cranberries, chocolate chips and toffee bits. The dough will be very dense.

Drop by spoonfuls 2 inches apart onto a cookie sheet lined with baking parchment. Bake for 12 to 15 minutes or until light brown. The cookies will continue to bake after being removed from the oven. Cool on the cookie sheet for 2 minutes. Remove to a wire rack to cool completely. Store in an airtight container. Makes 4 dozen cookies.

Iced Pumpkin Cookies

2 cups all-purpose flour

1 teaspoon baking powder

1 teaspoon baking soda

1 teaspoon (or more) ground cinnamon

1/8 teaspoon ground nutmeg or allspice (optional)

1 cup (2 sticks) butter, softened

1 cup canned pumpkin

1/2 cup granulated sugar

1/2 cup packed brown sugar

1 egg

1 teaspoon vanilla extract

Cream Cheese Icing

Preheat the oven to 375 degrees. Mix the flour, baking powder, baking soda, cinnamon and nutmeg in a bowl. Cream the butter, pumpkin, granulated sugar, brown sugar, egg and vanilla in a mixing bowl until light and fluffy, scraping the bowl occasionally. Fold in the flour mixture.

Drop by teaspoonfuls 2 inches apart onto a nonstick cookie sheet. Bake for 10 to 12 minutes or until light brown. Cool on the cookie sheet for 2 minutes. Remove to a wire rack to cool completely. Spread the Cream Cheese Icing over the top of each cooled cookie and store, covered, in the refrigerator. Makes 2 dozen cookies.

1 cup confectioners' sugar

4 ounces cream cheese, softened

1/4 cup (1/2 stick) butter, softened

1/2 teaspoon vanilla extract

CREAM CHEESE ICING

Cream the confectioners' sugar, cream cheese, butter and vanilla in a mixing bowl until of a spreading consistency, scraping the bowl occasionally. This recipe makes enough icing for 4 dozen cookies.

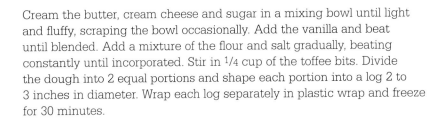

Toffee Crunch Cookies

2 cups (4 sticks) butter, softened

8 ounces cream cheese, softened

1¹/₄ cups sugar

2 tablespoons vanilla extract

4 cups all-purpose flour

1 teaspoon salt

3 (6-ounce) packages English toffee bits

Cream the butter, cream cheese and sugar in a mixing bowl until light and fluffy, scraping the bowl occasionally. Add the vanilla and beat until blended. Add a mixture of the flour and salt gradually, beating constantly until incorporated. Stir in ¹/₄ cup of the toffee bits. Divide the dough into 2 equal portions and shape each portion into a log 2 to 3 inches in diameter. Wrap each log separately in plastic wrap and freeze for 30 minutes.

Preheat the oven to 350 degrees. Unwrap the logs and coat with the remaining toffee bits. Cut each log into ¹/₄-inch slices and arrange the slices 2 inches apart on a cookie sheet lined with baking parchment. Bake for 15 to 18 minutes or until golden brown. Watch the cookies carefully, as they will brown quickly due to the amount of butter in the recipe. Cool on the cookie sheet for 2 minutes. Remove to a wire rack to cool completely. Store in an airtight container. Makes 5 dozen cookies.

LEMON POPPY SEED COOKIES

1 tablespoon fresh lemon juice

1 tablespoon almond extract

grated zest of 1 lemon

2 teaspoons poppy seeds

poppy seeds for coating

Prepare the Toffee Crunch Cookie dough as directed above, omitting the vanilla and toffee bits and adding the lemon juice, flavoring, lemon zest and 2 teaspoons poppy seeds. Proceed as directed above and roll the logs in additional poppy seeds after freezing. Slice, bake and store as directed above.

KAHLÚA PECAN COOKIES

1 cup pecans

1 teaspoon vanilla extract

1¹/₂ tablespoons Kahlúa

1 cup pecans, finely chopped

Toast 1 cup pecans and finely chop; see page 268. Prepare the Toffee Crunch Cookie dough as directed above, omitting the toffee bits, adding 1 cup toasted pecans, reducing the vanilla to 1 teaspoon and adding the liqueur. Coat the logs in 1 cup finely chopped pecans after freezing. Slice, bake and store as directed above.

Chocolate Brownies

2 ounces unsweetened chocolate

1 cup (2 sticks) butter, cubed and softened

4 eggs

2 cups granulated sugar

1 cup all-purpose flour

1 cup chopped pecans

confectioners' sugar to taste

Preheat the oven to 325 degrees. Heat the chocolate in a saucepan over low heat until melted, stirring frequently. Remove from the heat and stir in the butter until blended. Whisk the eggs in a bowl just until blended. Add the granulated sugar and flour to the eggs and stir just until incorporated. Fold in the chocolate mixture and pecans.

Spray the bottom of a 9×13-inch baking dish with nonstick cooking spray. Spread the batter evenly in the prepared dish and bake for 35 to 40 minutes or until the brownies pull from the sides of the baking dish. Immediately dust with confectioners' sugar. Cool in the baking dish on a wire rack. Makes 2 dozen brownies.

White Chocolate Cheesecake Squares

1³/₄ cups chocolate wafer crumbs

¹/₃ cup butter, melted

16 ounces white baking chocolate, chopped

16 ounces cream cheese, softened

¹/₂ cup sour cream

4 eggs

2 teaspoons vanilla extract

Preheat the oven to 300 degrees. Line a 9×13-inch baking pan with heavy-duty foil and spray with nonstick cooking spray. Combine the wafer crumbs and butter in a bowl and mix until crumbly. Reserve 2 tablespoons of the crumb mixture. Pat the remaining crumb mixture over the bottom of the prepared pan.

Heat the white chocolate in a saucepan over low heat until melted, stirring frequently. Remove from the heat and cool slightly. Beat the cream cheese and sour cream in a mixing bowl at medium speed until light and fluffy. Add the eggs 1 at a time, beating well after each addition. Stir in the white chocolate and vanilla. Spoon the batter into the prepared pan and bake for 30 minutes. Turn off the oven and let the cheesecake stand in the oven with the door closed for 30 minutes. Remove to a wire rack to cool.

Sprinkle the baked layer with the reserved crumb mixture. Chill, covered, for 8 hours or longer. Lift the cheesecake from the pan with the foil and discard the foil. Cut into squares and serve in individual paper baking cups if desired. Makes 4 dozen squares.

Walnut Dream Bars

1 cup (2 sticks) unsalted butter

$1/2$ cup granulated sugar

2 cups all-purpose flour

1 (1-pound) package light
   brown sugar

3 eggs

1 teaspoon vanilla extract

$1/4$ cup all-purpose flour

1 teaspoon salt

1 teaspoon baking powder

2 cups chopped walnuts

Confectioners' Sugar Icing

Preheat the oven to 350 degrees. Cream the butter and granulated sugar in a mixing bowl until light and fluffy, scraping the bowl occasionally. Add 2 cups flour gradually, beating constantly until combined. Press the dough over the bottom of a greased 12×18-inch baking pan and bake for 15 minutes. Maintain the oven temperature.

Combine the brown sugar, eggs and vanilla in a bowl and mix well. Stir in a mixture of $1/4$ cup flour, the salt and baking powder. Fold in the walnuts and spread over the baked layer. Bake for 20 minutes. Cool in the pan on a wire rack. Spread the Confectioners' Sugar Icing over the top and let stand until set. Cut into bars. Makes 5 dozen bars.

CONFECTIONERS' SUGAR ICING

2 cups confectioners' sugar, sifted

3 tablespoons milk

2 tablespoons butter, melted

1 teaspoon almond extract

Combine the confectioners' sugar, milk, butter and flavoring in a bowl and mix until of a spreading consistency.

Rhubarb Custard Bars

2 cups all-purpose flour

$^1/_4$ cup sugar

1 cup (2 sticks) butter or margarine,
   chilled and cubed

2 cups sugar

7 tablespoons all-purpose flour

1 cup heavy cream

3 eggs, beaten

5 cups finely chopped fresh or
   drained thawed frozen rhubarb

6 ounces cream cheese, softened

$^1/_2$ cup sugar

$^1/_2$ teaspoon vanilla extract

1 cup whipping cream, whipped

Preheat the oven to 350 degrees. Combine 2 cups flour and $^1/_4$ cup sugar in a bowl and mix well. Cut in the butter until crumbly. Pat the crumb mixture over the bottom of a greased 9×13-inch baking pan and bake for 10 minutes. Maintain the oven temperature.

Combine 2 cups sugar and 7 tablespoons flour in a bowl. Whisk in the heavy cream and eggs until blended and stir in the rhubarb. Spread the rhubarb mixture over the baked layer and bake for 40 to 45 minutes or until set. Let stand until cool.

Beat the cream cheese, $^1/_2$ cup sugar and the vanilla in a mixing bowl until smooth, scraping the bowl occasionally. Fold in the whipped cream. Spread the whipped cream mixture over the prepared layers and chill, covered, in the refrigerator. Cut into bars and store the leftovers in the refrigerator. Makes 2 dozen bars.

Angel Pecan Pie

1¹/₂ cups pecans

5 egg whites, at room temperature

1¹/₂ cups granulated sugar

1¹/₂ teaspoons vanilla extract

1¹/₂ cups butter cracker crumbs

1 cup whipping cream

2 tablespoons confectioners' sugar

white chocolate and/or semisweet
chocolate shavings or curls

12 long-stemmed strawberries

Preheat the oven to 350 degrees. Line the bottom and side of a 9-inch springform pan with baking parchment or foil, creasing the parchment or foil to fit. Spread the pecans in a single layer on a baking sheet and toast for 8 to 10 minutes or until light brown and fragrant, stirring occasionally. Cool and coarsely chop. Maintain the oven temperature.

Beat the egg whites in a mixing bowl at medium speed until soft peaks form. Add the granulated sugar 1 tablespoon at a time, beating constantly at high speed until stiff glossy peaks form. Beat in the vanilla and fold in the pecans and cracker crumbs. Spoon into the prepared pan and bake for 30 minutes. Cover loosely with foil and bake for 15 minutes longer. Cool in the pan on a wire rack. You may prepare to this point up to 2 days in advance and store, covered, at room temperature.

Remove the side of the pan and invert onto a plate. Remove the pan bottom and parchment paper and invert again onto a serving plate. Beat the whipping cream and confectioners' sugar in a mixing bowl until stiff peaks form and spread over the pie. Garnish with chocolate shavings and cut into wedges. Arrange the wedges on dessert plates and garnish each serving with a long-stemmed strawberry. Serves 12.

Apple Tart with Almond Cream

1 sheet puff pastry
1 egg yolk, beaten
Almond Cream
4 Granny Smith apples,
  peeled and cored
1/2 cup sugar
Butter Rum Sauce
vanilla ice cream

Preheat the oven to 375 degrees. Cut the puff pastry lengthwise into halves. Cut a 1/2-inch-wide strip from each of the long sides of the rectangles, forming 4 strips. Brush each pastry rectangle with some of the egg yolk. Place 1 strip on each long edge of both rectangles and arrange the pastry on a baking sheet lined with baking parchment. Brush the strips with some of the egg yolk. Spread the Almond Cream evenly down the centers of the pastries.

Cut the apples into halves and cut each half into 1/4-inch slices, leaving connected at 1 end. Press down on each apple half to fan out the slices. Arrange 4 apple halves over the Almond Cream on each pastry, fanning them down the length of the dough. Brush the apples with the remaining egg yolk and sprinkle with the sugar. Bake for 25 to 35 minutes or until golden brown. Remove to a wire rack and cool slightly.

Drizzle some of the warm Butter Rum Sauce on dessert plates. Cut each warm apple tart diagonally into 4 or 5 slices and arrange over the sauce. Top each with a scoop of vanilla ice cream and serve immediately. Serves 8 to 10.

Photograph for this recipe on facing page.

ALMOND CREAM

1/2 cup (1 stick) butter, softened
1/2 cup ground almonds
1/3 cup sugar
1/4 cup all-purpose flour
1 egg

Combine the butter, almonds, sugar, flour and egg in a food processor and process until smooth.

BUTTER RUM SAUCE

1/2 cup packed dark brown sugar
1/2 cup granulated sugar
1/2 cup heavy cream
5 tablespoons butter or margarine,
  softened
1 tablespoon rum

Combine the brown sugar, granulated sugar, heavy cream and butter in a saucepan. Bring to a boil and boil for 1 minute, stirring frequently. Remove from the heat and stir in the rum. Cover to keep warm.

Summer Cheddar Apple Pie

1/2 recipe Perfect Pie Pastry
   (page 271)
6 Golden Delicious or
   Granny Smith apples
1 cup sugar
2 tablespoons all-purpose flour
2 teaspoons grated lemon zest
1/2 teaspoon ground cinnamon
1/8 teaspoon salt
Cheddar Crumb Topping
sour cream or vanilla ice cream

Prepare the pie pastry and fit into a 9-inch pie plate; trim the edge. Preheat the oven to 400 degrees. Peel and slice the apples. Mix the sugar, flour, lemon zest, cinnamon and salt in a bowl. Add the apples to the sugar mixture and toss to coat.

Spoon the apple mixture into the pastry-lined pie plate and sprinkle with the Cheddar Crumb Topping. Bake for 40 to 45 minutes or until golden brown. Serve warm topped with sour cream or vanilla ice cream. Serves 6 to 8.

1/2 cup all-purpose flour
1/4 cup sugar
1/2 cup (2 ounces) shredded
   Cheddar cheese
1/4 cup (1/2 stick) butter

CHEDDAR CRUMB TOPPING

Combine the flour, sugar and cheese in a bowl and mix well. Cut in the butter until crumbly.

Crunchy Caramel Apple Pie

1/2 recipe **Perfect Pie Crust**
   (page 271)
1/2 **cup sugar**
3 **tablespoons all-purpose flour**
1 **teaspoon ground cinnamon**
1/8 **teaspoon salt**
6 **cups sliced cooking apples (Granny**
   Smith or Braeburn)
Brown Sugar Topping
1/2 **cup chopped pecans**
1/4 **cup caramel ice cream topping**

Prepare the pie pastry and fit into a 9-inch pie plate; trim the edge. Preheat the oven to 375 degrees. Combine the sugar, flour, cinnamon and salt in a bowl and mix well. Add the apples and toss to coat.

Spoon the apple mixture into the pastry-lined pie plate and sprinkle with the Brown Sugar Topping. Cover the edge of the pastry with foil.

Bake for 25 minutes and remove the foil. Bake for 25 to 30 minutes longer or until the crust is golden brown. Sprinkle with the pecans and drizzle with the caramel topping. Serves 6 to 8.

BROWN SUGAR TOPPING

1 **cup packed brown sugar**
1/2 **cup all-purpose flour**
1/2 **cup quick-cooking oats**
1/2 **cup (1 stick) butter, melted**

Combine the brown sugar, flour and oats in a bowl and mix well. Add the butter and stir until crumbly.

Apple Pie with Cream

1 recipe Perfect Pie Crust (page 271)
3/4 cup granulated sugar
1/4 cup packed brown sugar
2 tablespoons flour
2 tablespoons butter, melted
2 teaspoons ground cinnamon
3/4 teaspoon ground nutmeg
1/8 teaspoon salt
3 cups sliced peeled McIntosh apples
3 cups sliced peeled Granny Smith
  apples
1 egg, beaten
1 teaspoon heavy cream or water
1/2 cup heavy cream
ice cream

Prepare the pie pastry. Fit 1 of the pastries into a 9-inch pie plate. Preheat the oven to 400 degrees. Combine the granulated sugar, brown sugar, flour, butter, cinnamon, nutmeg and salt in a bowl and mix well. Add the apples and toss to coat. Spoon the coated apples into the pastry-lined pie plate.

Top with the remaining pastry, crimping the edge and cutting vents. Brush the pastry with a mixture of the egg and 1 teaspoon heavy cream and bake for 1 hour; tent with foil during the baking process to prevent overbrowning.

Turn off the oven and remove the pie. Pour 1/2 cup heavy cream through the vents in the top crust. Return the pie to the oven and let stand in the warm oven with the door closed for 20 minutes. Serve warm with ice cream. Serves 8.

Apricot Lavender Tart

1 unbaked (9-inch) pie shell

1/2 cup sugar

1/4 cup ground almonds

1 tablespoon butter

1 egg

2 pounds fresh apricots, sliced

8 to 12 ounces unsalted whole
   almonds

3 tablespoons lavender honey, heated

Preheat the oven to 500 degrees. Prick the bottom and side of the pie shell with a fork. Combine the sugar, ground almonds and butter in a bowl and mix well. Add the egg and stir until combined. Spread the almond mixture over the bottom of the pie shell.

Arrange the apricots in the almond mixture and sprinkle with the whole almonds. Bake for 10 minutes. Reduce the oven temperature to 400 degrees and bake for 40 minutes longer. Drizzle with the warm honey and broil just until caramelized. Serve warm or at room temperature. Serves 6 to 8.

Crème Brûlée Pie

1 unbaked (9-inch) pie shell
5 egg yolks
1/2 cup packed light brown sugar
1 1/2 cups half-and-half
1 cup heavy cream
1 teaspoon vanilla extract
1/4 cup packed light brown sugar

Preheat the oven to 400 degrees. Line the pie shell with baking parchment or foil and fill with pie weights or dried beans. Bake for 15 minutes. Let stand until cool. Remove the pie weights and foil. Reduce the oven temperature to 325 degrees. Blend the egg yolks and 1/2 cup brown sugar in a bowl with a wooden spoon. Do not use a whisk as this could make the custard grainy.

Heat the half-and-half and heavy cream in a saucepan until warm to the touch. Add 1/3 of the warm cream mixture to the egg yolk mixture and mix well. Gradually add the remaining warm cream mixture and vanilla and stir until blended.

Place the pie shell on a baking sheet. Pour the custard mixture into the pie shell. Place the baking sheet on the oven rack. Place a loaf pan filled with water in the oven to create steam. Bake for 45 minutes or just until the center is barely set. Remove to a wire rack to cool. Cover with plastic wrap and chill for 8 to 10 hours. Just before serving, sieve 1/4 cup brown sugar evenly over the top of the pie and broil until bubbly. Serve immediately. Serves 6 to 8.

Southern Sweet Potato Pie

1 recipe Perfect Pie Crust (page 271)
2 large sweet potatoes,
boiled and mashed
2 (12-ounce) cans evaporated milk
1 1/2 to 2 cups sugar
1 cup (2 sticks) salted butter, melted
6 eggs
2 teaspoons ground nutmeg
whipped cream

Prepare the pie pastry and fit into two 9-inch pie plates; trim the edges. Preheat the oven to 400 degrees. Combine the sweet potato pulp, evaporated milk, sugar, butter, eggs and nutmeg in a bowl and mix well.

Spoon 1/2 of the sweet potato filling into each pastry-lined pie plate. Bake for about 45 minutes or until a knife inserted in the centers comes out clean. Serve with whipped cream. Serves 16.

Double Chocolate Fried Pies

2/3 cup granulated sugar

2 tablespoons Dutch-processed
   baking cocoa

2 tablespoons cornstarch

1/16 teaspoon salt

2 cups milk

1 cup half-and-half

3 egg yolks, lightly beaten

6 ounces bittersweet chocolate,
   melted and cooled

1 tablespoon unsalted butter

2 teaspoons vanilla extract

vegetable oil for frying

Pie Pastry

confectioners' sugar

Sift the granulated sugar, baking cocoa, cornstarch and salt into a saucepan and mix well. Whisk in the milk, half-and-half and egg yolks. Stir in the chocolate. Bring to a boil over medium-high heat, stirring constantly with a wooden spoon. Reduce the heat to medium as the pudding begins to thicken and cook for 2 minutes or until the pudding coats the back of the spoon, stirring constantly. Strain through a sieve into a bowl, pressing with a spatula. Stir in the butter and vanilla. Let stand until cool.

Add enough oil to a skillet to measure about 1/2 to 1 inch deep and heat to 350 degrees. Roll the chilled pastry into eight 6-inch rounds on a lightly floured surface. Spoon about 2 to 3 tablespoons of the chocolate pudding in the center of each round. Moisten the edges of the rounds with water and fold over the filling to form a half-moon. Crimp the edges with a fork to seal. Fry the pies in hot oil until brown on both sides; drain. Dust the warm pies with confectioners' sugar and serve immediately. Makes 8 fried pies.

PIE PASTRY

3 cups all-purpose flour

1 teaspoon salt

3/4 cup shortening

1 egg

1/4 cup water

1 teaspoon white vinegar

Mix the flour and salt in a bowl. Cut the shortening into the flour mixture with a pastry blender until crumbly. Whisk the egg and water in a bowl until blended and sprinkle lightly over the flour mixture. Add the vinegar and stir gently with a fork just until moistened. Shape the pastry into a ball and wrap in plastic wrap. Chill for 1 hour or longer.

Breads & Brunch

THE DISH ON DALLAS

Breakfast, brunch, lunch, or dinner...eating out is a way of life in the Metroplex. Dallas/Fort Worth ranks second in the nation for per capita spending on eating out. That's not surprising since we have four times as many restaurants per person as New York City.

Ham and Vegetable Quiche recipe on page 252.

Cinnamon Raisin Biscuits

1¹/₂ cups all-purpose flour

1¹/₂ cups sifted cake flour

¹/₄ cup granulated sugar

1 tablespoon baking powder

1¹/₂ teaspoons ground cinnamon

1 teaspoon salt

³/₄ cup (1¹/₂ sticks) butter or
   margarine

1 cup raisins

1 cup milk

1¹/₂ tablespoons butter or margarine,
   melted

1 cup sifted confectioners' sugar

1¹/₂ tablespoons milk

Preheat the oven to 400 degrees. Combine the all-purpose flour, cake flour, granulated sugar, baking powder, cinnamon and salt in a bowl and mix well. Cut in ³/₄ cup butter until crumbly. Add the raisins and 1 cup milk and stir just until moistened.

Knead the dough 4 times on a lightly floured surface. Roll 1 inch thick and cut with a biscuit cutter. Arrange the rounds on a greased baking sheet and brush with 1¹/₂ tablespoons melted butter.

Bake for 15 minutes or until light brown. Mix the confectioners' sugar and 1¹/₂ tablespoons milk in a bowl until of a glaze consistency. Drizzle over the warm biscuits and serve immediately. Makes 15 biscuits.

Savory Buttermilk Biscuits

2 cups unbleached all-purpose flour

1 1/2 tablespoons baking powder

1 tablespoon sugar

1 teaspoon salt

3 tablespoons minced green onions

1/2 cup (1 stick) butter, softened

3/4 cup buttermilk

1 egg

1/4 cup (1 ounce) grated
   asiago cheese

3 tablespoons butter, melted
   (optional)

Preheat the oven to 400 degrees. Sift the flour, baking powder, sugar and salt into a bowl and mix well. Stir in the green onions. Cut in 1/2 cup butter with a pastry blender until crumbly. Whisk the buttermilk and egg in a bowl until blended and add to the crumb mixture along with the cheese, stirring just until moistened.

Knead the dough by hand on a lightly floured surface for 1 minute or until the dough adheres. Roll 1/2 inch thick and cut with a 2-inch cutter. Gently re-form any scraps of dough into a ball and reroll to cut additional biscuits.

Arrange the rounds 1 1/2 inches apart on an ungreased baking sheet. Place the baking sheet on the middle oven rack and bake for 9 minutes or until light brown. Brush the tops of the warm biscuits with 3 tablesoons melted butter and serve immediately. Makes 1 dozen biscuits.

Iron Skillet Corn Bread

1³/₄ cups plus 3 tablespoons
  cornmeal

1¹/₂ cups plus 1 tablespoon
  all-purpose flour

¹/₄ cup sugar

1¹/₂ tablespoons baking powder

2 teaspoons salt

¹/₄ teaspoon garlic powder

1¹/₂ cups buttermilk

³/₄ cup (1¹/₂ sticks) butter, melted

¹/₄ cup maple syrup

3 eggs

2 jalapeño chiles, seeded and minced

2 tablespoons (about) shortening

Place a 10-inch cast-iron skillet in the oven and preheat the oven to 400 degrees. Combine the cornmeal, flour, sugar, baking powder, salt and garlic powder in a bowl and mix well. Whisk the buttermilk, butter, maple syrup and eggs in a bowl until blended. Stir in the jalapeño chiles. Add the buttermilk mixture to the cornmeal mixture and stir just until combined.

Remove the hot skillet from the oven and coat with the shortening. Pour the batter into the prepared skillet and bake for 45 minutes or until a wooden pick inserted in the center comes out clean. Invert onto a wire rack and cut into wedges. Serve immediately. Serves 4 to 6.

Follow these steps when seasoning your cast-iron skillet. Preheat your oven to 350 degrees and line a baking sheet with foil. Wash a new cast iron-iron skillet in hot soapy water. Rinse and dry thoroughly. Rub the entire surface of the skillet with melted shortening or vegetable oil using a paper towel or small clean cloth. Arrange the baking sheet on the lower oven rack and place the skillet upside down on the top oven rack. Bake for one hour. Let stand until cool before storing.

Toasted Cheese Bread

1 loaf French bread
10 ounces Monterey Jack cheese,
   shredded
5 ounces mozzarella cheese,
   shredded
5 ounces Cheddar cheese, shredded
1¹⁄₂ cups mayonnaise
1¹⁄₂ to 3 teaspoons garlic powder
paprika to taste

Preheat the oven to 350 degrees. Cut the bread loaf horizontally into halves and arrange the halves cut side up on a baking sheet. Mix the Monterey Jack cheese, mozzarella cheese and Cheddar cheese in a bowl. Stir in the mayonnaise and garlic powder.

Spread the cheese mixture on the cut sides of the bread halves and sprinkle with paprika. Bake for 20 minutes. Broil for 2 minutes or until brown and bubbly. Slice each bread half into 6 to 8 slices and serve immediately. Makes 12 to 16 slices.

Bubble Bread

1 (25-ounce) package frozen dinner
 rolls, slightly thawed
1 (4-ounce) package vanilla pudding
 and pie filling mix
1/2 cup (1 stick) butter
1/3 cup granulated sugar
1/3 cup packed brown sugar
cinnamon to taste
1/2 cup chopped pecans

Cut the rolls into halves and gently stack in a bundt pan sprayed with nonstick cooking spray. Sprinkle the pudding mix over the rolls. Heat the butter, granulated sugar and brown sugar in a saucepan until blended, stirring occasionally. Drizzle over the rolls and sprinkle with cinnamon and pecans.

Grease a sheet of foil and place the foil greased side down over the rolls. Drape a tea towel over the top. Let stand at room temperature for 8 to 10 hours; do not chill.

Preheat the oven to 350 degrees and bake for 30 minutes. Cool in the pan for 5 minutes and carefully invert onto a serving platter. Serves 8 to 10.

Nutty Orange Coffee Cake

3/4 cup granulated sugar
1/2 cup pecans, chopped
2 teaspoons grated orange zest
3 ounces cream cheese
2 (10-count) cans refrigerated
 buttermilk biscuits, separated
1/4 to 1/3 cup butter, melted
1 cup confectioners' sugar, sifted
2 tablespoons fresh orange juice

Preheat the oven to 350 degrees. Mix the granulated sugar, pecans and orange zest in a bowl. Spoon about 3/4 teaspoon of the cream cheese in the center of each biscuit and fold over to enclose the filling. Press the edges to seal. Dip the filled biscuits in the butter and coat with the granulated sugar mixture.

Arrange the coated biscuits curved side down in a single layer in a lightly greased 12-cup bundt pan, spacing evenly. Do not stack. Arrange any remaining coated biscuits around the center of the pan. Drizzle with the remaining butter and sprinkle with the remaining granulated sugar mixture.

Bake for 35 to 40 minutes or until light brown. Immediately invert onto a serving platter and drizzle with a mixture of the confectioners' sugar and orange juice. Serves 6.

Apricot Almond Coffee Cake

3 cups all-purpose flour

1 tablespoon baking powder

1 teaspoon baking soda

1 teaspoon salt

1 cup sour cream

3/4 cup milk

1 1/2 cups granulated sugar

3/4 cup (1 1/2 sticks) butter, softened

2 eggs

1 teaspoon vanilla extract

1/2 cup packed brown sugar

3 tablespoons all-purpose flour

1 tablespoon butter, melted

1 (8-ounce) jar apricot preserves

1/4 cup almond paste

1/2 cup sliced almonds, toasted
   (page 268)

Preheat the oven to 350 degrees. Mix 3 cups flour, the baking powder, baking soda and salt together. Whisk the sour cream and milk in a bowl until blended. Beat the granulated sugar and 3/4 cup butter in a mixing bowl until creamy. Add the eggs and vanilla and beat until light and fluffy. Add the flour mixture and milk mixture alternately to the creamed mixture, mixing just until combined after each addition; do not overmix. This is the Basic Batter.

Mix the brown sugar, 3 tablespoons flour and 1 tablespoon butter in a bowl. Spoon 1/2 of the Basic Batter into a 9-inch springform pan sprayed with nonstick cooking spray. Layer with the brown sugar mixture and dot with the preserves and almond paste. Sprinkle with the almonds and top with the remaining Basic Batter. Bake for 50 to 60 minutes or until a wooden pick inserted in the center comes out clean.

3/4 cup sugar

3 eggs

1/2 cup fresh lemon juice
   (about 3 lemons)

grated zest of 1 1/2 lemons

6 tablespoons unsalted butter, chilled

1 1/2 cups shredded coconut, toasted

LEMON CURD COFFEE CAKE

Bring a shallow saucepan of water to a simmer. Combine the sugar and eggs in a heatproof mixing bowl and beat with an electric mixer fitted with a whisk attachment until light and fluffy. Add the lemon juice and lemon zest and beat until incorporated. Place over the simmering water and cook for 20 minutes or until the lemon curd coats the back of a spoon, whisking constantly. Remove from the heat and whisk in the butter. Cool slightly and chill in the refrigerator.

Preheat the oven to 350 degrees. Prepare the Basic Batter. Spoon 1/2 of the batter into a 9-inch springform pan sprayed with nonstick cooking spray. Layer with 1 1/2 cups of the lemon curd, 1 cup of the coconut and the remaining batter. Bake for 15 minutes and sprinkle with the remaining coconut. Bake for 45 to 50 minutes longer or until the coffee cake tests done. This version may require a longer baking time due to the lemon curd. The wooden pick will not come out clean.

1 1/2 cups chopped pecans

1 cup packed brown sugar

3 tablespoons all-purpose flour

3 tablespoons butter, melted

1 tablespoon ground cinnamon

TEXAS PECAN COFFEE CAKE

Preheat the oven to 350 degrees. Prepare the Basic Batter. Mix the pecans, brown sugar, flour, butter and cinnamon in a bowl. Spread 1/2 of the batter in a 9-inch springform pan sprayed with nonstick cooking spray. Layer with the pecan mixture and the remaining batter. Bake for 50 to 60 minutes or until a wooden pick inserted in the center comes out clean.

Sunday Morning Danish

1 (8-count) can crescent rolls or
    reduced-fat crescent rolls
16 ounces cream cheese or reduced-
    fat cream cheese, softened
1 cup sugar
1 egg yolk
1 teaspoon vanilla extract
1 (8-count) can crescent rolls or
    reduced-fat crescent rolls
1 egg white
$1/4$ cup sugar

Preheat the oven to 375 degrees. Unroll 1 can of crescent rolls and pat the dough over the bottom of a lightly greased 9×13-inch baking dish. Beat the cream cheese, 1 cup sugar, the egg yolk and vanilla in a mixing bowl until creamy, scraping the bowl occasionally. Spread the cream cheese mixture over the prepared layer.

Unroll 1 can of crescent rolls and arrange over the cream cheese mixture. Whisk the egg white in a bowl until foamy and brush over the top. Sprinkle with $1/4$ cup sugar and bake for 25 minutes. Cool slightly and cut into squares. Serve warm. Serves 8.

Applesauce Pecan Bread

4 cups all-purpose flour

2 teaspoons baking soda

1 teaspoon baking powder

1 teaspoon ground cinnamon

1/2 teaspoon ground nutmeg

1/2 teaspoon salt

2 cups sugar

2 cups applesauce

2/3 cup vegetable oil

4 eggs

2 or 3 Granny Smith or
    Golden Delicious apples,
    peeled and chopped

1 cup chopped pecans

Caramel Sauce

Preheat the oven to 350 degrees. Sift the flour, baking soda, baking powder, cinnamon, nutmeg and salt together. Beat the sugar, applesauce, oil and eggs in a mixing bowl at low speed until combined. Add the flour mixture gradually, beating constantly just until combined. Stir in the apples and pecans.

Spoon the batter into a greased and floured bundt pan and bake for 1 hour. Cool slightly in the pan and invert onto a serving platter. Just before serving, drizzle with the hot Caramel Sauce, or serve with homemade vanilla ice cream spiked with cinnamon. Serves 12 to 16.

CARAMEL SAUCE

1 cup packed light brown sugar

1/4 cup (1/2 stick) butter

1 cup heavy cream

1/2 cup chopped pecans

Bring the brown sugar and butter to a boil in a saucepan. Stir in the heavy cream and pecans and return to a boil. Boil for 3 to 4 minutes or until thickened, stirring frequently. Remove from the heat and cover to keep warm.

Decadent Banana Bread

1¹/₂ cups all-purpose flour

1 teaspoon baking soda

¹/₂ teaspoon salt

1 cup sugar

¹/₂ cup (1 stick) butter, softened

2 eggs

1 teaspoon vanilla extract

1 cup sour cream

1¹/₂ cups chopped pecans

2 ripe bananas, mashed

Coconut and Pecan Topping

Preheat the oven to 350 degrees. Sift the flour, baking soda and salt into a bowl and mix well. Beat the sugar, butter, eggs and vanilla in a mixing bowl until blended. Add the sour cream, pecans and bananas and mix well. Add the banana mixture to the flour mixture and stir just until moistened.

Spoon the batter into a greased and floured 5×9-inch loaf pan and bake for 1 hour or until a wooden pick inserted in the center comes out clean. Cool in the pan for 10 minutes and remove to a wire rack. Spoon the warm Coconut and Pecan Topping over the top of the warm loaf. You may bake in 3 miniature loaf pans. Serves 12.

²/₃ cup packed brown sugar

5 tablespoons butter

1 cup finely chopped pecans, toasted (page 268)

1 cup flaked coconut

COCONUT AND PECAN TOPPING

Combine the brown sugar and butter in a saucepan and cook over medium heat until blended, stirring frequently. Remove from the heat and stir in the pecans and coconut. Cover to keep warm.

234

Blueberry Streusel Muffins

1³/4 cups all-purpose flour

1/2 cup sugar

2³/4 teaspoons baking powder

³/4 teaspoon salt

2 teaspoons grated lemon zest

³/4 cup milk

1/3 cup vegetable oil

1 egg, lightly beaten

1 cup fresh or drained thawed
   frozen blueberries

1 tablespoon all-purpose flour

1 tablespoon sugar

Sugar and Cinnamon Topping

Preheat the oven to 400 degrees. Combine 1³/4 cups flour, 1/2 cup sugar, the baking powder, salt and lemon zest in a bowl and mix well. Make a well in the center of the flour mixture. Whisk the milk, oil and egg in a bowl until blended and add to the well. Stir just until moistened.

Toss the blueberries, 1 tablespoon flour and 1 tablespoon sugar in a bowl until coated. Fold the blueberry mixture into the batter. Fill miniature muffin cups 2/3 full and sprinkle with the Sugar and Cinnamon Topping. Bake for 18 minutes or until light brown. Immediately remove the muffins to a wire rack. Makes 1 dozen miniature muffins.

1/4 cup sugar

2¹/2 tablespoons all-purpose flour

1/2 teaspoon ground cinnamon

1¹/2 tablespoons butter or margarine

SUGAR AND CINNAMON TOPPING

Combine the sugar, flour and cinnamon in a bowl and mix well. Cut in the butter until crumbly.

Bran Muffins

2¹/₂ cups all-purpose flour

1³/₄ cups sugar

1 tablespoon baking soda

1 teaspoon salt

4 cups Raisin Bran

1 cup raisins (optional)

3³/₄ to 4 cups buttermilk

¹/₃ cup canola oil

2 eggs

Combine the flour, sugar, baking soda and salt in a bowl and mix well. Stir in the cereal and raisins. Whisk the buttermilk, canola oil and eggs in a bowl until blended. Add the flour mixture to the buttermilk mixture and stir just until moistened. Store, covered, in the refrigerator for 24 hours.

Preheat the oven to 350 degrees. Spoon the batter into paper-lined muffin cups and bake for 20 to 25 minutes or until the muffins test done. Makes 1 dozen large muffins.

Pineapple Carrot Muffins

2 cups all-purpose flour

1 cup sugar

2 teaspoons baking powder

1/2 teaspoon ground cinnamon

1/4 teaspoon ground ginger

1/4 teaspoon salt

1/2 cup shredded carrots

1/2 cup raisins

1/2 cup chopped pecans

1 (8-ounce) can crushed pineapple

1/4 cup (1/2 stick) margarine, melted

2 eggs, lightly beaten

1 teaspoon vanilla extract

Preheat the oven to 375 degrees. Combine the flour, sugar, baking powder, cinnamon, ginger and salt in a bowl and mix well. Stir in the carrots, raisins and pecans.

Combine the undrained pineapple, margarine, eggs and vanilla in a bowl and mix well. Add the pineapple mixture to the flour mixture and stir just until moistened. Spoon the batter into greased muffin cups and bake for 20 to 25 minutes or until the muffins test done. Makes 15 muffins.

Light-as-a-Feather Rolls

1 cup sour cream
1/2 cup (1 stick) unsalted butter
1/2 cup sugar
1 teaspoon salt
2 eggs
2 envelopes dry yeast
1/16 teaspoon sugar
1/2 cup warm (110 degrees) water
4 cups all-purpose flour
1/4 cup (1/2 stick) butter, melted

Combine the sour cream, 1/2 cup butter, 1/2 cup sugar and the salt in a microwave-safe bowl. Microwave for 2 minutes or until the butter melts. Stir and let stand until an instant-read thermometer inserted into the mixture registers 105 to 110 degrees. Combine the sour cream mixture with the eggs in a mixing bowl and beat until blended.

Dissolve the yeast and 1/16 teaspoon sugar in the warm water in a bowl. Let stand for 5 minutes. Add the yeast mixture to the egg mixture and mix well. Add the flour gradually, beating constantly until incorporated. The dough will be sticky. Place the dough in an oiled bowl, turning to coat the surface. Let rise, covered, in a warm environment for 2 hours.

Punch the dough down and shape into 2-inch balls, adding additional flour if needed to make an easily handled dough. Arrange the dough balls in muffin cups sprayed with nonstick cooking spray and let rise for 30 minutes. Preheat the oven to 350 degrees and bake for 15 minutes or until golden brown. Immediately brush with 1/4 cup melted butter and serve. Makes 2 dozen rolls.

CITRUS AND CREAM CHEESE ROLLS

8 ounces cream cheese, softened
1 3/4 cups confectioners' sugar
1 egg
1/4 teaspoon grated lemon or
**   orange zest**
1 1/2 tablespoons (or more)
**   warm water**
1/2 teaspoon vanilla, lemon or
**   almond extract**
Chambord or your favorite liqueur
**   to taste**

Prepare the Light-as-a-Feather Roll dough. Preheat the oven to 350 degrees. After the dough rises, punch down and roll into a 9×12-inch rectangle on a lightly floured surface. Beat the cream cheese, 1/4 cup of the confectioners' sugar, the egg and lemon zest in a mixing bowl until light and fluffy; spread over the rectangle. Roll tightly to enclose the filling, sealing the edge. Cut the roll into 4 equal portions and cut each portion into 3 equal slices, for a total of 12. Arrange the slices cut side down in a greased 9-inch baking pan or a 9×9-inch baking pan. Bake for 20 to 25 minutes. Drizzle the warm rolls with a mixture of the remaining 1 1/2 cups confectioners' sugar, the warm water, vanilla and liqueur.

PECAN STICKY ROLLS

2 tablespoons light corn syrup
1 1/2 tablespoons water
3 tablespoons butter, melted
1 3/4 cups packed brown sugar
1 tablespoon ground cinnamon
1/4 cup (1/2 stick) butter, melted
1/3 cup finely chopped pecans

Prepare the Light-as-a-Feather Roll dough. Preheat the oven to 350 degrees. After the dough rises, punch down and roll into a 9×12-inch rectangle on a lightly floured surface. Mix the corn syrup, water, 3 tablespoons butter and 3/4 cup of the brown sugar in a bowl and pour into a greased 9-inch baking pan or 9×9-inch baking pan. Mix the remaining 1 cup brown sugar, the cinnamon, 1/4 cup butter and the pecans in a bowl and spread over the rectangle. Roll tightly to enclose the filling and cut the roll into 4 equal portions. Cut each portion into 3 slices, for a total of 12. Arrange the slices cut side down in the prepared pan and bake for 25 to 30 minutes.

French Toast with Strawberries

12 slices French bread,
   1¹/2 inches thick

8 ounces cream cheese, softened

2 tablespoons sugar

1/2 teaspoon ground nutmeg

1/2 teaspoon ground cinnamon

1 cup half-and-half

6 eggs

Grand Marnier Sauce

Preheat the oven to 350 degrees. Make a horizontal slit in the tops of the bread slices to form a pocket. Beat the cream cheese, sugar, nutmeg and cinnamon in a mixing bowl until creamy. Spread about 1$1/2$ tablespoons of the cream cheese mixture in each pocket. Arrange 8 of the slices in a buttered 8×12-inch baking dish and the remaining 4 slices in a buttered 8×8-inch baking dish.

Beat the half-and-half and eggs in a mixing bowl until blended and pour over the bread slices, turning to coat. Bake for 35 minutes or until golden brown. Drizzle the warm Grand Marnier Sauce over the French toast and serve immediately. You may prepare up to 1 day in advance and store, covered, in the refrigerator. Bring to room temperature and bake as directed. Serves 8.

GRAND MARNIER SAUCE

1 cup sifted confectioners' sugar

2 tablespoons cornstarch

1/2 cup (1 stick) butter, melted

1/3 cup Grand Marnier

3 cups sliced fresh strawberries

Mix the confectioners' sugar and cornstarch in a medium saucepan. Add the butter and stir until smooth. Stir in the liqueur and cook over medium heat to the desired consistency, stirring constantly. Add the strawberries and cook for 1 minute longer, stirring frequently. Serve warm.

Cornmeal Pancakes with Corn Salsa

1 (10-ounce) package frozen corn

1 cup salsa

1/2 cup yellow cornmeal

1 tablespoon all-purpose flour

1 teaspoon sugar

1/2 teaspoon baking soda

1/2 teaspoon salt

1 cup buttermilk

2 egg yolks

2 egg whites

1/2 cup (2 ounces) shredded
   Cheddar cheese

1/2 cup sour cream

Microwave the corn in a microwave-safe dish for 2 minutes; drain. Or cook the corn with 1/2 cup boiling water in a saucepan for 1 minute or just until tender; drain. Mix 1/2 cup of the corn with the salsa in a bowl.

Sift the cornmeal, flour, sugar, baking soda and salt into a bowl and mix well. Whisk the buttermilk and egg yolks in a bowl until blended and stir into the cornmeal mixture. Beat the egg whites in a mixing bowl until stiff but not dry peaks form. Fold the egg whites into the cornmeal batter.

Preheat a skillet and spray the hot skillet with nonstick cooking spray. Pour 2 tablespoons of the batter into the hot skillet for each pancake and sprinkle with the remaining corn. Cook until the underside is golden brown and turn. Sprinkle with the cheese and cook until brown on the remaining side. Roll each pancake and top with 1 tablespoon of the corn salsa and a dollop of sour cream. Serve warm. Makes 4 to 6 pancakes.

Honey and Cinnamon Butter

**¹/₂ cup (1 stick) unsalted butter,
    softened**
1 tablespoon honey
¹/₄ teaspoon ground cinnamon
¹/₁₆ teaspoon ground nutmeg

Beat the butter in a mixing bowl using an electric mixer fitted with a whisk attachment for 30 seconds or until smooth. Add the honey, cinnamon and nutmeg and beat until incorporated. Spoon the butter into an 8-ounce ramekin and cover with waxed paper. Or shape the butter into a log and wrap with waxed paper or plastic wrap, securing the ends. Chill for 2 hours. You may prepare 2 to 3 days in advance and store in the refrigerator or freeze for up to 2 months.

CHOCOLATE BUTTER

1 tablespoon baking cocoa
4 teaspoons confectioners' sugar

Beat the butter as directed above. Omit the honey, cinnamon and nutmeg and add the baking cocoa and confectioners' sugar. Beat at medium speed until incorporated and store as directed above.

TOP SHELF BUTTER

1¹/₂ teaspoons fresh lime juice
1¹/₂ teaspoons tequila
1 teaspoon orange liqueur
1 teaspoon sugar
¹/₂ teaspoon grated lime zest
¹/₄ teaspoon grated orange zest

Mix the lime juice, tequila, liqueur and sugar in a bowl until the sugar dissolves. Beat the butter as directed above, omitting the honey, cinnamon and nutmeg. Add the lime juice mixture, lime zest and orange zest to the beaten butter and beat at medium speed until incorporated. Store as directed above.

243

Sweet compound butters add that special touch to any breakfast or brunch. Serve them on toast, pancakes, or your favorite biscuits.

Broiled Grapefruit

3 Texas Ruby Red grapefruit

3/4 cup citrus vodka (optional)

3 tablespoons light brown sugar

Reposition the top oven rack 3 to 4 inches from the top of the oven and preheat the broiler. Cut the grapefruit into halves and separate the pulp from the peel. Loosen each section with a sharp knife. Be careful not to pierce the bottom of the grapefruit to avoid losing all the juices.

Arrange the grapefruit halves cut side up on a baking sheet and drizzle each with 2 tablespoons of the vodka; some of the juice may be squeezed out. You may prepare to this point several hours in advance and store, covered, in the refrigerator. Sprinkle each half with 1 1/2 teaspoons of the brown sugar and broil for 3 to 4 minutes or until bubbly. Serves 6.

Grilled Blue Cheese Sandwiches

4 to 6 slices cinnamon raisin bread

1 ripe pear, peeled and thinly sliced

3 ounces Stilton cheese, crumbled

1 tablespoon butter

Layer 2 or 3 slices of the bread evenly with the pear and sprinkle with the cheese. Top with the remaining slices of bread to make sandwiches. Heat the butter in a skillet over medium-low heat until melted.

Arrange the sandwiches in the melted butter and cook, covered, for 2 minutes per side or until golden brown. Cut each sandwich diagonally into 4 portions and serve immediately. You may substitute 1 canned pear for the fresh pear. Makes 2 to 3 sandwiches.

Asparagus Gruyère Strudel

12 ounces fresh asparagus

salt to taste

1 pound mushrooms, thinly sliced

7 tablespoons butter, melted

2 teaspoons fresh lemon juice

1/3 cup walnuts, toasted and finely
   chopped (page 268)

2 tablespoons dry bread crumbs

12 sheets phyllo

1 cup (4 ounces) shredded
   Gruyère cheese

Snap off the woody ends of the asparagus spears. Cut the asparagus into uniform 6-inch-long spears. Cook the asparagus in boiling salted water in a saucepan for 4 to 8 minutes or to the desired degree of crispness; drain.

Sauté the mushrooms in 1 tablespoon of the butter in a skillet until the liquid evaporates. Stir in the lemon juice and sauté for 30 seconds longer. Remove from the heat and cool slightly. Mix the walnuts and bread crumbs in a bowl.

Preheat the oven to 375 degrees. Arrange 1 sheet of the phyllo on a hard surface, with the short side facing you. Cover the remaining sheets with waxed paper and a damp tea towel to prevent drying out. Lightly brush the phyllo with some of the remaining melted butter. Sprinkle with 1/6 of the walnut mixture. Top with another sheet of the phyllo and brush with some of the remaining butter. Sprinkle 1/6 of the cheese in a strip on the pastry, 2 inches from the edge facing you and leaving a 2-inch border on both sides. Layer 1/6 of the asparagus over the cheese and top with 1/6 of the mushrooms.

Roll the pastry as for a jelly roll to enclose the filling. Fold the left and right sides toward the center and continue rolling jelly roll fashion to the end. Place the packet seam side down on a baking sheet and brush lightly with some of the melted butter. Repeat the process with the remaining phyllo, remaining melted butter, remaining walnut mixture, remaining cheese, remaining asparagus and remaining mushrooms.

Bake for 25 minutes or until slightly puffed and golden brown. Serve immediately. You may assemble in advance and store, covered with plastic wrap, in the refrigerator until just before baking. Serves 6.

Camembert and Blue Cheese Egg Casserole

1 tablespoon butter

1 (20-ounce) package frozen hash
   brown potatoes

8 ounces thinly sliced turkey bacon,
   cut into 1/2-inch pieces

18 eggs

2 1/4 cups heavy cream

2 1/4 cups milk

1 teaspoon salt

1/8 teaspoon Tabasco sauce

pepper to taste

16 ounces Camembert cheese, rind
   removed and shredded or crumbled

8 ounces blue cheese, crumbled

1 tablespoon chopped fresh rosemary

Preheat the oven to 400 degrees. Coat a baking sheet with the butter. Spread the hash brown potatoes on the prepared baking sheet and bake until golden brown, turning occasionally. Remove the potatoes from the oven and reduce the oven temperature to 350 degrees.

Cook the bacon in a skillet until brown and very crisp, almost to the point of overcooking; drain. Whisk the eggs, heavy cream and milk in a bowl until blended. Stir in the salt, Tabasco sauce and pepper.

Spread the hash brown potatoes in a 9×13-inch baking pan and sprinkle with 1/2 of the bacon, 1/2 of the Camembert cheese and 1/2 of the blue cheese. Pour 1/2 of the egg mixture over the prepared layers. Top with the remaining bacon, remaining Camembert cheese, remaining blue cheese and remaining egg mixture.

Bake, covered with foil, for 50 minutes or until the eggs are set; remove the foil. Bake for 10 minutes longer or until brown. Sprinkle with the rosemary and serve immediately. Serves 20.

Chilaquiles

24 corn tortillas

vegetable oil for frying

2^1/2 cups roasted tomato sauce

^{1}/4 cup chicken broth (page 261)

^{1}/4 cup minced seeded pickled
jalapeño chiles

1 cup (4 ounces) shredded
Monterey Jack cheese

1 cup (4 ounces) shredded
Cheddar cheese

12 eggs

^{1}/2 cup heavy cream

^{1}/3 cup sour cream

Cut the tortillas into strips and let stand at room temperature for 30 minutes to dry. Pour enough oil into a skillet to measure ^{1}/2 inch deep and heat over medium heat. Fry the tortilla strips in the hot oil until almost crisp; drain.

Preheat the oven to 350 degrees. Process the tomato sauce, ^{1}/2 of the broth and the jalapeño chiles in a blender until smooth. Reserve ^{1}/2 cup of the sauce. Layer the tortilla strips, Monterey Jack cheese, Cheddar cheese and the remaining tomato sauce mixture ^{1}/2 or ^{1}/3 at a time in a greased 9×13-inch baking dish. Whisk the eggs and heavy cream in a bowl until fluffy and pour over the prepared layers.

Bake for 30 to 45 minutes or until set. Mix the sour cream with the remaining broth 1 tablespoon at a time in a bowl, stirring until the desired consistency is reached. Drizzle the sour cream mixture and reserved tomato sauce mixture over the top and serve immediately. Serves 12.

Chile-Cheese Egg Casserole

^{1}/2 cup all-purpose flour

1 teaspoon baking powder

^{1}/2 teaspoon salt

^{1}/2 cup (1 stick) butter, melted

10 eggs

1 (4-ounce) can diced green chiles,
drained

4 cups (16 ounces) shredded
Monterey Jack cheese

2 cups ricotta cheese

Preheat the oven to 350 degrees. Combine the flour, baking powder and salt in a bowl and mix well. Stir in the butter. Whisk the eggs in a bowl until blended. Add the flour mixture and green chiles to the eggs and mix well. Stir in the Monterey Jack cheese and ricotta cheese. Pour the egg mixture into a greased 9×13-inch baking pan and bake for 1 hour or until set. Serves 8 to 10.

Green Chile and Chorizo Breakfast Strata

14 to 16 ounces pork or beef chorizo,
    casings removed
2$^{1}/_2$ cups milk
5 eggs
1 teaspoon ground cumin
$^1/_2$ teaspoon salt
$^1/_4$ teaspoon ground pepper
6 slices sourdough bread, crusts
    trimmed
1$^3/_4$ cups (7 ounces) shredded hot
    pepper Monterey Jack cheese
2 (4-ounce) cans chopped mild green
    chiles, drained and patted dry
$^1/_2$ cup fresh cilantro, chopped
paprika to taste

Sauté the sausage in a large heavy skillet over medium-low heat for 15 minutes or until cooked through. Remove to a plate lined with paper towels to drain. Whisk the milk, eggs, cumin, salt and pepper in a bowl until blended.

Arrange 2 of the bread slices in a buttered 9×13-inch baking dish. Sprinkle with $^3/_4$ cup of the cheese, $^1/_2$ of the green chiles, $^1/_2$ of the cilantro and $^1/_2$ of the sausage. Pour $^1/_2$ of the egg mixture over the prepared layers. Top with 2 more bread slices, $^3/_4$ cup of the cheese, the remaining chiles, remaining cilantro, remaining sausage and $^1/_2$ of the remaining egg mixture. Layer with the remaining 2 bread slices and the remaining egg mixture and sprinkle with the remaining $^1/_4$ cup cheese and the paprika. Chill, covered, for 8 to 10 hours.

Preheat the oven to 350 degrees. Remove the cover and bake for 55 minutes or until puffed and golden brown. Serve immediately. You may bake in 8 ramekins. Serves 8.

Sunrise Frittata

1¹/₂ cups (¹/₂-inch pieces) potatoes

1 tablespoon vegetable oil

1¹/₂ cups finely chopped cooked ham

¹/₂ cup (2 ounces) shredded
   Cheddar cheese

9 eggs, lightly beaten

¹/₃ cup milk

1 (4-ounce) can diced green chiles,
   drained

¹/₄ cup finely chopped green onions

2 teaspoons snipped fresh oregano,
   or ¹/₂ teaspoon dried oregano,
   crushed

¹/₄ teaspoon salt

¹/₂ (7-ounce) jar roasted red bell
   peppers, drained and cut into
   thin strips

¹/₄ cup (1 ounce) shredded
   Cheddar cheese

1¹/₂ cups salsa

¹/₄ cup chopped fresh cilantro

sliced green onions (optional)

shredded Parmesan cheese (optional)

Preheat the oven to 350 degrees. Cook the potatoes in the oil in an ovenproof skillet over medium heat for 5 minutes, stirring occasionally. Cook, covered, for 5 minutes longer or until tender, stirring once. Remove from the heat and sprinkle with the ham and ¹/₂ cup Cheddar cheese.

Whisk the eggs, milk, green chiles, chopped green onions, oregano and salt in a bowl until mixed and pour over the potato mixture. Arrange the bell pepper strips in a spoke pattern over the top of the prepared layers. Bake for 25 to 30 minutes or just until a knife inserted in the center comes out clean. Sprinkle with ¹/₄ cup Cheddar cheese and let stand for 5 minutes.

Mix the salsa and cilantro in a saucepan and simmer until heated through, stirring occasionally. Sprinkle the frittata with sliced green onions and Parmesan cheese and cut into wedges. Serve immediately with the salsa mixture. Serves 4 to 6.

Chicken Pecan Quiche

1 cup all-purpose flour

1 cup (4 ounces) shredded sharp
   Cheddar cheese

3/4 cup chopped pecans

1/2 teaspoon salt

1/4 teaspoon paprika

1/3 cup vegetable oil

1 cup sour cream

1/2 cup chicken broth

1/4 cup mayonnaise

3 eggs, beaten

2 cups chopped roasted or
   smoked chicken

1/2 cup (2 ounces) shredded sharp
   Cheddar cheese

1/4 cup minced onion

1/4 teaspoon dried whole dill weed

3 drops of hot sauce

pecan halves (optional)

Preheat the oven to 350 degrees. Combine the flour, 1 cup cheese, chopped pecans, salt and paprika in a bowl and mix well. Add the oil and stir until crumbly. Reserve 1/4 cup of the crumb mixture. Press the remaining crumb mixture over the bottom and up the side of a 9-inch quiche pan. Prick the bottom and side with a fork and bake for 10 minutes. Remove from the oven and reduce the oven temperature to 325 degrees.

Whisk the sour cream, broth, mayonnaise and eggs in a bowl until blended. Stir in the chicken, 1/2 cup cheese, the onion, dill weed and hot sauce. Spoon the chicken mixture into the baked crust and sprinkle with the reserved crumb mixture. Top with pecan halves and bake for 45 minutes. Serves 6 to 8.

Ham and Vegetable Quiche

1 recipe Savory Tart Crust (page 272)
1 tablespoon chopped fresh thyme
1¹/₂ cups assorted wild mushrooms,
    chopped
1 to 2 tablespoons butter
1¹/₂ cups trimmed fresh spinach,
    chopped
1 cup half-and-half
4 eggs
8 ounces cooked ham, cut into
    ¹/₄-inch pieces
8 ounces Gruyère cheese, shredded
¹/₄ teaspoon freshly grated nutmeg
¹/₄ teaspoon freshly ground pepper
¹/₁₆ teaspoon salt

Preheat the oven to 400 degrees. Prepare the Savory Tart Crust, adding the thyme. Pat the dough over the bottom and up the side of a 3-inch-deep tart pan or a 9-inch pie plate. Line with baking parchment and weight with dried beans or pie weights. Bake for 10 minutes. Let cool and remove the pie weights and baking parchment. Maintain the oven temperature.

Sauté the mushrooms in the butter in a skillet until tender. Remove the mushrooms to a plate using a slotted spoon, reserving the pan drippings. Sauté the spinach in the reserved pan drippings just until wilted. Whisk the half-and-half and eggs in a bowl until blended. Stir in the mushrooms, spinach, ham, cheese, nutmeg, pepper and salt.

Pour the egg mixture into the baked crust and bake for 35 to 40 minutes or until a knife inserted in the center comes out clean. Cool for 5 to 10 minutes before serving. Serves 6 to 8.

Photograph for this recipe on page 224.

252

Tostada Quiche

1 unbaked (9-inch) deep-dish pie shell
8 ounces ground beef
¹/₄ cup chopped onion
2 tablespoons chopped green chiles
1 to 2 tablespoons taco seasoning mix
1¹/₂ cups (6 ounces) shredded
    Cheddar cheese or Monterey Jack
    cheese
1¹/₂ cups half-and-half
3 eggs, lightly beaten
¹/₂ teaspoon salt
¹/₈ teaspoon pepper

Preheat the oven to 375 degrees. Prick the side and bottom of the pie shell with a fork or line with baking parchment or foil and fill with pie weights or dried beans. Bake for 7 minutes. Maintain the oven temperature.

Combine the ground beef, onion, green chiles and taco seasoning mix in a medium skillet and mix well. Cook over medium heat until the ground beef is brown and the onion is tender, stirring occasionally; drain. Layer the cheese and ground beef mixture in the pie shell.

Whisk the half-and-half, eggs, salt and pepper in a bowl until blended but not foamy and pour over the prepared layers. Bake for 45 minutes or until a knife inserted near the center comes out clean. Let stand for 10 minutes before serving. Garnish each serving with shredded lettuce, chopped tomatoes, black olives, guacamole, sour cream and salsa. Serves 6.

Cheese Grits

1 quart milk

1/2 cup (1 stick) plus 3 tablespoons butter

1 cup quick-cooking grits

10 ounces sharp Cheddar cheese, shredded

1 teaspoon seasoned salt

1 teaspoon Tabasco sauce

1 teaspoon paprika

1/2 teaspoon pepper

1 egg, beaten

Preheat the oven to 350 degrees. Combine the milk and butter in a saucepan and bring almost to a boil, stirring occasionally. Sprinkle the grits over the hot milk mixture and simmer for 5 to 10 minutes or until thickened, stirring occasionally. Remove from the heat and stir in the cheese, seasoned salt, Tabasco sauce, paprika and pepper. Blend in the egg and beat with an electric mixer for 5 minutes.

Spoon the grits mixture into a greased 8×12-inch baking dish and bake for 35 to 45 minutes or until the top is golden brown. Tent with foil if needed to prevent overbrowning. Serves 6 to 8.

First 3 ingredients of Cheese Grits

4 ounces Gruyère cheese, grated

4 ounces Parmesan cheese, grated

1/2 teaspoon cayenne pepper

1 egg, beaten

1 small can artichoke hearts, drained and chopped

4 ounces prosciutto, thinly sliced and chopped

2 ounces Parmesan cheese, grated

TUSCAN CHEESE GRITS

Cook the grits as directed above until thickened. Remove from the heat and stir in the Gruyère cheese, 4 ounces Parmesan cheese and the cayenne pepper. Blend in the egg. Beat as directed above and stir in the artichokes and prosciutto. Bake as directed, sprinkling with 2 ounces Parmesan cheese 15 minutes before the end of the baking process.

First 3 ingredients of Cheese Grits

6 ounces sharp Cheddar cheese, shredded

2 ounces Gruyère cheese, grated

2 ounces Swiss cheese, shredded

1 teaspoon Greek seasoning

1 or 2 garlic cloves, roasted (page 131)

2 drops of Tabasco sauce

2 drops of Worcestershire sauce

1 egg, beaten

2 ounces Parmesan cheese, grated

FOUR-CHEESE GRITS

Cook the grits as directed above until thickened. Remove from the heat and stir in the Cheddar cheese, Gruyère cheese, Swiss cheese, Greek seasoning, garlic, Tabasco sauce and Worcestershire sauce. Blend in the egg. Beat as directed above. Bake as directed, sprinkling with the Parmesan cheese 15 minutes before the end of the baking process.

Cranberry Pudding Tamales with Tequila Orange Curd

Award-winning chef, author, and PBS-TV host, Stephen Pyles is an innovator. As the first Texan inducted into Who's Who of Food and Wine in America, his food ventures have changed the direction of Southwestern food and taken it to new culinary heights.

3³/₄ cups fresh cranberries, sorted

1 cup ground pecans

1 cup sugar

3 tablespoons all-purpose flour

³/₄ teaspoon ground cinnamon

¹/₄ teaspoon ground allspice

¹/₄ teaspoon ground ginger

1¹/₂ cups finely ground bread crumbs

1 cup gingersnap cookie crumbs

³/₄ cup sugar

1 tablespoon baking powder

¹/₂ teaspoon salt

³/₄ cup (1¹/₂ sticks) unsalted butter, melted and cooled

³/₄ cup milk

3 eggs, lightly beaten

4 (12×36-inch) banana leaves

Tequila Orange Curd (page 255)

Cranberry Glaze (page 255)

Process the cranberries in a food processor until coarsely chopped. Combine the chopped cranberries and pecans in a bowl and mix well. Stir in 1 cup sugar, the flour, cinnamon, allspice and ginger. Combine the bread crumbs, cookie crumbs, ³/₄ cup sugar, the baking powder and salt in a bowl and mix well. Stir in the butter, milk and eggs. Add the bread crumb mixture to the cranberry mixture and mix well. Chill, covered, for 30 minutes or longer.

Soften the banana leaves over an open flame for 10 seconds on each side, being careful not to scorch the leaves. Cut each leaf crosswise into four 9×12-inch portions and arrange on a hard surface. Divide the cranberry mixture into 16 equal portions. Spoon 1 portion in the center of each banana leaf and spread into a 4-inch square, leaving at least a 1¹/₂-inch border at the end and a ³/₄-inch border along the long sides.

To fold, pick up the two long sides of the banana leaf and bring together; the leaf will surround the filling. Tuck 1 side under the other and fold the flaps on each end underneath the tamale. Repeat until all of the tamales are shaped. Arrange the tamales in a steamer set over gently boiling water and steam, tightly covered, for 20 to 25 minutes. Remove the tamales and slice to expose the cranberry pudding.

Drizzle some of the Tequila Orange Curd on each of 8 plates. Arrange 2 tamales on each plate and spoon some of the Cranberry Glaze over the top of each serving. Serves 8.

TEQUILA ORANGE CURD

3/4 cup fresh orange juice

1 cup milk

1 cup heavy cream

1 vanilla bean, split lengthwise
into halves

6 egg yolks

2/3 cup sugar

1 tablespoon gold tequila

1 teaspoon grated orange zest

3/4 cup sour cream or crème fraîche,
chilled

Pour the orange juice into a saucepan and cook over high heat until reduced to 1/4 cup. Remove from the heat and set aside. Bring the milk, heavy cream and vanilla bean to a boil. Remove from the heat and cover. Let infuse for 15 minutes.

Place the egg yolks in a bowl. Add the sugar gradually, whisking constantly. Continue to whisk until the yolks have lightened in color. Return the milk mixture to a boil and pour through a strainer into the yolk mixture, stirring constantly; discard the vanilla bean.

Return the egg yolk mixture to the saucepan and cook over low heat, stirring constantly with a wooden spoon. Scrape down the side and bottom of the pan and continue to cook for 5 to 10 minutes longer or until a candy thermometer inserted in the mixture registers 185 degrees and the mixture has thickened. Remove from the heat and place over an ice bath. Stir in the tequila, orange zest, reduced orange juice and sour cream. Chill, covered, in the refrigerator. Serves 8

CRANBERRY GLAZE

1 cup cranberry juice

1 cup sugar

1 cup cranberries

Combine the cranberry juice and sugar in a saucepan and mix well. Cook over medium heat until the sugar dissolves, stirring constantly and brushing down any sugar crystals that cling to the side of the pan with a brush dipped in cold water. Bring to a boil and boil until a candy thermometer in the mixture registers 250 degrees, gently swirling the pan. Stir in the cranberries. Remove from the heat and let stand until cool. Chill, covered, in the refrigerator. Serves 8

Not-Just-for-Breakfast
Hash Brown Casserole

1 (20-ounce) package frozen hash
    brown potatoes, thawed
2¹/2 cups (10 ounces) shredded
    Cheddar cheese
2 cups sour cream
1 (10-ounce) can cream of
    chicken soup
¹/2 cup (1 stick) butter, melted
1 teaspoon salt
¹/2 teaspoon pepper
1¹/2 cups cornflake crumbs
¹/4 cup (¹/2 stick) butter, melted

Preheat the oven to 350 degrees. Combine the potatoes, cheese, sour cream, soup, ¹/2 cup butter, the salt and pepper in a bowl and mix well. Spoon the potato mixture into a greased 9×13-inch baking dish. Toss the cornflake crumbs with ¹/4 cup butter in a bowl until coated and sprinkle over the prepared layer.

Bake for 45 minutes or until brown and bubbly. You may prepare up to 1 day in advance and store, covered, in the refrigerator. Bake just before serving. Serve as a side dish with beef tenderloin. Serves 8 to 10.

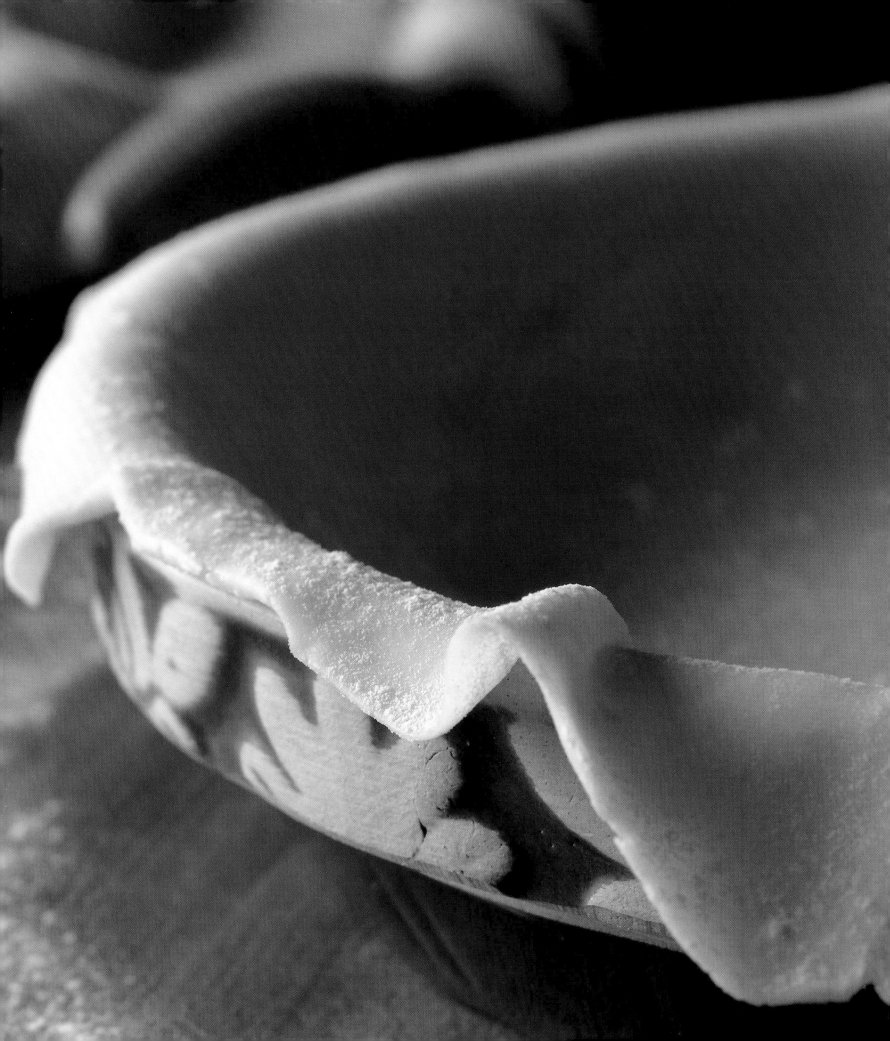

Basics

THE DISH ON DALLAS

Future chefs and hospitality professionals can attend
one of the many degreed programs in the area to
learn everything from the basics to the exquisite.
The same goes for the "foodie" who loves cooking
workshops. Dallas offers approximately thirty different
classes a week through local culinary businesses
and organizations, such as the American Institute of
Wine & Food and local restaurants.

Perfect Pie Crust recipe on page 271.

Simple Syrups

1 cup sugar
1 cup water
1 vanilla bean

VANILLA BEAN SYRUP

Combine the sugar and water in a 1-quart saucepan and mix well. Add the vanilla bean and cook over medium-high heat just until the mixture comes to a boil. Reduce the heat and simmer for 5 minutes or until the sugar dissolves, stirring occasionally. Remove from the heat.

Remove the vanilla bean and split into halves. Scrape the seeds into the syrup mixture using a sharp knife. The vanilla bean may be rinsed, patted dry and stored in an airtight container for future use. Cool the syrup and pour into an airtight container. Store in the refrigerator for up to 2 weeks. Drizzle over fresh summer berries, like the blackberries found in Dallas.

1¹/₂ cups packed fresh mint
4 slices fresh ginger

GINGER MINT SYRUP

Combine equal parts of water and sugar with the mint and ginger. Cook as directed above. Cool and strain through a fine sieve into an airtight container, discarding the solids. Store as directed above.

zest of 1 large Texas Ruby Red
grapefruit
zest of 1 Texas orange

CITRUS SIMPLE SYRUP

Combine equal parts of water and sugar with the grapefruit zest and orange zest. Cook as directed above. Cool and strain into an airtight container, discarding the solids. Store as directed above. When zesting citrus fruits, be careful not to remove the white pith with the zest, as the white pith will make the syrup bitter.

Chicken Stock

1 **pound chicken parts**

6 **cups water**

1 **large unpeeled yellow onion,**
  cut into 6 wedges

3 **ribs celery with leaves,**
  coarsely chopped

2 **carrots, coarsely chopped**

2 **bay leaves**

1^1/$_2$ **teaspoons salt**

5 **peppercorns**

Combine the chicken, water, onion, celery, carrots, bay leaves, salt and peppercorns in a large stockpot and bring to a boil over high heat. Reduce the heat and simmer, covered, for 1 hour.

Discard the chicken, onion, celery, carrots and bay leaves. Skim the fat off the surface of the stock and strain into a bowl through a fine sieve lined with cheesecloth. Store, covered, in the refrigerator for up to 3 days or freeze for future use. Makes 5 cups.

The Perfect Hard-Cooked Egg

10 to 12 eggs

cold water

Gently place the eggs in a stockpot large enough to accommodate the eggs and add enough cold water to completely cover. Use a stockpot that is large enough to accommodate the eggs, but not so large that it allows the eggs to bump during the boiling process.

Bring the eggs to a rolling boil over high heat. Remove from the heat and let stand, covered, for 18 minutes. Drain and rinse with cold water to cool.

Hard-cooked eggs may be stored in the refrigerator for 7 to 10 days. Leftover egg whites and egg yolks may be stored, covered, in the refrigerator for up to 4 days. Cover the egg yolks with water to prevent drying out. Egg whites may be frozen for up to 1 year. Makes 10 to 12 hard-cooked eggs.

Poached Chicken

4 cups chicken stock or water

2 whole chicken breasts with skin and bones

Pour enough stock over the chicken in a stockpot to cover. Bring to a boil over medium-high heat. Reduce the heat and simmer for 3 to 5 minutes. Remove from the heat and cover. Let stand until the chicken is completely cool. Remove the breast meat, discarding the skin and bones.

Use the poached chicken in your favorite recipes. To shred the chicken quickly for chicken salad or enchiladas, coarsely chop the chicken and place in a food processor. Pulse until the desired consistency.
Makes 2 cups.

Roasted Poultry

Simply great food begins with a love of the season's freshest fruits and vegetables, prepared and served with the best of care. Michael Lane Cuisine utilizes only the freshest ingredients to prepare full-flavored meals complete with all the thoughtful details and finishing touches. His experience at The Mansion on Turtle Creek in Dallas and Cafe Annie in Houston has helped influence his creativity and passion for fine cuisine. Michael is also a graduate of the Culinary Institute of America and has been cooking for twelve years.

poultry of choice (chicken, pheasant, turkey)
3 or 4 sprigs of fresh sage, chopped
1 bunch parsley, chopped
salt and pepper to taste
1 onion, coarsely chopped
4 to 6 garlic cloves, coarsely chopped
1 large carrot, coarsely chopped
2 ribs celery, coarsely chopped
5 or 6 sprigs of thyme
3 or 4 sprigs of rosemary
2 or 3 sprigs of basil

Preheat the oven to 350 degrees. Rinse the poultry and cut off any excess fat. Rub the sage and parsley over the outside surface of the poultry and sprinkle with salt and pepper. Mix the onion, garlic, carrot, celery, thyme, rosemary and basil in a bowl and stuff the poultry with the onion mixture.

Arrange the poultry on a roasting rack in a roasting pan. Bake until the juices run clear after being pierced with a fork. Remove the poultry from the rack and place on a serving platter. Remove the vegetable mixture from the cavity and stir into the roasting juices. Use as a base for gravy. Variable servings.

Marinara Sauce

3 tablespoons olive oil
1 carrot, peeled and chopped
1 small yellow onion, chopped
4 garlic cloves, chopped
2 (32-ounce) cans imported plum
   tomatoes
10 basil leaves
1 tablespoon sugar
salt and pepper to taste

Heat the olive oil in a large saucepan over medium heat. Add the carrot and onion to the hot oil and sauté until the onion is tender. Stir in the garlic and cook for 1 to 2 minutes, stirring frequently. Mix in the undrained tomatoes and reduce the heat to low.

Simmer for about 10 minutes, stirring occasionally. Stir in the basil, sugar, salt and pepper. Taste and adjust the seasonings if desired.

Process the tomato mixture in a blender or with a hand blender to the desired consistency. Store in an airtight container in the refrigerator for up to 1 week or freeze for up to 6 months. Serve over hot cooked pasta or use in your favorite Italian dishes. Makes 3 cups.

265

For roasted chiles or peppers, grill chiles or peppers on an indoor grill or broil until the skins are charred and blackened. Immediately place in a nonrecycled paper bag or sealable plastic bag and seal tightly. Let steam for 15 to 20 minutes. Remove the skins with your fingers, discarding the seeds. Do not remove the skins under running water or rinse the chiles or peppers after skin removal as this will greatly reduce the roasted flavor.

Penne à la Vodka

16 ounces penne

4 cups Marinara Sauce (page 265)

3/4 cup vodka

1 cup frozen peas, thawed

1/2 cup cream, at room temperature

4 ounces prosciutto, thinly sliced and julienned

3/4 cup (3 ounces) freshly grated Parmigiano-Reggiano cheese

freshly ground pepper to taste

Cook the pasta using the package directions. Drain and set aside. Heat the Marinara Sauce in a saucepan over medium heat, stirring occasionally. Add the vodka and simmer for 5 minutes, stirring occasionally. Stir in the peas and bring to a slight simmer. Add the cream and mix well. Stir in the prosciutto and cheese and add the pasta. Simmer just until heated through, stirring occasionally. Season to taste with pepper. Serves 6 to 8.

Baked Ziti

2 to 3 tablespoons olive oil

16 ounces ziti

1 cup ricotta cheese

1/2 cup (2 ounces) grated Parmesan or Romano cheese

1 egg, beaten

1/4 cup cream

1 to 2 tablespoons chopped fresh parsley

1/16 teaspoon freshly grated nutmeg

1/16 teaspoon salt

1/16 teaspoon freshly ground pepper

8 ounces mozzarella cheese, shredded

5 cups Marinara Sauce (page 265)

1/2 cup (2 ounces) grated Parmesan or Romano cheese

Preheat the oven to 400 degrees. Coat a 9×13-inch baking dish with the olive oil. Cook the pasta using the package directions until al dente. Drain and set aside. Mix the ricotta cheese, 1/2 cup Parmesan cheese, the egg, cream, parsley, nutmeg, salt and pepper in a bowl. Add the pasta to the ricotta cheese mixture and toss to mix. Fold in the mozzarella cheese.

Heat the Marinara Sauce in a saucepan over low heat. Reserve about 1/2 to 3/4 cup of the sauce. Pour the remaining sauce over the pasta mixture and mix gently. Spoon the pasta mixture into the prepared baking dish and drizzle with the reserved sauce. Sprinkle with 1/2 cup Parmesan cheese and bake for 20 minutes or until bubbly. Let stand for 4 minutes before serving. Serves 8 to 10.

Basic Cream Sauce

2 tablespoons unsalted butter
1 tablespoon all-purpose flour
1 cup half-and-half
salt and white pepper to taste

Heat the butter in a heavy saucepan over medium-low heat. Mix in the flour and cook for 1 to 2 minutes to form a roux, stirring constantly. Do not allow the roux to color. Remove from the heat and whisk in 1/4 cup of the half-and-half. Return to the heat and whisk in the remaining 3/4 cup half-and-half.

Increase the heat and bring the half-and-half mixture to a boil, stirring frequently. Reduce the heat to low and cook for 4 to 5 minutes, whisking constantly. Season to taste with salt and white pepper. Makes 1 cup.

For **Cheese Sauce,** add 4 ounces of Gruyère cheese, Cheddar cheese or Swiss cheese to the Basic Cream Sauce. Add 1/8 teaspoon dry mustard if adding Cheddar cheese.

For **Béchamel Sauce,** substitute chicken broth for the half-and-half in the Basic Cream Sauce.

For **Hot Thousand Island Sauce,** add a mixture of 1/4 cup mayonnaise and 1/4 cup chili sauce to the hot Basic Cream Sauce.

For additional variations, refer to the Vegetable Saucery chart on page 273.

Hollandaise

3 egg yolks
2 tablespoons fresh lemon juice
1/2 cup (1 stick) butter
1/4 teaspoon salt

Whisk the egg yolks and lemon juice in the top of a double boiler until blended. Place over simmering water and whisk in 3 tablespoons of the butter. Simmer until the butter melts, whisking constantly. Whisk in 3 more tablespoons of the butter and simmer until the butter melts, whisking constantly.

Add the remaining 2 tablespoons butter and simmer until the mixture thickens, whisking constantly. Remove from the heat and stir in the salt. Makes 2/3 cup.

Basic Cake Batter

1 cup sugar

6 eggs

¹/₂ cup (1 stick) butter, melted

1 cup sifted cake flour, sifted

¹/₂ teaspoon vanilla or almond extract

Preheat the oven to 350 degrees. Grease the bottom of two 9-inch cake pans and line the bottoms with baking parchment. Grease the baking parchment and sides of the pans.

Combine the sugar and eggs in a heatproof bowl and place the bowl over a saucepan of simmering water. Simmer for 4 to 5 minutes, whisking constantly. Remove from the heat and beat with an electric mixer at high speed for 6 to 8 minutes or until the mixture triples in bulk and reaches the ribbon stage. Drizzle the batter from a spoon and a ribbonlike pattern should form. Beat at medium speed for 2 minutes longer. Add the butter gradually, beating constantly at low speed for 30 seconds. Fold in all the flour just until incorporated and stir in the vanilla.

Spoon the batter evenly into the prepared pans and bake for 25 minutes or until a wooden pick inserted in the center comes out clean, rotating the pans if necessary halfway through the baking process. Cool in the pans on a wire rack for 15 minutes. Run a knife around the edge of both layers and invert onto a wire rack to cool completely. Citrus flavorings and citrus zest may be substituted for the extracts. Makes 2 (9-inch) cake layers.

There are two methods that can be used when toasting nuts, the stovetop method or oven method. Choose the method that works best for you. The stovetop method is best for a small amount of nuts, and you are less likely to forget about them.

For the stovetop method, heat the nuts in a large skillet over medium-high heat, stirring occasionally with a wooden spoon. Toast approximately five to seven minutes or until golden brown and fragrant, stirring frequently. The skillet will not need any oil due to the high fat content of the nuts. Immediately pour the nuts onto another surface, such as a wooden cutting board, to stop the toasting process.

For the oven method, spread the nuts in a single layer on a baking sheet with sides. Toast at 375 degrees for seven to ten minutes or until golden brown and fragrant, stirring or shaking the baking sheet one or more times.

Homemade Ice Cream with Vanilla Beans

2 vanilla beans

2 cups half-and-half

6 egg yolks

3/4 cup sugar

1 cup heavy cream

Split the vanilla beans into halves and scrape the seeds. Combine the half-and-half, vanilla pods and vanilla seeds in a saucepan and bring to a boil over medium-high heat. Remove from the heat and let stand for 5 minutes. Remove the pods.

Lightly beat the eggs yolks in a bowl. Add the sugar and whisk until the mixture is pale yellow in color. Whisk the half-and-half mixture into the egg yolk mixture and return to the saucepan. Cook over medium heat for 10 minutes or until the custard coats the back of a wooden spoon, whisking constantly. Run your finger down the back of the spoon and the line should remain.

Strain the custard through a fine sieve into a bowl and stir in the heavy cream. Press plastic wrap directly onto the surface of the custard and chill for 8 to 10 hours. Freeze in an ice cream maker using the manufacturer's directions for a soft ice cream or spoon into a freezer container and freeze for a very firm ice cream. Add mix-ins at the soft stage. Makes 6 cups.

Perfect Pie Crust

**3/4 cup (1¹/₂ sticks) unsalted butter,
  chilled**

2¹/₂ cups all-purpose flour

1 teaspoon salt

1 teaspoon sugar

2 tablespoons shortening

4 to 8 tablespoons ice water

all-purpose flour for dusting

1 egg, beaten

2 teaspoons water

Cube the butter and chill until needed. Combine 2¹/₂ cups flour, the salt and sugar in a bowl and mix well. Cut in the chilled butter and shortening with a fork or pastry blender until crumbly. Drizzle the ice water 2 tablespoons at a time over the crumb mixture and incorporate, continuing to add the water just until the dough adheres and is no longer crumbly.

Divide the dough into 2 equal portions and shape each portion into a ball. Flatten each ball into a disc between sheets of plastic wrap. Wrap separately in plastic wrap and chill in the refrigerator.

Dust a hard work surface with flour. Place 1 of the dough portions on the floured surface and sprinkle with additional flour. Roll the dough ¹/₈ inch thick with a rolling pin, flipping and rotating the dough every couple of rolls and dusting with additional flour as needed.

Roll the dough onto the rolling pin to lift and fit into a 9-inch pie plate. Cut off the excess and pinch the edge under to form a lip. Crimp the edge with a fork or between fingers to form a decorative edge and brush the edge with a mixture of the egg and 2 teaspoons water. Roll the remaining dough portion for a top crust or freeze for future use. Brush the top crust with the egg wash. Makes 1 (2-pastry) pie crust.

Photograph for this recipe on page 258.

271

Savory Tart Crust

10 tablespoons unsalted butter,
  chilled

1$^1/_2$ cups all-purpose flour

$^1/_2$ teaspoon salt

1 egg yolk

2 tablespoons cold water

Cut the butter into $^1/_2$-inch cubes and chill until needed. Combine the flour and salt in a food processor and pulse until combined. Sprinkle the butter over the flour mixture and pulse until crumbly. Whisk the egg yolk and cold water in a small bowl until blended. Drizzle the egg yolk mixture over the crumb mixture and pulse until a dough forms and adheres.

Shape the dough into a large disc and wrap in plastic wrap or waxed paper. Chill for 2 hours or longer or freeze for up to 1 month. Thaw in the refrigerator. Roll the dough $^1/_8$ inch thick between sheets of waxed paper. Fit into an ungreased tart pan or quiche pan and chill for 30 minutes.

Preheat the oven to 350 degrees. Line the shell with foil or baking parchment and fill with pie weights. Bake for 10 minutes, remove the pie weights and foil and fill with a tart or quiche filling. Bake using the recipe directions. Makes 1 crust.

Vegetable Saucery

The word *sauce* comes from the French, meaning a condiment or relish to make food more appetizing. Historically, sauces were used to mask the taste of tainted food caused by the lack of proper refrigeration. Times have definitely changed. Today a basic cream sauce is used not only as an accompaniment to vegetables, but as a versatile base for many pasta recipes. By adding a few simple ingredients, a basic cream sauce can turn everyday seafood or white meats into gourmet dishes. Experiment with your favorite seasonings or herbs…the possibilities are endless. The Basic Cream Sauce recipe is featured on page 267. Use this chart to create a variety of sauces.

Variations

Sauce	Add to basic sauce	Use with
Cheese	1/2 cup sharp Cheddar cheese 2 drops of Worcestershire sauce	broccoli, brussels sprouts, cabbage, cauliflower
Curry	2 to 3 teaspoons curry powder 1/8 teaspoon ginger	asparagus, carrots, mushrooms, squash
Dill	1 to 2 teaspoons dill weed	cauliflower, green beans
Mushroom	1/2 cup sautéed mushrooms	broccoli, peas, spinach
Mustard	1 to 2 tablespoons prepared mustard or Dijon mustard	bok choy, green beans, onions, tomatoes
Parsley	2 tablespoons chopped parsley	peas, potatoes
Tomato	1/4 cup chili sauce Dash of Tabasco sauce	eggplant, onions, peppers, zucchini

Equivalents

When the recipe calls for	Use

Baking
$1/2$ cup butter	4 ounces
2 cups butter	1 pound
4 cups all-purpose flour	1 pound
$4^1/2$ to 5 cups sifted cake flour	1 pound
1 square chocolate	1 ounce
1 cup semisweet chocolate chips	6 ounces
2 cups granulated sugar	1 pound

Cereal/Bread
1 cup fine dry bread crumbs	4 to 5 slices
1 cup soft bread crumbs	2 slices
1 cup small bread cubes	2 slices
1 cup fine cracker crumbs	28 saltines
1 cup crushed cornflakes	3 cups, uncrushed
4 cups cooked macaroni	8 ounces, uncooked
$3^1/2$ cups cooked rice	1 cup, uncooked

Dairy
1 cup shredded cheese	4 ounces
1 cup cottage cheese	8 ounces
1 cup sour cream	8 ounces
1 cup whipped cream	$1/2$ cup heavy cream
$2/3$ cup evaporated milk	1 (5-ounce) can
$1^2/3$ cups evaporated milk	1 (12-ounce) can

Fruit
4 cups sliced or chopped apples	4 medium
1 cup mashed bananas	3 medium
2 cups pitted cherries	4 cups, unpitted
$2^1/2$ cups shredded coconut	8 ounces
4 cups cranberries	1 pound
3 to 4 tablespoons lemon juice plus 1 tablespoon grated lemon zest	1 lemon
$1/3$ cup orange juice plus 2 teaspoons grated orange zest	1 orange
4 cups sliced peaches	8 medium

Meats
4 cups chopped cooked chicken	1 (5-pound) chicken
3 cups chopped cooked meat	1 pound, cooked
2 cups cooked ground meat	1 pound, cooked

When the recipe calls for	Use

Nuts

1 cup chopped nuts . . . . 4 ounces, shelled or
1 pound, unshelled

Vegetables

2 cups cooked green beans . . . . 1/2 pound fresh or
1 (16-ounce) can
2 1/2 cups lima beans or red beans . . . . 1 cup dried, cooked
4 cups shredded cabbage . . . . 1 pound
1 cup grated carrot. . . . . 1 large
8 ounces fresh mushrooms . . . . 1 (4-ounce) can
1 cup chopped onion . . . . 1 large
4 cups sliced or chopped potatoes. . . . . 4 medium
2 cups canned tomatoes . . . . 1 (16-ounce) can

Metric Equivalents

Liquid

1 teaspoon = 5 milliliters
1 tablespoon = 15 milliliters
1 fluid ounce = 30 milliliters
1 cup = 250 milliliters
1 pint = 500 milliliters

Dry

1 quart = 1 liter
1 ounce = 30 grams
1 pound = 450 grams
2.2 pounds = 1 kilogram

Measurement Equivalents

1 tablespoon = 3 teaspoons
2 tablespoons = 1 ounce
4 tablespoons = 1/4 cup
5 1/3 tablespoons = 1/3 cup
8 tablespoons = 1/2 cup
12 tablespoons = 3/4 cup
16 tablespoons = 1 cup
1 cup = 8 ounces or 1/2 pint
4 cups = 1 quart
4 quarts = 1 gallon

1 (6 1/2- to 8-ounce) can = 1 cup
1 (10 1/2- to 12-ounce) can = 1 1/4 cups
1 (14- to 16-ounce) can = 1 3/4 cups
1 (16- to 17-ounce) can = 2 cups
1 (18- to 20-ounce) can = 2 1/2 cups
1 (29-ounce) can = 3 1/2 cups
1 (46- to 51-ounce) can = 5 3/4 cups
1 (6 1/2- to 7 1/2-pound) can or
Number 10 = 12 to 13 cups

Herbs

Use fresh whole herbs when possible. When fresh herbs are not available, use dried whole herbs that can be crushed just while adding. Store herbs in airtight containers away from the heat of the stove. Fresh herbs may be layered between paper towels and microwaved on High for two minutes or until dry.

Basil: Can be chopped and added to cold poultry salads. If the recipe calls for tomatoes or tomato sauce, add a touch of basil to bring out a rich flavor.

Bay leaf: The basis of many French seasonings. It is added to soups, stews, marinades, and stuffings.

Bouquet garni: A bundle of parsley, thyme, and bay leaves tied together and added to stews, soups, or sauces. Other herbs and spices may be added to the basic herbs.

Chervil: One of the traditional fines herbes used in French cooking. (The others are tarragon, parsley, and chives.) It is good in omelets and soups.

Chives: Available fresh, dried, or frozen, chives can be substituted for fresh onion or shallot in almost any recipe.

Garlic: One of the oldest herbs in the world, it must be handled carefully. For best results, press or crush the garlic clove.

Marjoram: An aromatic herb of the mint family, it is good in soups, sauces, stuffings, and stews.

Mint: Use fresh, dried, or ground with vegetables, desserts, fruits, jelly, lamb, or tea. Fresh sprigs of mint make attractive aromatic garnishes.

Oregano: A staple savory herb in Italian, Spanish, Greek, and Mexican cuisines. It is very good in dishes with a tomato foundation, especially in combination with basil.

Parsley: Use this mild herb as fresh sprigs or dried flakes to flavor or garnish almost any dish.

Rosemary: This pungent herb is especially good in poultry and fish dishes and in such accompaniments as stuffings.

Saffron: Use this deep-orange herb, made from the dried stamens of a crocus, sparingly in poultry, seafood, and rice dishes.

Sage: This herb is a perennial favorite with all kinds of poultry and stuffings.

Tarragon: One of the fines herbes. Goes well with all poultry dishes, whether hot or cold.

Thyme: A widely used herb, thyme is usually used in combination with bay leaf in soups, stews, and sauces.

Acknowledgments

We thank the following for supporting the Junior League of Dallas:

Cebolla Fine Flowers
Elephant Walk
Jimmie Henslee
Ali Jones
Cathy Kincaid

Darren Looker
Peacock Alley
Rue 1
Kathleen Schlichenmaier
Sur La Table

Trinity District Antiques
Uncommon Market
Carole Walter

Recipe Testers

Becky Abbott
Susan Anderson
Jennifer Archers
Elenora Asbury
Jennifer Atkins
Jeanie Jenkins Bateman
Pamela Beal
Alisha Bell
Leslie Bellows
Suzanne Boyd-Chapman
Nicole Brewer
Frances Bright
Frances Bruns
Dian Bumpas
Mary Bush
Sandra Carlton
Peggy Carr
Ann Carruth
Liz Cook
Melissa Cooksey
Betty Sanford Crawford
Leslie Cuthrell
Joecely Dabeau
Patsy Denman
Mary Ann Denton
Brian Dooley

Karen Douning
Deidre Dowd
Katharine Felder
Judy Ferguson
Patricia Fink
Lynne Frawley
Pauline Gatto
Tisha Ghormley
Jennifer Graham
Catherine Gravel
Lisa Turner Grissom
Martha Groves
Rhonda Hanrahan
Holland Hayden
Cindy Hazelbaker
Susanne Hilou
Heidi Hollomon
Laura Holt
Priscilla Horn
Anne Gannett Howard
Judy Huff
Kathy Jackson
Tara Jiranek
Shanna Johnston
Carole Jordon
Rachel Karnes

Elizabeth Keating
Bernadine Kirchhof
Jana Koenig
Alicia Koo
Michele Kovsky
Maureen Kuntz
Margaret Landis
Kimberly Lane
Catherine Linden
Sheila Long
Amy Lott
D'Ann Love
Carla McClanahan
Sharon McGowan
Brigette Miller
Susan Millet
Carin Moeller
Dana Moore
Marcia Mootz
Lisa Morris
Susan Nowlin
Ann O'Boyle
Roz Palasota
Trista Perot
Amy Pithan
Kathleen Power

Amy Robb
Debbie Ryan
Betsie Sears
Mary Shelton
Ann Simpson
Linda D. Slaughter
Bettye Slaven
Janet K. Smith
Vicki Smith
Debbie Browne Snell
Lyndal Stephens
Abby Suddart
Jane Switzer
Betsy Tanis
Susie Taylor
Kirsten Toben
Kirin Vieira
Mary Helen Vollmer
Amanda Wallace
Linda Wells
Katie West
Kelly Whittredge
Cayla Woodruff
Sharon Wooton
Liana Yarckin
Cathy Zavodny

277

Recipe Contributors

Melissa Allan
Karin Allison
Linda Altick
Margaret Arrington
Elenora Asbury
Laura Assyia
Jenifer Atkins
Sherri Zillgitt Baer
Kelly Baisden
Emy Lou Baldridge
Susan Baldwin
Sallye Kay Coleman Bales
Janice Barger
Missy Barras
Tamara Morris Beachum
Pricilla Bell
Leslie Bellows
Anne Bentley
Elizabeth Beshear
Carolyn Bess
Julie Blackmon
Locie Boggs
Suzanne Boyd-Chapman
Jaclyn Braddy
Kelly Braddy
Kim Brannon
Marsha Braswell
Amy Brechin
Nicole Metzger Brewer
Carolyn Brannan Bright
Deanna Brown
Alison Bryant
Ellen Bryant
Elaine Brzezinski
Janey Buck
Mary Hope Burns
Mrs. Paul R. Burton
Pam Busbee
Kristina Bush
Monique Callagy
McCall Cameron
Catherine Campbell
Susan Candy

Sandra Haynes Carlton
Mary-Elizabeth Carrell
Karen Votteler Carreon
Christie Carter
Jill Chambless
Rebecca Chambless
Julie Clark
Wendy Cobb
Brenda Cohenour
Mary Ann Collins
Tracy Constantino
Maggie Cooke
Melissa E. Cooksey
Whitney Cortner
Evelyn Costolo
Eun-Sang Covin
Barbara Cox
Mary Tullie Critcher
Blair Crossley
Sally Grayson Cullum
Carol Dalton
Ginger Fite Daniel
Beth Darr
Doris Davis
Luaren A. DeBoever
Mersine Patts Defterios
Mary Ann Denton
Tiffany Dixon
Devon Doby
Holly Dawson Driggers
Judy McClain Duncan
Denise Dunlap
Nancy Dean Egan
Susan Eldredge
Elizabeth Emerson
Stacy Eppers
Junior Esquivel
Shannon Estes
Laurie Ewing
Kathleen Berry Fawcett
Leigh Ann Feagan
Marcy Feldman
Jane Ann Ferguson

Judy Ferguson
Tiffany Finn
Jane Fitch
Tanya Foster
Margie Francis
Lynne Frawley
Elizabeth Fritz
Susan Floyd Frymire
Diane Fullingim
Elizabeth Reding Gambrell
Jessica Garner
Pauline Gatto
Michael Gaule
Wendy Gaule
Betsy Gekiere
Sharilyn Getz
Susan Geyer
Cara Ginsberg
Christina Godbey
Julia Good
Jennifer Graham
Beverly Grant
Catherine H. Gravel
Elizabeth M. Greenwood
Lisa Turner Grissom
Martha Groves
Elizabeth Gunby
Nancy Cramer Gurevtiz
Polly Hall
Elizabeth Hammer
Hadley Hammons
Rhonda Hanrahan
Sarah Hardin
Susan Harvey
Heather Haskins
Scott Hatfield
Stacy Hawkins
J. B. Hayes
Charlotte Hickey
Carol Jamison Hildebrand
Heidi Holt Hill
Kristianne Hinkamp
Jane Hoffman

MaryAnn Holder-Browne
Cindy Holliday
Lee K. Holmberg
Mrs. James H. Holmes III
Laura Holt
Mary Ann Holt
Jan Hopkins
Mary Louise Hopson
Rhonda Houston
Jeannie Hubert
Eileen Hudnall
Shannan Humphries
Nell Anne Hunt
Stephanie Bradford Hunt
Elizabeth Hunter
Teffy Jacobs
Amy Jent
Jeanette Johnson
Kristen Johnson
Shannon Johnston
Angela Jones
Jessics Martin Jones
Summer Jones
Rachel Karnes
Rebekah Hamilton Kay
Diana Kayser
Elizabeth Keating
Laura Keck
Whitney Kielwasser
Meredith Kim
Erica Kimble
Bernardine Kirchhof
Kathey Hannah Kivell
Cheryl Klima
Christine Kobeck
Alicia Koo
Barbara W. Kurilecz
Paige Lackey
Janis Lamoreaux
Karen Lancaster-Brown
Kimberly Lane
LeAnne Langholz
Kate Lavelle

Leslie Lehr
Marylyn Leonard
Margaret Lesesne
Martha Levy
Cindy Lindsley
Allison Freeman Logan
Jennifer Lohse
Sheila Long
Fernand Louvat
Erin Lundie
Alison Malone
Jeanette Mann
Lucie Mansfield
Brenda Mauldin Mason
Shelley Mason
Elizabeth Mateja
Brenda Mauldin
Ruth A. May
Carla McClanahan
Meredy McClure
Kate Anderle McCoy
Paige McDaniel
Kelley McDonald
Susie McDonough
Terry McKee
Nancy McMahon
Carmen McMillan
Lucy McRae
Melissa McRoberts
Sherry McWhorter
Kirsten Merritt
Lesley Metz
Brigette K. Miller
Kristi Miller
Patti Miller
Kim Moats
Carin Moeller
Diane Mooney
Nancy Moore
Lee Mootz
Marcia Garrett Mootz
Renee Morales
Pat Morris

Elysia Moschos
Carey Mosley
Rachel Mulry
Suzanna Nash
Martha Nichols-Pecceu
Christina Nihira
Allison Nolan
Libby Norwood
Cynthia Nowak
Chris A. Ogden
Garnett Ogden
Lisa Olden
Valerie L. Orgera
Cindy Orlandi
Pam Perella
Paula Pettigrew
Leanne Pettit
Linda Phelps
Amber Pick
Donna C. Pierce
Kelly Pittman
Maria Martineau Plankinton
Kate Hoak Power
Mrs. Robert C. Prather, Sr.
Stephanie Prince
Karen Prothro Puckett
Kathryn Quest
Jane Quinn
Seema Qureshi
Kendall Ramirez
Alyson Ray
Gem-Ann Regan
Patricia Riatti
Amy Richard
Julie Wakser Richter
Michelle Rickman
Nancy Greenwood Riddle
Kelly Rigas
Amy Robb
Susan Roberds
Carmina Robuck
Lisa Rogers
Stephanie Rogers

Debra Ropp
Neall Grinnan Rose
Audra Roswell
Jeane Rovillo
Amanda Sanguinet
Elizabeth Sawyer
Kay Schaffer
Laura Schieber
Ginger Gillison Schlather
Traci Schuh
Christy Schwall
Elizabeth Scrivner
Betsie Sears
Suzette D'Ayson Shelmire
Susan E. Skaggs
Alicia M. Slay
Dorothy Smith
Janet Smith
Kate Smith
Margaret Ann Smith
Marilee Smith
Patricia Franklin Smith
Vicki Smith
Holly Holt Soetenga
Mrs. Walter F. Sosnowski
Marilyn Spencer
Alison Stacy
Lyndal S. Stephens
Denise Stewart
Kathleen Stewart
Tricia Stewart
Drew Bass Stull
Jane Switzer
Betsy Tanis
Shirley Tart
Anna Marie Johnson Teague
Byrd Teague
Roxanne Tedford
Haley Teegarden
Alexandra Teodoro
Neely Thrash
Kirsten Toben
JoAnn Tobey

Randee Travis
Terri Tygart
Monica Urbaniak
Bettye Williams
  Vanderwoude
Susan Vice
Molly Villasana
Susan McNabb Voigt
Mary Helen Vollmer
Amanda Wallace
Tracy Wallingford
Judy Walters
Amanda Ward
Carol Watson
Sarah Wechsler
Lynette Willis Weisheit
Katie West
April Graf Wharton
Laura Wheat
Janey White
Lori Whitlow
Lisa Wiegert
Diane Pou Wilcox
Sabrina Wilhoit
Emily Williams
Kelli Williams
Erin Willis
Ann Winniford
Heidi Wolf
Alicia Wood
Elizabeth Woodard
Adrienne Wooldridge
Dale Wooton
Jennifer Wooton
Sharon Wootton
Sally Wrightman
Liana Yarckin
Bayla Wakser Yess
Cathy Zavodny
Rene Zvolanek

279

Index

Accompaniments. *See also* Salsa;
   Sauces, Savory; Sauces, Sweet
Ancho Mayonnaise, 164
Arugula Mayonnaise, 78
Avocado Crème Fraîche, 71
Baked Hazelnuts, 104
Charred Tomato Chutney, 159
Chive Butter, 125
Chocolate Butter, 243
Cilantro Cream, 94
Crème Fraîche, 109
Dijon and Peppercorn Butter, 125
Fried Tortilla Strips, 72
Ginger-Cilantro Lime Butter, 80
Honey and Cinnamon Butter, 243
Jalapeño Lime Butter, 125
Maple Jalapeño Cream, 134
Peach Jalapeño Chutney, 154
Pepper Jam, 55
Pico de Gallo, 24
Quick Herbed Mustard, 34
Squash Pickles, 133
Top Shelf Butter, 243

Appetizers. *See also* Dips; Spreads
Artichoke Stuffed with Brie, 56
Blue Cheese Popovers, 25
Camembert Pastry Platter, 54
Chicken Phyllo Pockets, 38
Chiquito Risotto, 35
Crisp Scallops and Creamed
   Sweet White Corn, 43
Designer Crab Purses, 42
Fried Green Tomatoes, 33
Gorgonzola-Stuffed Endive, 26
Grilled Shrimp with
   Basil Pistachio Sauce, 45
Marinated Olives, 28
Pears with Goat Cheese and
   Prosciutto, 27
Pepper Jam, 55
Pita Chips, 28
Poached Salmon with
   Horseradish Sauce, 39
Reuben Strudel, 37
Roasted Garlic, 131

Shrimp 'n' Caper Bites, 32
Shrimp Wrapped in Bacon with
   Jalapeño, 44
South-of-the-Border Bruschetta, 24
Steak Satay with Cilantro, 36
Steamed Mussels with Chorizo, 40
Sweet Tomato Tart, 34
Tomato Basil Bruschetta, 24
Vegetarian Spring Rolls, 30
Wild Mushroom Bruschetta, 24

Apple
Apple Pie with Cream, 220
Applesauce Pecan Bread, 233
Apple Tart with Almond
   Cream, 217
Crunchy Caramel Apple
   Pie, 219
Fall Spice Cake, 197
Margarita Coleslaw, 98
Red Appletini, 14
Summer Cheddar Apple Pie, 218

Apricot
Apricot Almond Coffee Cake, 231
Apricot Lavender Tart, 221

Artichokes
Angry Pasta for Manic Mondays, 175
Artichoke Stuffed with Brie, 56
Hot Feta Artichoke Dip, 46
Tuscan Cheese Grits, 253
Verde Vegetable Salad, 106

Asparagus
Asparagus, Fennel and
   Radish Salad, 43
Asparagus Gruyère Strudel, 245
Asparagus with Champagne
   Vinaigrette, 119
Asparagus with Fresh Parmesan
   Cheese, 114
Hot Asparagus Sandwiches, 76
Sliced Sirloin Salad with
   Blue Cheese Dressing, 91
Verde Vegetable Salad, 106

Avocado
Avocado Caviar Mousse, 51
Avocado Crème Fraîche, 71
Avocado Feta Salsa, 47
Corn Bread Salad, 99
Fiesta Salsa, 48
Fresh Herb Tortilla Soup, 72
Layered Avocado Salad, 86
Layered Black Bean Salad, 97
Texas Two-Step Guacamole, 46
Tomatillo and Avocado Salsa, 49

Bacon/Pancetta
Arugula and Parmesan Salad, 96
Basil-Stuffed Chicken with
   Caper Sauce, 157
Butternut Squash Bisque with
   Lobster Dumplings, 67
Camembert and Blue Cheese
   Egg Casserole, 246
Caramelized Grouper, 163
Chutney Cheese Ball, 50
Corn Bread Salad, 99
Dainty BLTs, 77
Layered Black Bean Salad, 97
Sautéed Okra, 132
Shrimp Wrapped in Bacon with
   Jalapeño, 44
Traditional Green Beans, 115
Turnip Greens Soup, 74

Banana
Banana Pudding, 187
Decadent Banana Bread, 234

Beans
Chili Mac, 63
Corn Bread Salad, 99
Dallas Chalupas, 149
Fava Beans, 147
Green Beans and Tomatoes in
   White Wine, 116
Grilled Barbecued Chicken Salad
   Pizza, 158
Layered Black Bean Salad, 97
Sesame Long Beans, 117

Southwest Chicken Salad, 93
Steak and Big Bean Chili with
    Homemade Biscuits, 63
Traditional Green Beans, 115
Verde Vegetable Salad, 106
Wicked White Chili, 64

Beef. *See also* Veal
Authentic Texas Chili, 62
Beef Tenderloin with
    Mustard Cream Sauce, 143
Beer-Marinated Steaks with
    Peppercorn Sauce, 144
Chili Flank Steak, 145
Chili Mac, 63
Do-Ahead Brisket, 146
Flank Steak with Wine and Shallots, 145
Marinated Flank Steak, 145
Mushroom-Crusted Beef Tenderloin
    with Balsamic Jus, 142
Open-Faced Corned Beef Bagels, 82
Reuben Strudel, 37
Sliced Sirloin Salad with
    Blue Cheese Dressing, 91
Steak and Big Bean Chili with
    Homemade Biscuits, 63
Steak Satay with Cilantro, 36
Tostada Quiche, 252

Beets
Arugula and Roast Beet Salad, 95
Grapefruit with Red Leaf Lettuce, 88

Beverages. *See also* Syrups
Ice Ring, 20
Lime Phosphate, 17
Lone Star Sweet Tea, 21
Nectarine Basil Lemonade, 16
Orange Frosty, 19
Summer Lemonade, 17

Beverages, Alcoholic
Bloody Mary, 12
Bloomer Droppers, 12
Classic Vodka Martini, 14
Mexitini, 11
Morning Cooler, 21
Peach Margarita, 10
Peppermint Martini, 14
Prickly Pear Margarita, 10
Red Appletini, 14
The Best Margarita, 10

Vodka Freeze, 15
White Wine Sangria, 15

Beverages, Punch
Cranberry Raspberry Punch, 20
Holiday Party Punch, 20
Sunshine Punch, 19

Blueberry
Blueberry Buckle, 183
Blueberry Streusel Muffins, 235
Farmer's Market Berry Soup, 60

Breads. *See also* Coffee Cakes
Cornmeal Pancakes with
    Corn Salsa, 241
French Toast with Strawberries, 240
Toasted Cheese Bread, 229

Breads, Biscuits
Cinnamon Raisin Biscuits, 226
Homemade Biscuits, 63
Savory Buttermilk Biscuits, 227

Breads, Corn Bread
Corn Bread Salad, 99
Iron Skillet Corn Bread, 228

Breads, Loaves
Applesauce Pecan Bread, 233
Decadent Banana Bread, 234

Breads, Muffins
Blueberry Streusel Muffins, 235
Bran Muffins, 236
Pineapple Carrot Muffins, 237

Breads, Yeast
Citrus and Cream Cheese Rolls, 238
Homemade Biscuits, 63
Light-as-a-Feather Rolls, 238
Pecan Sticky Rolls, 238

Broccoli
Rosemary Broccoli, 120
Verde Vegetable Salad, 106

Brunch. *See also* Breads; Egg Dishes
Asparagus Gruyère Strudel, 245
Broiled Grapefruit, 244
Cranberry Pudding Tamales with
    Tequila Orange Curd, 254

Grilled Blue Cheese Sandwiches, 244
Not-Just-for-Breakfast Hash Brown
    Casserole, 256

Cabbage
Chicken Salad with
    Peanut Dressing, 92
Grilled Jicama Slaw, 164
Margarita Coleslaw, 98
Open-Faced Corned Beef Bagels, 82
Reuben Strudel, 37
Spring Salad with English Peas, 98

Cakes
Basic Cake Batter, 268
Bavarian Layer Cake, 196
Classic Chocolate Cake, 202
Coconut Sour Cream Cake, 200
Fall Spice Cake, 197
Happy Hour Rum Cake, 201
Quatro Leches, 198

Candy
Blue Ribbon Toffee, 205
Perfect Pralines, 204

Carrots
Carrot Bisque, 61
Carrots with Shallot Rings, 113
Chicken and Dumplings, 155
Chicken Salad with
    Peanut Dressing, 92
Cointreau Carrots, 121
Cowboy Mashed Potatoes, 131
Pineapple Carrot Muffins, 237
Spicy Noodle Salad, 90
Spicy Veggie Couscous, 137
Thick-as-Fog Pea Soup, 66
Vegetarian Spring Rolls, 30
Wild Rice Spinach Timbales, 147

Cheesecakes
Chocolate Pecan Crust, 181
Graham Cracker
    Cheesecake Crust, 181
Lemon Cheesecake with
    Raspberry Sauce, 179
Lemon Shortbread Crust, 181
Pumpkin Cheesecake with
    Praline Sauce, 180
White Chocolate Cheesecake
    Squares, 212

281

Cherry
Ice Ring, 20
Pork with Cherry Cream Sauce, 148
Traditional Green Beans, 115

Chicken
Basil-Stuffed Chicken with
  Caper Sauce, 157
Chicken à la Crescents, 77
Chicken and Dumplings, 155
Chicken Pecan Quiche, 250
Chicken Phyllo Pockets, 38
Chicken Salad, 93
Chicken Salad with
  Peanut Dressing, 92
Chicken Stock, 261
Chicken with Charred
  Tomato Chutney, 159
Crispy Oven-Fried Chicken, 156
Curried Chicken Salad, 93
Deep-in-the-Heart-of-Texas
  Backyard Barbecue Chicken, 154
Fresh Herb Tortilla Soup, 72
Green and White Chicken
  Enchiladas, 160
Grilled Barbecued Chicken Salad
  Pizza, 158
Grilled Honey Cilantro
  Chicken Sandwiches, 83
Poached Chicken, 263
Slow-Cooker Sticky Chicken, 155
Southwest Chicken Salad, 93
Tomatillo Chicken Enchiladas, 161
Wicked White Chili, 64

Chiles
Ancho Mayonnaise, 164
Baked Chiles Rellenos, 122
Chilaquiles, 247
Chile-Cheese Egg Casserole, 247
Corn Salsa, 167
Cowboy Mashed Potatoes, 131
Cream of Poblano with
  Crostini, 68
Fiesta Salsa, 48
Fresh Herb Tortilla Soup, 72
Green Chile and Chorizo
  Breakfast Strata, 248
Green Chile Casserole, 123
Grilled Pork Chops, 151
Iron Skillet Corn Bread, 228
Jalapeño Dressing, 97

Jalapeño Lime Butter, 125
Maple Jalapeño Cream, 134
Monterey Jack Cilantro Salsa, 47
Pepper Jam, 55
Risotto with Roasted Southwestern
  Chiles and Corn, 139
Shrimp Wrapped in Bacon with
  Jalapeño, 44
South-of-the-Border
  Bruschetta, 24
Southwest Chicken Salad, 93
Spicy Jalapeño Ranch
  Dressing, 107
Squash Pickles, 133
Sunrise Frittata, 249
Texas Two-Step Guacamole, 46
Tomatillo and Avocado
  Salsa, 49
Tomatillo Gazpacho with
  Lobster, 71
Tomatillo Sauce, 161
Wicked White Chili, 64

Chili
Authentic Texas Chili, 62
Chili Mac, 63
Steak and Big Bean Chili with
  Homemade Biscuits, 63
Wicked White Chili, 64

Chocolate
Bavarian Layer Cake, 196
Blue Ribbon Toffee, 205
Chocolate Anglaise, 189
Chocolate Brownies, 212
Chocolate Butter, 243
Chocolate Fudge Frosting, 202
Chocolate Pecan Crust, 181
Chocolate Sauce, 190
Chocolate Soufflés with
  Crème Anglaise, 189
Classic Chocolate Cake, 202
Cowboy Cookies, 207
Double Chocolate Fried Pies, 223
Kahlúa Brownie Torte, 195
The Love Cookie, 209
Warm Chocolate Molten with
  Chocolate Sauce, 190
White Chocolate Cheesecake
  Squares, 212
White Chocolate
  Crème Brûlée, 178

Coconut
Chutney Cheese Ball, 50
Coconut and Pecan
  Topping, 234
Coconut Sour Cream Cake, 200
Cowboy Cookies, 207
Lemon Curd Coffee Cake, 231

Coffee Cakes
Apricot Almond Coffee Cake, 231
Bubble Bread, 230
Lemon Curd Coffee Cake, 231
Nutty Orange Coffee Cake, 230
Sunday Morning Danish, 232
Texas Pecan Coffee Cake, 231

Cookies
Biscochitos, 206
Cowboy Cookies, 207
Ginger Molasses Cookies, 208
Iced Pumpkin Cookies, 210
Kahlúa Pecan Cookies, 211
Lemon Poppy Seed Cookies, 211
Oatmeal Wafer Crisps, 208
The Love Cookie, 209
Toffee Crunch Cookies, 211

Cookies, Bar
Chocolate Brownies, 212
Rhubarb Custard Bars, 214
Walnut Dream Bars, 213
White Chocolate
  Cheesecake Squares, 212

Corn
Corn Bread Salad, 99
Cornmeal Pancakes with
  Corn Salsa, 241
Corn Salsa, 167
Corn Soufflé, 126
Cowboy Mashed Potatoes, 131
Crawfish and Corn Chowder, 65
Creamed Summer Corn, 127
Crisp Scallops and
  Creamed Sweet White Corn, 43
Fiesta Salsa, 48
Grilled Barbecued Chicken Salad
  Pizza, 158
Grilled Sweet Corn on the Cob, 124
Layered Black Bean Salad, 97
Risotto with Roasted Southwestern
  Chiles and Corn, 139

Crab Meat
Baked Lobster with
Crab Meat Stuffing, 170
Citrus Crab Salad
Tea Sandwiches, 81
Designer Crab Purses, 42
Southwestern Crab Cake Salad, 94

Cranberry
Cranberry Dressing, 102
Cranberry Glaze, 255
Cranberry Pudding Tamales with
Tequila Orange Curd, 254
Cranberry Raspberry Punch, 20
Fresh Cranberry Sorbet, 194
Gorgonzola and Pecan Tart, 174
Margarita Coleslaw, 98
Raspberry Vinaigrette, 87
The Love Cookie, 209

Crawfish
Crawfish and
Corn Chowder, 65
Crawfish Pie, 172

Crusts/Pastry
Chocolate Pecan Crust, 181
Graham Cracker
Cheesecake Crust, 181
Lemon Shortbread Crust, 181
Perfect Pie Crust, 271
Pie Pastry, 223
Savory Tart Crust, 272

Desserts. *See also* Cakes; Candy;
Cheesecakes; Cookies;
Frostings/Glazes/Icings;
Pies/Tarts, Dessert; Puddings;
Sauces, Sweet
Blackberry Crisp, 182
Blueberry Buckle, 183
Chocolate Soufflés with
Crème Anglaise, 189
Easy Mexican Flan, 186
Grilled Peaches, 193
Kahlúa Brownie Torte, 195
Peach Crisp with
Toffee Pecan Topping, 185
Praline Crème Brûlée, 178
Rhubarb Crunch, 184
Simple Syrups, 260
Tiramisu, 191

Vanilla Crème Brûlée, 178
Warm Chocolate Molten with
Chocolate Sauce, 190
White Chocolate
Crème Brûlée, 178

Desserts, Frozen
Cinnamon Ice Cream, 195
Fresh Cranberry Sorbet, 194
Homemade Ice Cream with
Vanilla Beans, 270
Orange Rosemary Sorbet, 194
Ruby Red Grapefruit Sorbet, 194

Dips. *See also* Salsa
Hot Feta Artichoke Dip, 46
Texas Two-Step
Guacamole, 46

Egg Dishes. *See also* Quiches
Camembert and Blue Cheese
Egg Casserole, 246
Chilaquiles, 247
Chile-Cheese Egg
Casserole, 247
Green Chile and Chorizo
Breakfast Strata, 248
Sunrise Frittata, 249
The Perfect Hard-Cooked
Egg, 262

Eggplant
Roasted Vegetables, 138
Tamarind Vegetables, 136

Fish. *See also* Salmon; Sea Bass
Baja Fish Tacos, 164
Caramelized Grouper, 163
Sautéed Sole with
Chardonnay Sauce, 169

Frostings/Glazes/Icings. *See also*
Cakes
Caramelized Meringue, 199
Chocolate Fudge Frosting, 202
Confectioners' Sugar
Icing, 213
Cranberry Glaze, 255
Cream Cheese
Frosting, 196, 200
Cream Cheese Icing, 210
Rum Glaze, 201

Fruit. *See also* Apple; Apricot;
Avocado; Banana; Blueberry;
Cherry; Coconut; Cranberry;
Grapefruit; Lemon; Orange;
Peach; Pear; Pumpkin; Raspberry;
Salads, Fruit; Strawberry
Blackberry Crisp, 182
Holiday Party Punch, 20
Lime Phosphate, 17
Morning Cooler, 21
Nectarine Basil Lemonade, 16
Pineapple Carrot Muffins, 237
Prickly Pear Margarita, 10
Sunshine Punch, 19
Vodka Freeze, 15
White Wine Sangria, 15

Grains. *See also* Rice
Cheese Grits, 253
Four-Cheese Grits, 253
Polenta with Roasted
Vegetables, 138
Tuscan Cheese Grits, 253

Grapefruit
Broiled Grapefruit, 244
Caramelized Grouper, 163
Grapefruit with
Red Leaf Lettuce, 88
Ruby Red Grapefruit Sorbet, 194
White Wine Sangria, 15

Ham/Prosciutto
Ham and Vegetable Quiche, 252
Pears with Goat Cheese and
Prosciutto, 27
Penne à la Vodka, 266
Steamed Mussels with Chorizo, 40
Sunrise Frittata, 249
Thick-as-Fog Pea Soup, 66
Turkey Ham Rolls, 79
Tuscan Cheese Grits, 253
Wild Mushroom Bruschetta, 24

Jicama
Grilled Barbecued Chicken Salad
Pizza, 158
Grilled Jicama Slaw, 164

Lamb
Rosemary Pesto Lamb with
Wild Rice Spinach Timbales, 147

283

Lemon
    Caramelized Grouper, 163
    Lemon Butter Sauce, 171
    Lemon Cheesecake with
        Raspberry Sauce, 179
    Lemon Curd Coffee Cake, 231
    Lemon Poppy Seed Cookies, 211
    Lemon Shortbread Crust, 181
    Lemon Vinaigrette, 96
    Nectarine Basil Lemonade, 16
    Summer Lemonade, 17
    Sunshine Punch, 19

Lobster
    Baked Lobster with
        Crab Meat Stuffing, 170
    Butternut Squash Bisque with
        Lobster Dumplings, 67
    Tomatillo Gazpacho with
        Lobster, 71

Mushrooms
    Asparagus Gruyère Strudel, 245
    Asparagus with Champagne
        Vinaigrette, 119
    Balsamic Jus, 142
    Ham and Vegetable Quiche, 252
    Mushroom-Crusted Beef Tenderloin
        with Balsamic Jus, 142
    Mushroom-Stuffed Tomatoes, 135
    Risotto with Wild Mushroom
        Ragu, 139
    Rosemary Pesto Lamb with
        Wild Rice Spinach Timbales, 147
    Three-Mushroom Soup, 66
    Veal Stroganoff, 146
    Vegetarian Spring Rolls, 30
    Wild Mushroom Bruschetta, 24

Nuts. *See* Pecans; Walnuts

Okra
    Fried Okra, 132
    Sautéed Okra, 132

Orange
    Caramelized Grouper, 163
    Nutty Orange Coffee
        Cake, 230
    Orange Frosty, 19
    Orange Rosemary Sorbet, 194
    Tequila Orange Curd, 255

Pasta
    Angry Pasta for
        Manic Mondays, 175
    Baked Ziti, 266
    Brie and Tomato Pasta, 174
    Chili Mac, 63
    Marinara Sauce, 265
    Penne à la Vodka, 266
    Shrimp with White Wine and
        Dill Sauce, 173
    Spicy Noodle Salad, 90
    Spicy Veggie Couscous, 137

Pastry. *See* Crusts/Pastry

Peach
    Bloomer Droppers, 12
    Grilled Peaches, 193
    Peach Crisp with
        Toffee Pecan Topping, 185
    Peach Jalapeño Chutney, 154
    Peach Margarita, 10

Pear
    Camembert Pastry Platter, 54
    Grilled Blue Cheese Sandwiches, 244
    Margarita Coleslaw, 98
    Mixed Greens with Pears and
        Raspberry Vinaigrette, 87
    Pears with Goat Cheese and
        Prosciutto, 27
    Spinach and Pear Salad with
        Rosemary Vinaigrette, 102

Peas
    Penne à la Vodka, 266
    Spring Salad with English
        Peas, 98
    Thick-as-Fog Pea Soup, 66

Pecans
    Angel Pecan Pie, 215
    Applesauce Pecan Bread, 233
    Blue Ribbon Toffee, 205
    Brandy Cheese Ball, 50
    Bubble Bread, 230
    Caramel Sauce, 233
    Cheese Ball, 50
    Chicken Pecan Quiche, 250
    Chocolate Brownies, 212
    Chocolate Pecan Crust, 181
    Chutney Cheese Ball, 50

Coconut and Pecan Topping, 234
Cowboy Cookies, 207
Cranberry Pudding Tamales with
    Tequila Orange Curd, 254
Crunchy Caramel Apple Pie, 219
Decadent Banana Bread, 234
Fall Spice Cake, 197
Gorgonzola and Pecan Tart, 174
Kahlúa Pecan Cookies, 211
Mixed Greens with Pears and
    Raspberry Vinaigrette, 87
Nutty Orange Coffee Cake, 230
Pecan-Crusted Salmon, 166
Pecan Sticky Rolls, 238
Perfect Pralines, 204
Pineapple Carrot Muffins, 237
Praline Crème Brûlée, 178
Praline Sauce, 180
Sweet and Spicy Pecans, 87
Texas Pecan Coffee Cake, 231
Toffee Pecan Topping, 185

Pies/Tarts, Dessert
    Angel Pecan Pie, 215
    Apple Pie with Cream, 220
    Apple Tart with Almond
        Cream, 217
    Apricot Lavender Tart, 221
    Crème Brûlée Pie, 222
    Crunchy Caramel Apple
        Pie, 219
    Double Chocolate Fried
        Pies, 223
    Perfect Pie Crust, 271
    Southern Sweet Potato
        Pie, 222
    Summer Cheddar Apple
        Pie, 218

Pies/Tarts, Savory. *See also* Quiches
    Crawfish Pie, 172
    Gorgonzola and Pecan Tart, 174
    Savory Tart Crust, 272
    Sweet Tomato Tart, 34

Pork. *See also* Bacon/Pancetta;
    Ham/Prosciutto; Sausage
    Creole Chops, 150
    Dallas Chalupas, 149
    Grilled Pork Chops, 151
    Pork with Cherry Cream Sauce, 148
    Tangy Texas Ribs, 153

Potatoes. *See also* Sweet Potatoes
Boursin Potatoes, 129
Camembert and Blue Cheese
Egg Casserole, 246
Cowboy Mashed Potatoes, 131
Mashed Potatoes with
Roasted Garlic, 131
Not-Just-for-Breakfast Hash Brown
Casserole, 256
Oven-Roasted Four-Potato Salad, 101
Sunrise Frittata, 249
The Best Mashed Potatoes, 131
Thick-as-Fog Pea Soup, 66

Poultry. *See also* Chicken; Turkey
Roasted Poultry, 264

Puddings
Banana Pudding, 187
Bread Pudding with
Whiskey Sauce, 188

Pumpkin
Iced Pumpkin Cookies, 210
Pumpkin Cheesecake with
Praline Sauce, 180

Quiches
Chicken Pecan Quiche, 250
Ham and Vegetable Quiche, 252
Tostada Quiche, 252

Raspberry
Cranberry Raspberry Punch, 20
Farmer's Market Berry Soup, 60
Raspberry Sauce, 179
Raspberry Vinaigrette, 87

Rhubarb
Rhubarb Crunch, 184
Rhubarb Custard Bars, 214

Rice
Chiquito Risotto, 35
Classic Risotto, 139
Green Chile Casserole, 123
Risotto with Roasted Southwestern
Chiles and Corn, 139
Risotto with Wild Mushroom
Ragu, 139
Turkey and Wild Rice Cream Soup, 73
Wild Rice Spinach Timbales, 147

Salads
Baked Hazelnuts, 104
Corn Bread Salad, 99
Fried Tortilla Strips, 72
Spicy Noodle Salad, 90
Sweet and Spicy Pecans, 87

Salads, Dressings
Asian Dressing, 90
Best-Ever Blue Cheese Dressing, 108
Blue Cheese Dressing, 91
Buttermilk Ranch Dressing, 107
Celery Seed Dressing, 109
Cranberry Dressing, 102
Cucumber Ranch Dressing, 107
Dijon Vinaigrette, 26
Garlic Parmesan Dressing, 27
Jalapeño Dressing, 97
Lemon Vinaigrette, 96
Mustard Vinaigrette, 88
Peanut Dressing, 92
Raspberry Vinaigrette, 87
Rosemary Vinaigrette, 102
Spicy Jalapeño Ranch
Dressing, 107
Verde Dressing, 106

Salads, Fruit
Grapefruit with
Red Leaf Lettuce, 88
Layered Avocado Salad, 86
Mixed Greens with Pears and
Raspberry Vinaigrette, 87
Spinach and Pear Salad with
Rosemary Vinaigrette, 102

Salads, Main Dish
Chicken Salad, 93
Chicken Salad with Peanut
Dressing, 92
Curried Chicken Salad, 93
Sliced Sirloin Salad with
Blue Cheese Dressing, 91
Southwest Chicken Salad, 93
Southwestern Crab Cake
Salad, 94

Salads, Vegetable
Arugula and Parmesan Salad, 96
Arugula and Roast Beet Salad, 95
Asparagus, Fennel and Radish
Salad, 43

Celeriac Slaw, 171
Crispy Goat Cheese on
Vine-Ripened Tomatoes, 103
Grapefruit with Red Leaf Lettuce, 88
Grilled Jicama Slaw, 164
Layered Black Bean Salad, 97
Margarita Coleslaw, 98
Marinated Cucumbers, 128
Mixed Greens with Pears and
Raspberry Vinaigrette, 87
Oven-Roasted Four-Potato
Salad, 101
Spinach and Pear Salad with
Rosemary Vinaigrette, 102
Spring Salad with
English Peas, 98
Stacked Tomato Salad, 104
Verde Vegetable Salad, 106

Salmon
Pecan-Crusted Salmon, 166
Poached Salmon with
Horseradish Sauce, 39
Salmon with Horseradish, 162
Smoked Salmon Spread, 53
Smoked Salmon
Tea Sandwiches, 80

Salsa
Avocado Feta Salsa, 47
Corn Salsa, 167
Fiesta Salsa, 48
Monterey Jack Cilantro Salsa, 47
Tomatillo and Avocado Salsa, 49

Sandwiches
Chicken à la Crescents, 77
Citrus Crab Salad
Tea Sandwiches, 81
Dainty BLTs, 77
Grilled Blue Cheese
Sandwiches, 244
Grilled Honey Cilantro
Chicken Sandwiches, 83
Hot Asparagus Sandwiches, 76
Open-Faced Corned Beef
Bagels, 82
Smoked Salmon
Tea Sandwiches, 80
Smoked Turkey
Tea Sandwiches, 78
Turkey Ham Rolls, 79

Sauces, Savory
Balsamic Jus, 142
Basic Cream Sauce, 267
Basil Pistachio Sauce, 45
Béchamel Sauce, 267
Caper Sauce, 157
Cheese Sauce, 267
Ginger Dipping Sauce, 31
Hollandaise, 267
Horseradish Sauce, 39
Hot Thousand Island Sauce, 267
Lemon Butter Sauce, 171
Marinara Sauce, 265
Mustard Cream Sauce, 143
Peanut Dipping Sauce, 31
Peppercorn Sauce, 144
Rosemary Pesto, 147
Tomatillo Sauce, 161
Whole Grain Mustard Sauce, 56

Sauces, Sweet
Arequipe Sauce, 199
Butter Rum Sauce, 217
Caramel Sauce, 197, 233
Chocolate Anglaise, 189
Chocolate Sauce, 190
Crème Anglaise, 189
Grand Marnier Sauce, 240
Praline Sauce, 180
Raspberry Sauce, 179
Tequila Orange Curd, 255
Three Leches Sauce, 199
Whiskey Sauce, 188

Sausage
Angry Pasta for
    Manic Mondays, 175
Green Chile and Chorizo
    Breakfast Strata, 248
Steamed Mussels with Chorizo, 40

Sea Bass
Miso-Marinated Sea Bass, 168
Polenta-Crusted Sea Bass, 167

Seafood. *See* Fish; Shellfish

Shellfish. *See also* Crab Meat;
    Crawfish; Lobster; Shrimp
Crisp Scallops and
    Creamed Sweet White Corn, 43
Steamed Mussels with Chorizo, 40

Shrimp
Grilled Shrimp with
    Basil Pistachio Sauce, 45
Grilled Shrimp with
    Spicy Garlic Paste, 172
Shrimp 'n' Caper Bites, 32
Shrimp with White Wine and
    Dill Sauce, 173
Shrimp Wrapped in Bacon with
    Jalapeño, 44

Side Dishes. *See also* Grains;
    Pies/Tarts, Savory
Baked Chiles Rellenos, 122
Crab Meat Stuffing, 170
Fried Green Tomatoes, 33
Green Chile Casserole, 123
Lobster Dumplings, 67
Marinated Cucumbers, 128
Mushroom-Stuffed Tomatoes, 135
Spicy Veggie Couscous, 137
Wild Rice Spinach Timbales, 147

Soups. *See also* Chili
Butternut Squash Bisque with
    Lobster Dumplings, 67
Carrot Bisque, 61
Chicken Stock, 261
Crawfish and Corn Chowder, 65
Cream of Poblano with Crostini, 68
Farmer's Market Berry Soup, 60
Fire and Ice Tomato Soup with
    Dainty BLTs, 69
Fresh Herb Tortilla Soup, 72
Fried Tortilla Strips, 72
Thick-as-Fog Pea Soup, 66
Three-Mushroom Soup, 66
Tomatillo Gazpacho with
    Lobster, 71
Turkey and Wild Rice
    Cream Soup, 73
Turnip Greens Soup, 74

Spinach
Crisp Scallops and
    Creamed Sweet White Corn, 43
Green and White Chicken
    Enchiladas, 160
Ham and Vegetable Quiche, 252
Spinach and Pear Salad with
    Rosemary Vinaigrette, 102
Wild Rice Spinach Timbales, 147

Spreads
Avocado Caviar Mousse, 51
Brandy Cheese Ball, 50
Cheese Ball, 50
Chutney Cheese Ball, 50
Hot Onion Soufflé, 57
Smoked Salmon Spread, 53
Sun-Dried Tomato Spread, 52

Squash
Butternut Squash Bisque with
    Lobster Dumplings, 67
Southwestern Squash, 132
Squash Pickles, 133

Strawberry
Cranberry Raspberry Punch, 20
Farmer's Market Berry Soup, 60
Grand Marnier Sauce, 240

Sweet Potatoes
Oven-Roasted Four-Potato
    Salad, 101
Southern Sweet
    Potato Pie, 222
Tamarind Vegetables, 136
Twice-Baked Blue Cheese
    Sweet Potatoes, 134

Syrups
Citrus Simple Syrup, 260
Ginger Mint Syrup, 260
Vanilla Bean Syrup, 260

Texas Favorites
Authentic Texas Chili, 62
Avocado Feta Salsa, 47
Baja Fish Tacos, 164
Baked Chiles Rellenos, 122
Biscochitos, 206
Blue Ribbon Toffee, 205
Brandy Cheese Ball, 50
Brussels Sprouts a Tejas, 112
Chilaquiles, 247
Citrus Simple Syrup, 260
Corn Bread Salad, 99
Cornmeal Pancakes with
    Corn Salsa, 241
Cowboy Cookies, 207
Cowboy Mashed Potatoes, 131
Cranberry Pudding Tamales with
    Tequila Orange Curd, 254

Deep-in-the-Heart-of-Texas
   Backyard Barbecue Chicken, 154
Double Chocolate Fried Pies, 223
Easy Mexican Flan, 186
Fiesta Salsa, 48
Fresh Herb Tortilla Soup, 72
Green and White Chicken
   Enchiladas, 160
Green Chile and Chorizo
   Breakfast Strata, 248
Grilled Peaches, 193
Iron Skillet Corn Bread, 228
Jalapeño Lime Butter, 125
Kahlúa Pecan Cookies, 211
Layered Avocado Salad, 86
Layered Black Bean Salad, 97
Lone Star Sweet Tea, 21
Margarita Coleslaw, 98
Mexitini, 11
Monterey Jack Cilantro Salsa, 47
Perfect Pralines, 204
Praline Crème Brûlée, 178
Prickly Pear Margarita, 10
Quatro Leches, 198
Red Appletini, 14
Risotto with Roasted Southwestern
   Chiles and Corn, 139
Ruby Red Grapefruit Sorbet, 194
South-of-the-Border Bruschetta, 24
Southwest Chicken Salad, 93
Southwestern Crab Cake Salad, 94
Spicy Jalapeño Ranch Dressing, 107
Tangy Texas Ribs, 153
Texas Pecan Coffee Cake, 231
Texas Two-Step Guacamole, 46
Tomatillo and Avocado Salsa, 49
Tomatillo Chicken Enchiladas, 161
Top Shelf Butter, 243

Tomatillos
Corn Salsa, 167
Tomatillo and Avocado Salsa, 49
Tomatillo Gazpacho with
   Lobster, 71
Tomatillo Sauce, 161

Tomatoes
Angry Pasta for Manic
   Mondays, 175
Avocado Feta Salsa, 47
Baked Chiles Rellenos, 122
Brie and Tomato Pasta, 174

Charred Tomato Chutney, 159
Chiquito Risotto, 35
Corn Bread Salad, 99
Corn Salsa, 167
Crawfish and Corn Chowder, 65
Creole Chops, 150
Crispy Goat Cheese on
   Vine-Ripened Tomatoes, 103
Dainty BLTs, 77
Fiesta Salsa, 48
Fire and Ice Tomato Soup with
   Dainty BLTs, 69
Fresh Herb Tortilla Soup, 72
Fried Green Tomatoes, 33
Green Beans and Tomatoes in
   White Wine, 116
Grilled Barbecued Chicken Salad
   Pizza, 158
Layered Black Bean Salad, 97
Marinara Sauce, 265
Monterey Jack Cilantro Salsa, 47
Mushroom-Stuffed Tomatoes, 135
Pico de Gallo, 24
Roasted Plum Tomatoes, 137
South-of-the-Border Bruschetta, 24
Stacked Tomato Salad, 104
Steamed Mussels with
   Chorizo, 40
Sun-Dried Tomato Spread, 52
Sweet Tomato Tart, 34
Texas Two-Step Guacamole, 46
Tomatillo Gazpacho with Lobster, 71
Tomato Basil Bruschetta, 24

Toppings
Brown Sugar Topping, 182, 219
Cheddar Crumb Topping, 218
Cinnamon Crumb Topping, 183
Coconut and Pecan Topping, 234
Oat and Brown Sugar Topping, 184
Sugar and Cinnamon Topping, 235
Toffee Pecan Topping, 185

Tortillas
Baja Fish Tacos, 164
Chilaquiles, 247
Fresh Herb Tortilla Soup, 72
Fried Tortilla Strips, 72
Green and White Chicken
   Enchiladas, 160
Grilled Jicama Slaw, 164
Tomatillo Chicken Enchiladas, 161

Turkey
Smoked Turkey Tea Sandwiches, 78
Turkey and Wild Rice Cream Soup, 73
Turkey Ham Rolls, 79

Veal Stroganoff, 146

Vegetables. *See also* Artichokes;
   Asparagus; Beans; Beets; Broccoli;
   Cabbage; Carrots; Corn; Eggplant;
   Jicama; Mushrooms; Okra; Peas;
   Potatoes; Rhubarb; Salads,
   Vegetable; Spinach; Squash;
   Sweet Potatoes; Tomatillos;
   Tomatoes; Zucchini
Brussels Sprouts a Tejas, 112
Roasted Vegetables, 138
Tamarind Vegetables, 136
Turnip Greens Soup, 74

Walnuts
Asparagus Gruyère Strudel, 245
Camembert Pastry Platter, 54
Chicken à la Crescents, 77
Gorgonzola-Stuffed Endive, 26
Walnut Dream Bars, 213

Zucchini
Fiesta Salsa, 48
Roasted Zucchini, 137
Spicy Veggie Couscous, 137
Squash Pickles, 133

287

Dallas Dish

Junior League of Dallas, Inc.
8003 Inwood Road
Dallas, Texas 75209

Junior League
of Dallas

Proceeds from the sale of this book will allow the League to continue to fund important community projects. Our focus areas are Arts and Cultural Enrichment, Education, Family Preservation, Health, Poverty Intervention and Violence Intervention.

Name _____

Address _____

City _____ State _____ Zip _____

Telephone _____

E-mail _____

Your Order	**Qty**	**Total**
Dallas Dish at $32.00 per book	_____	$ _____
Shipping/Handling at $6.00 per book	_____	$ _____
Total		$ _____

Method of Payment:
[   ] American Express   [   ] MasterCard   [   ] VISA
[   ] Check payable to Junior League of Dallas, Inc.

Account Number _____ Exp. Date _____

Cardholder Name _____

Signature _____

You may order online at www.jld.net or call 1.800.931.8821.

Photocopies will be accepted.